Designing the Compassionat

Designing the Compassionate City outlines an approach to urban design that is centred on an explicit recognition of the inherent dignity of all people. It suggests that whether we thrive or decline—as individuals or as a community—is dependent on our ability to fulfil the full spectrum of our needs. This book considers how our surroundings help or hinder us from meeting these needs by influencing both what we can do and what we want to do; either inspiring us to lead healthy, fulfilled lives or consigning us to diminished lives tainted by ill health and unfulfilled potential.

Designing the Compassionate City looks at how those who participate in designing towns and cities can collaborate with those who live in them to create places that help people to accumulate the life lessons, experiences and achievements, as well as forge the connections to meet their needs, to thrive and to fulfil their potential. The book explores a number of inspiring case studies that have sought to meet this challenge and examines what has worked and what hasn't. From this, some conclusions are drawn about how we can all participate in creating places that leave a lasting legacy of empowerment and commitment to nurturing one another. It is essential reading for students and practitioners designing happier, healthier places.

Jenny Donovan is the Principal of the Melbourne-based urban design practice, Inclusive Design. She set up the practice to focus on and advocate for urban design that emphasizes improved social outcomes. Her work spans urban and landscape design, social and environmental planning and neighbourhood renewal in Australia, the UK, Palestine, Ireland, Ethiopia, Kosovo and Sri Lanka.

"In an age of global markets and instantaneous international communication, it's easy to assume that where we live and how we interact with our physical surroundings is becoming less important to our personal fulfilment and societal contribution. In fact, the opposite is the case—contact with nature and contact with our neighbours is consistently shown to underpin our health and happiness. This book offers important and timely insights into the need to design cities that recognise our fundamental biological and psychological needs and the built characteristics that might help us meet these needs."

—*Graham Duxbury, Chief Executive, Groundwork UK*

"For students and practitioners of urbanism, Jenny Donovan restores faith in the potential of people to 'spread their wings'—given a little time, space and help—to create places which nurture life in the round. This stimulating handbook speaks of 'inherent dignity', 'emotional capital', and 'the importance of belonging'. A door bangs open when we think of weighing hope and happiness and 'the uniqueness of everyone's perspective' with the grinding commercial viability issues to which the built environment professions have been subjected in recent years."

—*David Lock CBE, founder of David Lock Associates*

Designing the Compassionate City
Creating Places Where People Thrive

Jenny Donovan

Routledge
Taylor & Francis Group

NEW YORK AND LONDON

First published 2018
by Routledge
711 Third Avenue, New York, NY 10017

and by Routledge
2 Park Square, Milton Park, Abingdon, Oxon, OX14 4RN

Routledge is an imprint of the Taylor & Francis Group, an informa business

© 2018 Taylor & Francis

Library of Congress Cataloging-in-Publication Data
A catalog record for this book has been requested

ISBN: 978-1-138-56270-7 (hbk)
ISBN: 978-1-138-18387-2 (pbk)
ISBN: 978-1-315-64555-1 (ebk)

Typeset in Sabon
by Apex CoVantage, LLC

Contents

Figures

All figures by author unless indicated otherwise.

Acknowledgements

Thanks to Stephen Ingrouille and my parents whose support and belief in me were the foundations that made this project possible. To Stephen thanks too for his patience and keen editorial eye.

To Graham Duxbury, Father Bob Maguire, Donna Petsinis, Dominique Hes, Melissa Kennedy, Mike Biddulph, Finlay McNabb, Mark Sheppard, Fiona Gormann, Des McKenna, Clare Reddington, Andrew McKay, Laura Hansen, Julian Dobson, Kerry Irwin, Erin Marslen, Bonnie Rosen, Douglas Nuttall, Emily Ballantyne Brodie, Maria and Brian, thank you for being so generous with your time in talking over emerging ideas.

To Belinda Strickland, Gregory Dunn, Judy Schwartz Haley, Aoife Doherty and Phil Rogers, thank you for the kind use of your pictures and your time in discussing the ideas they show.

To the principled, inspiring and often brave people behind the projects covered in this book, you have achieved some amazing things. Thank you for sharing the passion you have brought to these projects, your insights and honest reflections. I feel very privileged to have been given access to your ideas and I hope the words and pictures in these pages do them justice.

To John Hoey, Suzanne Lavery and Jean Brown in Northern Ireland and Paul Lonsdale, Phil Millar, Philippa Hay and Rachael Welfare in New Zealand, thank you for your insights into how disasters of nature and human nature that have broken other people can be met face on and their socially destructive impacts challenged.

Thank you to my former colleagues Frank D'hondt, Fiona McCluney, Pren Domjioni, Asmaa Ibrahim and Nabil Awad at UN Habitat. It was good for the soul to work with you and give expression to our shared belief that planning can be used as an instrument of social justice. Thank you also to Israa Tabib and her mother for their kindnesses and for demonstrating that it is possible to live lives of great dignity and creativity even in very difficult circumstances.

To Paul Downton and Sue Gilbey in Adelaide, thank you for your time and kindness. Your enthusiasm, faith in your project and determination to see it through were inspirational.

To Elton Jorgji, Eranda Janku and Dr Aliaj Besnik in Albania, I will remember your generosity of spirit for a long time.

To Paul Hocker and Ken Greenway in London, your ideas, kindness and commitment to creating circumstances where humanity can flower was inspiring.

To Ros Porter, all at the Father Bob Foundation in Melbourne, to Jesse Jorg, Cathelijn de Reede and Hans Karssenberg in Amsterdam, your unwavering belief in the possibility of a better world and creativity in finding ways to make it happen have left a deep impression on me.

Thank you.

To you all, despite being yet another researcher, you all made me feel very welcome.

Thanks too to Krystal LaDuc, Nicole Solano and all at Routledge for your faith in this project and your patience with me.

I dedicate this book to all these above and all those working determinedly and often unthanked on thousands of projects big and small who are demonstrating how creativity and compassion can come together to realize a better world.

1 Introduction

When we design, build, manage, occupy or even just pass through a place, we change it. Whether we are conscious of it or not these changes can embellish, adorn, colour, tint or taint that place in the eyes of the people who share it. This book suggests these diverse actions embed messages in the built environment that influence the people who receive them to see and use a place in particular ways. Some of these messages will be subtle, created by designed characteristics that gently encourage or deter certain choices. Some of these messages will be anything but subtle, created by hard edges such as barriers and gates, reinforced by threats that enforce or prohibit what we experience and where we go (Figure 1.1). When we embed these designed messages in the built environment, we play a part in framing the range of experiences that others enjoy, endure or miss out on that will over time affect the trajectory of their lives.

This book considers how urban design—in its broadest sense—can align these messages to help people to meet their needs, thrive and fulfil their potential.

Nurturing and the Neglectful Places

Like any other influence on our lives, the messages we receive from our surroundings can be good or bad. They are good when they help us to do all the things we need to do to enjoy fulfilled lives. They are bad when they misdirect or deter us from doing these things. As the book will suggest, places rich in these 'good' messages nurture the people who experience them. Their inhabitants find it relatively easy to stay healthy, connect with one another and forge the bonds of family, friendships and community. They are inspired by surroundings that are beautiful and enjoy experiences that they find interesting and fun. Their choice of opportunities is wide and their ability to understand the choices available to them is cultivated.

In such a place people can accumulate experiences, fond memories, life lessons, self-organize, overcome challenges and gather insights that will help them thrive. They can draw reassurance from the knowledge that others in the community are looking out for them and their family. They will feel permitted, even encouraged, to express themselves and carve their own niche in their community. They can develop skills and nurture their own 'islands of competence' to borrow a term from Robert Brooks (2003) that can bolster a sense of self-worth. They are able to enjoy a degree of satisfaction from their contribution to work, family and social life and earn the respect of their peers. Their opinions about the character of their area and its future are sought and considered in what gets built. The levers of power are visible to them and they understand the levers they can pull, along with the responsibilities that come from pulling those levers. Their home, neighbourhood and community provide a

Figure 1.1 Some of the Messages We Receive From Our Surroundings

refuge from life's stresses. These things are a good financial and emotional investment and reflect well on them in the eyes of the wider community. They feel able to bring up children who can benefit from the advantages that come from independent outdoor play and have the best chances of developing the life skills that will serve them well as they grow up. Misfortune that brings with it disability does not deny them opportunities to participate. In such a place older people benefit from the accumulated benefits of an active, stimulated life and a public realm that they interpret as acceptably safe so they can stay healthy and engaged for longer, enjoying more years of healthy life.

On the other hand in a neglectful place the 'helpful messages' that facilitate these outcomes are absent or obscured by contra messages inviting people to choose unhealthy, isolating and unsustainable behaviours. People who live in such places are disadvantaged by their surroundings and the behaviours those environments encourage. These may consign people to diminished lives where the impacts that they have on each other is adversely influenced by the dysfunctional relationship between people and place.

The people who live, work or seek to learn in such places may find themselves isolated from opportunity behind multiple and reinforcing barriers. These barriers are usually not intended as such and the shackles that limit people's lives aren't always physical. Instead they are made by distance, prejudice, lack of awareness or social stratification, reinforced by a qualitatively inadequate physical environment. The people disadvantaged by these neglectful surroundings often find it difficult to do anything about it as the levers of power are obscured and if they can be found they are discouraged from pulling them.

Neglectful places require people to drive or be driven to get anywhere they need to go. If the inhabitants of these places do have a car and can drive they are dependent on an expensive, dangerous, polluting, resource inefficient, increasingly vulnerable, and time-consuming and mood-deflating mode of transport that imposes isolated and sedentary lifestyles. If they can't drive or don't have access to a car—8.6 per cent of Australian households (.idcommunity 2011, sourced from ABS 2011) and 9.2 per cent of US households (American Association of State Highway and Transportation Officials 2013)—then they are trapped, unable to access opportunities.

Human nature being what it is, people will often overcome these difficulties and thrive, irrespective of the bad influences in their surroundings. However if our incremental design, management or behavioural choices combine to make it more difficult for some to meet their needs and prohibitively difficult for others, we are creating arbitrary and unjust urban environments. It diminishes us all when some people's lives are being stifled by their surroundings, denied opportunities to fulfil their potential and fully participate in, and contribute to, society (Figure 1.2).

Living in the neglectful city   Living in the compassionate city

Figure 1.2 The Challenges of Living in the Neglectful or Compassionate City

As this book will explore, these neglectful messages and barriers are concentrated amongst those already disadvantaged. This reflects the observations of Mai Stafford of the Medical Research Council in the UK and Sir Michael Marmot, director of the University College London Institute of Health Equity, who concluded that "*being relatively poor may be a barrier to taking a fully active part in society*" in their UK study on neighbourhood deprivation and health (2003). Sir Marmot further developed this view in his influential report *Fair Society Healthy Lives* (2010) which found that "*People living on a low income in deprived urban areas are more likely to experience worse health and be less physically active*" (reported in CABE 2010).

Furthermore those living in more deprived areas are less likely to find opportunity to escape or recover from the stresses of urban life that consequently can build up to toxic levels (Lederbogen et al. 2011). They are more likely to suffer the profound health problems that come from loneliness (Valtorta et al. 2016), inactivity (Australian Government Department of Health 2011), and problems of insecurity and violence (Muggah 2012), and to be stigmatized by their association with that place or activity (Hess 2012). They are more vulnerable to diabetes, heart disease, obesity, mental health problems, alcohol and drug abuse, and violence (Friel 2009). The causes of this are many and their interplay complex and they extend far beyond urban design. However "*there is a reciprocal relationship between urban social conditions and the built environment*", according to Dr Sharon Friel (2011). The quality of the physical environment and the choices it offers play an important part in determining if people are able to meet their needs or not (Friel et al. 2009).

This inequity is profoundly unfair and is an important and growing issue: "*While city populations have tended to become wealthier than their rural counterparts, they have become increasingly unequal*" (Friel 2011). This is not just an ethical matter, it is a matter of practical efficiency and self-interest for all. People who live in more equal societies tend to be happier. Morgan Kelly's (2006) study of crime and inequality found a strong relationship between inequality and violent crime (though not to property crime). Inequality.org quotes research from the World Bank that found that high levels of inequality negatively affect the health of the affluent as well as the poor (Inequality.org undated). Wilkinson and Pickett (2010) found that social inequity erodes trust, leads to increased anxiety and illness in all sections of the community, and encourages excessive consumption. They concluded that the healthiest and more resilient societies were not always the wealthiest but they were the ones where wealth was more equitably shared in absolute terms.

This is not a simple matter with a simple urban design fix. The complex relationship between people and place means that rarely can we say if we 'do x then y will happen'. Design is far from destiny. As this book will explore, each of us has a different sensitivity and ability or desire to respond to the messages we receive from our surroundings. As such when we intervene in other people's surroundings, we do not make a certain outcome happen; we can however make particular outcomes more or less likely. For example, designing (and then building) a footpath may facilitate people to walk; it doesn't mean that everyone who could walk on that path will choose to do so. However some will, their choices swayed by their own interpretation of the invitation offered by their surroundings.

Unfortunately despite the undoubted good intentions of those engaged in urban design, the 'causal pathways' between what gets built and social outcomes are often not adequately explored in the design process (Haigh 2013). Experience suggests these pathways are either assumed, disregarded in the pursuit of other objectives or deemed unknowable and put in the 'too hard basket'.

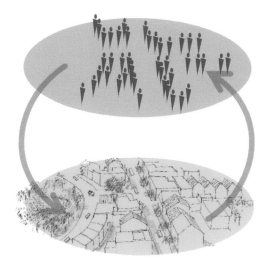

We impact upon our surroundings by the development choices we make but also by the way we manage the things we create, the way we move through them, how we use them, whether we chose to care for them or neglect them....

... in turn our surroundings impact us by the choice of opportunities they offer us, the degree they reflect our values and the degree they expose us to risks such as pollution or danger

Figure 1.3 The Relationship Between People and Place

About This Book

This book has been written to offer a practitioner's perspective on this important issue. *Designing the Compassionate City* looks at how urban design—in its broadest sense—can influence many aspects of people's lives: how they feel, what they can do and what they want to do, amongst many other things. It recognizes that our interventions change the balance of power in the spaces we create, giving unwritten licence to some users and activities and discouraging others.

This book seeks to explore how we might tailor our interventions to become a better reflection of our underlying humanity and was written from the perspective that urban design is a social investment. It leaves a legacy that impacts the social fabric of the town or city it is embedded within and changes by a small or large degree the momentum of that community (Figure 1.3).

The Inspiration for This Book

Before I could articulate it I intuitively felt that our surroundings influenced the quality of our lives. Growing up in very urban London with frequent trips to rural County Wexford in Ireland, I was fascinated by the way that different places provoked different emotional responses. Some places brought happiness whilst others had the opposite effect. The places that felt 'happy' were diverse and could be found in the city or the country. Hence these places often looked very different but felt equally comfortable, interesting and welcoming. In contrast other places, usually urban in character, cultivated fear and cast strangers as potential enemies. Tension, anger or fear sat oppressively over these areas, fun was harder to find and parents discouraged children from playing outside. More often than not these places were grim and depressing. Opportunities of any kind were sparse and unappealing and the experiences they offered were often scary or distressing.

Yet sometimes the places that provoked these contrasting responses were very close to one another. I remember the contrast between the little houses on little streets such as ours

Figure 1.4 Contrasting West London Streetscapes That Seemed to Cultivate Contrasting Social Outcomes

(Figure 1.4) and the heroic development projects of the post war era that partly replaced them (Figure 1.5)—projects such as the tower blocks that dotted the horizon from where we lived, the huge sprawling housing estates not far away and the new towns that ringed the major cities.

For those living in many (but by no means all) of these major urban renewal and development projects, it seemed that life was harder and hope that things could get better seemed to be more difficult to maintain. That is not to say that the bonds of humanity, the friendships and a sense of community didn't survive or even flourish in those places, they self-evidently did. My experience as a play leader organizing games for children in a park in a West London housing estate as a student vacation job reaffirmed this for me. However it also led me to feel that this was a testament to people's resilience and adaptability. These people flourished *despite* their surroundings. If a place could be attributed human characteristics, such places might be described as neglectful, unresponsive and uncaring. To my eyes the places these estates and new towns partly replaced, the little terraced houses overlooking narrow streets, although far from perfect, seemed so much more of a nurturing, more human place to live.

This interest inspired me to study town planning. Through my studies I noticed that as well as the obvious benefits of planning, there were often social costs. The wholesale intervention in the settings for people's lives—the clearance and rebuilding that I observed in London—had been advocated, designed and built by professionals who were motivated by a desire to make the city a better place. Their intent had been noble and they were as well read and trained as I aspired to be, but their efforts had left a mixed legacy. Living in some housing estates allowed people to flourish whilst other apparently very similar ones didn't. It was obvious that the architecture, planning and landscape were not the only factors that influenced whether people thrived but at the same time they were an important influence on people's chances in life.

To me this arbitrary distribution of benefits and problems seemed unfair and presented a serious flaw in the way planning was undertaken. That is not to say this led me to believe that the idea of planning was fundamentally flawed. A moment's study of the history of urbanization and the human cost of uncontrolled development is enough to see that 'the

Figure 1.5 Contrasting West London Streetscapes That Seemed to Cultivate Contrasting Social
Outcomes

market', left alone, is much worse at delivering places that support people's well-being.
For example the rapid uncontrolled urbanization of the industrial revolution in the UK
contributed to a dramatic fall in life expectancy, in the case of Liverpool falling to 25 years
when their rural compatriots lived to 45 years (Haley 1978). The question seemed to me
not should we intervene, but how can we intervene better? This made me think, what could
we learn from the patchily successful planning of the past? What was it about the way that
people, buildings and spaces interacted that meant some places supported people whilst
others didn't? It seemed that when we intervene in the public realm, we are intervening
in a very complex system where others had intervened, for a range of different reasons
and with differing capacities, insights and degrees of comprehensiveness. It struck me this
was like someone tinkering with a machine that they do not understand properly that had
already been tinkered with using an outdated manual with pages missing. The diversity and
complexity of humanity means that we can never know exactly how people will respond to
our interventions and the outcomes of those interventions will always be something of an
experiment. However that doesn't mean we shouldn't try and learn as much as possible so
we might design places that were at least *more likely* to help people to thrive.

Through my professional life I have come across many inspiring projects that have thoughtfully addressed the relationship between people and their surroundings. This has offered me a few insights into some of the mechanisms by which people's urban surroundings become traps or refuges, catalysts or inhibitors of fulfilment. It has also revealed some insights that might be helpful in understanding how well-meant interventions have gone wrong, leading to unforeseen and sometimes detrimental outcomes. It is to share these insights that I have written this book in the hope that others may find it helpful to apply themselves, their skills and insights to the task of designing places where people thrive.

The Beliefs Behind This Book

The philosophical foundations for this book are that:

- Everyone, born or not yet born, has *inherent dignity*, deserving of our respect and consideration and has an inalienable right to seek to fulfil their own potential;
- The design of our towns and cities and the social processes they cultivate play a part in moulding people's lives by framing the opportunities open to them.

Consequently if we alter the settings within which other people lead their lives, we have a responsibility to consider the impact this will have on them, ensuring we do nothing that diminishes their ability to fulfil their potential and everything to support it.

Inherent Dignity

A commitment to recognizing the dignity of all people is not merely an abstract ethical position, it is a cornerstone of human well-being and is reflected in the preamble of the Universal Declaration of Human Rights. This states that *"recognition of the inherent dignity and of the equal and inalienable rights of all members of the human family is the foundation of freedom, justice and peace in the world"* (UN 1948). Inherent dignity might be visualized as a spark of unique worth and potential within each person. This spark is dimmed or brought up to its fullest brightness according to the ability of that person to access the opportunities and experiences they require to meet their needs and develop their abilities. Consequently the compassionate city seeks to empower its inhabitants to meet their needs and explore and develop their abilities. This is a perspective with parallels in *Building Better Places*, a report of Select Committee on National Policy for the Built Environment by the UK House of Lords, which stated: *"striving to develop a built environment where all people can live well and make a full contribution to society should be a key objective for decision makers"* (House of Lords 2016).

Right to Choose How to Participate

This commitment to inherent dignity also leads to the conclusion that, as a default position, everyone has a right (assuming competence) to make their own choices about their path to well-being and how they can best participate in society. This requires giving people a wide range of appealing choices so they can select the particular healthy/fun/enlightening/sustainable behaviour that suits them best and makes the adoption of that choice one of personal preference rather than imposition. For example where behavioural changes are required—as it is in car-dependent neighbourhoods that impose sedentary, isolated lifestyles—the compassionate city should seek to address this by attracting people to active transport rather than demanding they stop driving. In other words it should be more 'carrot' than 'stick'. This aligns with the conclusions of Neil Thin (2012), who found that the benefits of changing behaviours contribute more to people's well-being when they are freely chosen rather than enforced.

It follows from this that it is not adequate to just quantitatively embed the opportunities for people to meet their needs into their surroundings if those opportunities are insufficiently appealing. If the past (unhelpful) behaviours are still felt of as preferable then why would people change behaviour? For example providing access to an unattractive, exposed play area, even one with many different play apparatuses, may make play possible but it is unlikely to make it competitive against screen-based entertainment (Hemmings 2007). Consequently in the compassionate city where people have the right to do everything or nothing, we need to create surroundings that make needs-fulfilling activity not just *possible* but *preferable*.

Emotional Capital

Another reflection of this commitment to the inherent dignity is a recognition that people who live, work or otherwise experience an area will care about it and accumulate insights and experiences that the designer will not have. These insights and the emotional responses they trigger matter to people; they generate emotional capital. This is the *"shared sense of trust, safety, and reciprocity that promotes involvement and commitment"* (McGrath and Buskirk, undated.). Although the term 'emotional capital' is more often used by economists and sociologists to explain people's loyalty to organizations or brands, it is also a useful way to look at a person's commitment to their surroundings and the people around them. This can be a very powerful motivating force, compelling people to take action to make things better or protect what they value.

The Importance of Being Connected

Human beings are social creatures with a profound need to connect who thrive best in complex social structures. This book reflects the belief it is both reassuring and rewarding to forge connections with one another that *"make us feel that we matter, that we are engaged with others and that we are embedded in networks of mutual appreciation and care"* according to Australian social researcher Jane Frances Kelly (Kelly et al. 2012). In her informative report "Social Cities" for the Australian social policy research centre the Grattan Institute, she observes the true importance of belonging and being connected becomes apparent when it is missing. Loneliness can be severely damaging, bringing with it *"serious health consequences, with a similar impact to high blood pressure, lack of exercise, obesity, or smoking"* (Kelly et al. 2012).

She goes on to quote fieldwork from the Young Foundation (a UK social policy research centre) that reveals young people go *"without food in order to keep their mobile phones topped up, leading the Foundation's former chief executive, Geoff Mulgan, to conclude that 'the human need for connectedness' outweighs 'almost everything else'."*

The Importance of Health

Health and its absence frames human potential. Unhealthy people are less happy (Guo and Hu 2011), do less well at school (Zhang et al. 2014) and have lower levels of attainment in the labour force (Currie et al. 2008). The stifling effect of ill health echoes through generations, passing from parent to child (Currie et al. 2008). The book reflects the view that good health is *"a state of complete physical, mental and social well-being and not merely the absence of disease or infirmity"* (United Nations 1948). The book was written from the perspective that the experience of living in the city should offer a person many of the things they need to support their physical and emotional health and impose few things that diminish it.

The Importance of Hope

Hope is often overlooked but when hope dies so does motivation. This book reflects the belief that realizable hope is a critical precondition to motivate people to do what is required to achieve improvement and safeguard against deterioration. An absence of hope deters people from setting goals and encourages people to give up, leaving problems unsolved and left in the 'too hard basket', seemingly intractable. The profound effects of hope and its absence were explored by Dominque Hes and Chrisna du Plessis in their insightful and deeply thoughtful book *Designing for Hope* (2015). They contend that to challenge the despair and despondency that can result from the apparent prevailing momentum of history—taking us down a path of climate change and resource depletion—we need the innovation born of hope, quoting Raymond Williams: *"to be truly radical is to make hope possible, rather than despair convincing"*. Hes's and du Plessis's work suggests that designers' ability to visualize their way around problems and create inspiring images of the future can provide people with a direction and focus that can make a belief in a better future a more influential factor in their quality of life. However hope is a fragile thing: it needs careful cultivation and when it is based on unrealistic expectations or is raised only to be dashed it can be bitterly disappointing and discourage future involvement.

The importance of hope and the critical part that the planning process can play in it was demonstrated to me in the aftermath of the devastating earthquakes of 2010–2011 in Canterbury, New Zealand, by Rob Kerr of Waimakamara District Council. The sudden destruction and loss of so many layers of community life negated previous hopes and left people with very little ability to visualize a better future. Instead they were focussed on what they had lost. This sense of loss and lack of hope brought with it significant psychological distress that proved hard to shift. *"Repairing the roads and buildings would be the easy bit"*, Rob told me (pers. corr. 2013). However, his experience of the recovery and rebuilding demonstrated to him the importance of the planning process in cultivating hope. It provided survivors with reassuring evidence that the worst was past and allowed them to look into the future with a degree of confidence. In doing so it released them from the past and its trauma. As Rob put it: *"a good plan supported by good visualisations is worth a thousand hours of counselling"*. He found that the process they had chosen and refined, with its sensitivity to the psychological processes of the survivors and explicit recognition of hope, helped to cultivate the belief that what was lost or would have to change was going to be replaced with something better. He told me, *"Before the earthquakes people came to planning meetings to voice their fear of what could be, whereas afterwards people came to find hope in what could be."*

The Importance of Happiness

According to UN Secretary-General Ban Ki-Moon (2014): *"Happiness is neither a frivolity nor a luxury. It is a deep-seated yearning shared by all members of the human family. It should be denied to no-one and available to all,"* a view shared by Neil Thin, who stated:

"*Happiness is more than just a desirable personal objective that can be discarded for more important objectives, it is a social and public good and is a matter of importance to all of humanity*" (Thin 2012). Happiness is a good state in its own right but also brings with it many other desirable outcomes that one would wish to use to support people to thrive: "*Numerous studies show that happy individuals are successful across multiple life domains, including marriage, friendship, income, work performance, and health*" (Lyubomirsky et al. 2005). Building up a stock of happy memories can protect people against ill health (Siahpush et al. 2008) and has been linked to reducing the effects of stress, supporting heart health (Davidson et al. 2010) and supporting the immune system (Cohen et al. 2003).

What happiness actually consists of however is contested and has long been the focus of attention of poets, philosophers, politicians and psychologists. The author adopts the views of Huta and Ryan (2009) that happiness has two components: hedonia (seeking pleasure and comfort) and eudaimonia (seeking to express and develop the best in oneself). C. D. Ryff (1989) stated that eudaimonic well-being is about "*belonging and benefiting others, flourishing, thriving and exercising excellence*". Huta and Ryan (2009) concluded that "*hedonia and eudaimonia occupy overlapping and distinct niches within a complete picture of well-being, and their combination may be associated with the greatest well-being.*" Eudaimonia might come from visiting a friend's house to help them move, fix something for them or take the time to listen to their concerns and support them through difficult times. Hedonia might come from visiting them for a party. From this perspective happiness isn't just smiles, pleasure and comfort. Discomfort and effort can contribute to happiness when they help us achieve eudaimonic well-being, when they are investments in helping others and give us opportunity to do the right thing. However, fun is an equally essential part of our well-being. It seems apparent that hedonia and eudaimonia overlap; experiences can be fun and satisfying, as people who play team sports or volunteer for a cause important to them will attest. Thus from this point of view happiness spans a life of meaning—striving to fulfil one's potential in relation to others'—and enjoyment.

Cascading from these beliefs are a series of other philosophical positions that are also reflected in this book.

Broad Responsibilities of Urban Designers

Those people who call themselves professional urban designers are only one of the groups of players who influence the world other people share, but their role is important. The Urban Design Group (in the UK) tells us, "*What gets urban designers out of bed in the morning is the challenge of creating a place that will be used and enjoyed by a wide range of different people for different purposes, not only now but in years to come*" (undated). As such, professional urban designers are dedicated to considering the social impacts of their work and have (hopefully) the training and experience to draw informed conclusions about these impacts. Furthermore urban designers influence the form of masterplans and the content and priorities of design guidance which guide development decisions that involve commitments of vast amounts of resources. Thus the outcomes of our handiwork will be experienced by many people and will probably be around a long time. In the UK it is estimated that "*90% of the buildings and infrastructure that will exist in 30 years have already been built*" (House of Lords 2016). In helping to make such an indelible mark on the landscape, urban designers have been given a great privilege and responsibility. The places we help create frame other people's choices about what they can do and want to do way into the future. Hence our actions will almost definitely impact upon people unknown to us or not yet born.

Recognition of the Uniqueness of Everyone's Perspective

> *Every man is influenced by his fellows, dead and living, but his mind is his own and its functioning is necessarily an individual affair.*
>
> (Emerson 1963)

In any shared environment our experience of our surroundings will overlap with many other people who will be looking on those surrounding in a similar way. However despite these broad similarities everyone's picture of their surroundings will vary in detail, reflecting their unique perspectives about whether their surroundings help or hinder them to do all the things they need to do. Consequently this book stresses the importance of listening, of understanding these perspectives and of applying creative design skills to find solutions that resonate with as wide a variety of these perspectives as possible.

Recognition of the Complex Nature of Cities

Cities are not just inanimate compositions of buildings and spaces. Cities are complex and ever-evolving systems animated by the people and the wider biological community that occupy them. Affect one of these variables and you affect the others, often in unexpected ways. This complexity denies perfect knowledge and masks impacts by obscuring cause and effect. As Charles Montgomery (2013) points out, interventions made by well-meaning, well-informed and educated people nonetheless often detrimentally affect people's lives through many *"unintended consequences"*. He cites the examples of how interventions designed to make roads safer through such measures as road widening and the removal of street-side trees actually encouraged faster speeds, which in turn led to more accidents and an increased likelihood that those accidents would be fatal.

The Importance of Compassion

For most of humanity, one of the cardinal points of our values is compassion, the *"concern we feel for another being's welfare"* (Keltner undated). Evolution has taught us we do better when we co-operate and consider others (Goetz et al. 2010) and we have become *"hardwired for compassion"* according to Donna Petsinis (pers. corr. 2015). This commitment to collective well-being is reflected in our *"desire to uphold ethical norms"* (Bowles and Gintis 2011) and is not only an expression of ethical values but is intrinsically rewarding: *"A strong correlation exists between the well-being, happiness, health, and longevity of people who are emotionally and behaviourally compassionate"* (Post 2005). Furthermore, *"people think that cooperating is the right thing to do and enjoy doing it, and they dislike unfair treatment and enjoy punishing those who violate norms of fairness"* (Bowles and Gintis 2011).

This book reflects the view that this perspective resonates with most planners, architects and others who intervene in the settings within which other people lead their lives. It is taken as read that many such professionals are drawn to this field, at least in part, by a desire to create places that contribute to the lives of the people who experience their handiwork. For this perspective, 'good design' in the built environment responds not just to the physical landscape, the needs of the client and planning code requirements but it also responds to the social landscape. It considers people who haven't contributed financially to the development nor exercise formal power over it but are still impacted by it. Consequently this book reflects a belief that for many designers their sense of what represents good design may change with their understanding of the link between built form and social impact.

The Scope of This Book

This book considers the differences that urban design can make to people's lives and seeks to identify the types of interventions that best facilitate people to meet their needs. This book does not seek to comprehensively address all of the aspects that influence the relationship between people and their surroundings. That relationship is too complex and informed by too many other variables (Haigh 2013) that extend well beyond the scope of urban design to make such a claim. The book embeds itself in the social context within which urban design interventions are made. It considers issues such as social inclusion, public health, safety and sustainability that are influenced by the design of the built environment. Following Jan Gehl's advice, *"First life, then spaces, then buildings—the other way around never works"* (quoted in Project for Public Spaces undated), this book has been written with an emphasis on the perspective of the users of the public realm and their ability to contribute to each other's quality of life. The book doesn't peer inside the buildings that define the public realm other than to consider their impact and responsibilities to the public realm. Some very important issues such as housing, healthcare and education are only very lightly touched upon, despite the undoubtedly profound impact they have on a city's ability to nurture its inhabitants. Beyond recognizing the importance of these and other issues, the urban design focus of this book requires that they are left for others to address.

Although this book is written from a professional urban designer's perspective, I hope it is of interest to anyone concerned about social outcomes in urban areas and the quality of the built environment. This book suggests a way of looking at the built environment that might help people to question whether their towns and cities nurture or neglect their inhabitants. By drawing people's attention to this issue and inviting them to consider their interventions in this light, it is hoped to provide a means that may help people apply their insights and invest their emotional capital in making places more nurturing for the people who experience them.

Designing the compassionate city does not seek to promote a single, consistent aesthetic beyond some characteristics established by underlying physiological and emotional needs. No such single aesthetic exists. Beauty is indeed very much in the eye of the beholder. The sense of what represents aesthetic perfection varies by culture, class, experience and personal taste, amongst many other variables (Porteous 1990; Green 2010). This book does not seek to impose an aesthetic or say anyone's sense of what they find visually appealing is right or wrong. However that is not to say beauty is unimportant. As this book will suggest experiencing the inspiration of beauty is a basic human need, it just can't be reduced down to a simple universal equation or list. Thus the images and ideas contained in this book reflect my own aesthetic values, albeit for the most part having been tested for conformance with the values of the clients and the communities affected. Consequently what the compassionate city might look like when viewed through the lens of another culture may be very different in appearance to my interpretations of projects outlined in these pages. However it is suggested that, despite these differences, the compassionate city—wherever in the world it would be found—would still need to facilitate underlying and universal human needs.

It is recognized that throughout this book the word 'community' is used loosely. Place and communities are not bound in a strict 'one place = one community' relationship. The concept is far more amorphous than that: *"In fact, the concept of 'community' means different things for different people in different circumstances"* (Marsh et al. 2018). People can belong to one or more communities and a single place can be home to many communities. A sense of community can arise through anything shared; it does not have to be geography.

Faith, employment, allegiance to a movement or even a shared support of a sporting code or club can all create a sense of common interest and shared purpose. Consequently, in any given place, there will probably be people who identify themselves as members of different communities and who bring multiple interpretations about what that place means to them. Consequently when the word 'community' is used in this book, it is shorthand for all users who experience a place and encompasses the diversity of perspectives they may hold.

This book is also not the last word. It is a practitioner's perspective and was written to add to the discussion about what represents good design. It is hoped that some of the insights may prove helpful, that the examples of projects covered in the book may inspire and that the lessons learnt and recounted in the studies help people avoid pitfalls and unnecessary difficulties. It makes no claim to scientifically prove its thesis.

Chapters 1 to 5 present the ideas that underpin the book, the relationship between people and place, and what it means to live in nurturing or neglectful surroundings. They consider how we embed and interpret messages in our surroundings and how those messages influence other people's ability to meet their needs. They suggest that in addition to the quantitative paucity of opportunity in disadvantaged communities, these people are also often disadvantaged by a qualitative paucity. Their surroundings only half-heartedly invite them to take up those opportunities that do exist. I will suggest that this inequitable distribution of the encouragements we get from our surroundings creates a steep 'social gradient of invitation' akin to the social gradient of health that compounds disadvantage. This part of the book concludes by suggesting an abstract model of the compassionate city that considers the optimum relationship between people and place and allows us to realize our individual and collective potential.

Chapters 6 to 14 look at the stories of a number of projects that have been undertaken explicitly to enhance the relationship between people and place. They include projects that changed the physical fabric of the city, the way people think about and use their surroundings, and the administrative framework which governs the rights and responsibilities to land and the people who occupy it. These studies outline the project, its goals, the key design characteristics that were employed to achieve those goals and the lessons learnt from those experiences—what worked and what didn't work.

Chapters 15 to 19 take stock of the lessons learnt from these projects and others, as well as seeks to make some observations about what this all means for an urban designer. They outline the barriers to achieving these goals, as well as the principles, processes and product characteristics that may help us overcome these barriers and achieve a more compassionate city, mindful of the constraints/limitations of all parties.

References

American Association of State Highway and Transportation Officials (2013) *Commuting in America 2013: The National Report on Commuting Patterns and Trends.* Accessed June 2016, http://traveltrends.transportation.org/Documents/B7_Vehicle%20and%20Transit%20Availability_CA07-4_web.pdf

Australian Government Department of Health (2011) *The Health Consequences of Physical Inactivity and the Benefits of Physical Activity 2011.* Accessed July 2016, www.health.gov.au/internet/publications/publishing.nsf/Content/phd-physical-rec-older-disc~chapter-

Bowles, S, and Gintis, H (2011) A cooperative species. In *A Cooperative Species: Human Reciprocity and Its Evolution.* Princeton, NJ: Princeton University Press. Accessed July 2016, http://EconPapers.repec.org/RePEc:pup:chapts:9474-1

Brooks, R (2003) *Self-Worth, Resilience and Hope: The Search for Islands of Competence*. Accessed July 2016, www.cdl.org/articles/self-worth-resilience-and-hope-the-search-for-islands-of-competence/

Cohen, S, Doyle, WJ, Turner, RB, Alper, CM, and Skoner, DP (July–August 2003) Emotional style and susceptibility to the common cold. *Psychosomatic Medicine* 65(4): 652–7. Accessed July 2016, www.ncbi.nlm.nih.gov/pubmed/12883117

Commission for Architecture and the Built Environment (2010) *Community Green*. London: CABE.

Currie, C, Nic Gabhainn, S, Godeau, E, Roberts, C, Smith, R, Currie, D, Picket, W, Richter, M, Morgan, A, and Barnekow, V (Eds.) (2008) *Inequalities in Young People's Health: Health Behaviour in School-Aged Children*. International Report From the 2005/2006 Survey Child and Adolescent Health Research Unit, University of Edinburgh. Accessed November 2016, www.euro.who.int/__data/assets/pdf_file/0005/53852/E91416.pdf

Davidson, K, Mostofsky, E, and Whang, W (May 2010) Don't worry, be happy: Positive affect and reduced 10-year incident coronary heart disease: The Canadian Nova Scotia Health Survey. *European Heart Journal* 31(9): 1065–70. www.ncbi.nlm.nih.gov/pmc/articles/PMC2862179/

Emerson, T (1963) *Toward a General Theory of the First Amendment*. Faculty Scholarship Series. Paper 2796. http://digitalcommons.law.yale.edu/fss_papers/2796

Friel, S (2011) *The Determinants of Urban Healthy Equity*. LSE Cities. Accessed October 2016, https://lsecities.net/media/objects/articles/the-determinants-of-urban-healthy-equity/en-gb/

Friel, S, and The Australian National Preventative Health Task Force & Australian National University & University College, London. Dept. of Epidemiology and Public Health (2009) *Health Equity in Australia: A Policy Framework Based on Action on the Social Determinants of Obesity, Alcohol and Tobacco*. Canberra: Australian National Preventative Health Taskforce.

Goetz, J, Dacher, K, and Emiliana, S (2010) Compassion: An evolutionary analysis and empirical review. *Psychological Bulletin* 136(3): 351–74. PMC. Web. Accessed 23 February 2016. www.ncbi.nlm.nih.gov/pmc/articles/PMC2864937/

Green, R (2010) *Coastal Towns in Transition*. Clayton, Australia: CSIRO Publishing.

Guo, T, and Hu, L (2011) *Economic Determinants of Happiness*. https://arxiv.org/abs/1112.5802

Haigh, F (2013) Characteristics of health impact assessments reported in Australia and New Zealand 2005–2009. *Australian and New Zealand Journal of Public Health* 37(6) 534–46.

Haley, B (1978) *The Healthy Body and Victorian Culture*. Cambridge, MA: Harvard University Press.

Hemmings, P (2007) Renegotiating the primary school: Children's emotional geographies of sport, exercise and active play. *Children and Geographies* 5: 353–71. Accessed June 2016, www.tandfonline.com/doi/citedby/10.1080/14733280701631817?scroll=top&needAccess=true

Hes, D, and du Plessis, C, (2015) *Designing for Hope: Pathways to Regenerative Sustainability*. New York: Routledge.

Hess, A (2012) Race, class, and the stigma of riding the bus in America. *The Atlantic Citylab*. Accessed May 2016, www.citylab.com/cityfixer/2012/07/race-class-and-stigma-riding-bus-america/2510/

House of Lords (2016) *Building Better Places, a Report of Select Committee on National Policy for the Built Environment*. HL Paper 100, House of Lords.

Huta, V, and Ryan, R (2009) Pursuing pleasure or virtue: The differential and overlapping well-being benefits of hedonic and eudaimonic motives. *Journal of Happiness Studies* 11: 735–62.

.idcommunity (2011) *Community Profile*. http://profile.id.com.au/australia/*car-ownership*?BMID=50

Inequality.org (undated) *Inequality and Health*. http://inequality.org/inequality-health/

Kelly, J-F, Breadon, P, Davis, C, Hunter, A, Mares, P, Mullerworth, D, and Weidmann, B (2012) Social Cities. Melbourne: Grattan Institute.

Kelly, M (2006) Inequality and crime. *Review of Economics and Statistics* 82(4): 530–9. Posted Online March 13, 2006. doi:10.1162/003465300559028. Accessed July 2016, http://irserver.ucd.ie/bitstream/handle/10197/523/kellym_article_pub_004.pdf

Keltner, D (undated) *The Compassionate Instinct*. Berkeley: University of California. http://greatergood.berkeley.edu/article/item/the_compassionate_instinct/

Ki-moon, B (2014) *Secretary-General's Message for International Day of Happiness*. United Nations. Accessed May 2016, www.un.org/sg/en/content/sg/statement/2014-03-20/secretary-generals-message-international-day-happiness

Lederbogen, F, Kirsch, P, Haddad, L, Streit, F, Tost, H, Schuch, P, Wüst, S, Pruessner, J, Rietschel, M, Deuschle, M, and Meyer-Lindenberg, A (June 23rd, 2011) City living and urban upbringing affect neural social stress processing in humans. *Nature* 474: 498–501. doi:10.1038/nature10190

Lyubomirsky, S, King, L, and Diener, E (November 2005) The benefits of frequent positive affect: Does happiness lead to success? *Psychological Bulletin* 131(6): 803–55. Accessed May 2016, www.ncbi.nlm.nih.gov/pubmed/16351326

Marmot, M (2010) *Fair Society Healthy Lives*. London: University College London.

Marsh, G, Ahmed, I, Mulligan, M, Donovan, J, Barton, S (Eds.) (forthcoming) *Community Engagement in Post-Disaster Recovery*. New York: Routledge.

McGrath D and Van Buskirk Bill (n.d.) Social and Emotional Capital in Education: Cultures of Support for At Risk Students. Accessed March 2012, http://faculty.ccp.edu/dept/viewpoints/jde/support.htm

Montgomery, C (2013) *Happy City*. London: Penguin Books.

Muggah, R (2012) *Researching the Urban Dilemma: Urbanization, Poverty and Violence*. International Development Research Centre, Ottowa, Canada. Accessed May 2016, www.idrc.ca/sites/default/files/sp/Images/Researching-the-Urban-Dilemma-Baseline-study.pdf

Petsinis, D (2015) *Personal Correspondence*, May 2015.

Porteous, JD (1990) *Landscapes of the Mind: Worlds of Sense and Metaphor*. Toronto, Canada: University of Toronto Press.

Post, SJ (2005) Altruism, happiness, and health: It's good to be good. International Journal of Behavioral Medicine 12(2): 66–77. Accessed May 2016, http://ggsc-web02.ist.berkeley.edu/images/uploads/Post-AltruismHappinessHealth.pdf

Project for Public Spaces (undated) *Jan Gehl*. www.pps.org/reference/jgehl/

Ryff, CD (1989) Happiness is everything, or is it? Explorations on the meaning of psychological well-being. *Journal of Personality and Social Psychology* 57: 1069–81. Accessed May 2016, http://ggsc-web02.ist.berkeley.edu/images/uploads/Post-AltruismHappinessHealth.pdf

Siahpush, M, Spittal, M, and Singh, GK (September–October 2008) Happiness and life satisfaction prospectively predict self-rated health, physical health, and the presence of limiting, long-term health conditions. *American Journal of Health Promotion* 23(1): 18–26. doi:10.4278/ajhp.061023137. Accessed May 2016, www.ncbi.nlm.nih.gov/pubmed/18785370

Stafford, M, and Marmot, M (2003) Neighbourhood deprivation and health: Does it affect us all equally? International Journal of Epidemiology 32(3): 357–66. doi:10.1093/ije/dyg084. Accessed May 2016, www.ncbi.nlm.nih.gov/pubmed/12777420

Thin, N (2012) *Social Happiness: Research Into Policy and Practice*. Bristol: Policy Press.

United Nations (1948) *United Nations Universal Declaration of Human Rights*. www.un.org/en/universal-declaration-human-rights/

Urban Design Group (undated) *Urban Design as a Career*. Accessed January 2016, www.udg.org.uk/careers

Valtorta, N, Kanaan, M, Gilbody, S, Ronzi, S, and Hanratty, B (2016) Loneliness and social isolation as risk factors for coronary heart disease and stroke: Systematic review and meta-analysis of longitudinal observational studies. *Heart*. doi:10.1136/heartjnl-2015-308790. Accessed November 2016, http://heart.bmj.com/content/102/13/1009

Wilkinson, R, and Pickett, K (2010) *The Spirit Level: Why More Equal Societies Almost Always Do Better*. London: Penguin Books.

Zhang, D, Giabbanelli, P, Arah, O, and Zimmerman, F (July 2014) Impact of different policies on unhealthy dietary behaviors in an urban adult population: An agent-based simulation model. *American Journal of Public Health*, 104(7): 1217–22. doi:10.2105/AJPH.2014.301934. Accessed May 2016, www.ncbi.nlm.nih.gov/pubmed/24832414

2 Human Needs

Creating places that facilitate people to meet their needs is the central challenge of designing the compassionate city. So what are these needs? According to Len Doyal and Ian Gough, needs are "*certain essentials that allow us to continue and enhance our existence*" (1991). As Douglas Nuttall puts it, they are "*are aspects of human nature (biology, psychology) that are invariant within the population—everyone needs to eat, sleep, be loved, etc.*" (pers. corr. 2015). Adopting this view, the compassionate city is one that is designed to give its inhabitants the best chance of looking around and finding all the opportunities and experiences they require to meet these needs and avoid the "*degradation of the self, family, or community*" (Nuttall 2015, pers. corr.) that would result if denied such opportunities.

Of what then do these needs comprise? Many authors have given careful thought to this question and arrived at a range of different conclusions. It is beyond the scope of this book to give an in-depth analysis of these diverse perspectives or to arrive at a unified theory of human needs. However it is important to broadly get a sense of what each of us require to thrive so that we might better consider how our surroundings can help us to meet these needs.

Each of the philosophers, economists and psychologists who have commented on needs have cut the cake differently but fundamentally most recognize the primacy in normal circumstances of fulfilling basic physiological imperatives (food, water, shelter) to support life. Meeting these needs allows us to focus on meeting other needs that make life worthwhile. They also largely share the conclusion that it is only when all needs are met that it is possible for people to fulfil their potential. Typically they tell us that these needs and their relationships are universal and apply to everyone, irrespective of culture. However most acknowledge that the preferred way of meeting these needs will vary according to the availability of local resources and the personal and cultural values of the individual.

Here are a few of the different perspectives on needs:

Abraham Maslow made a helpful and influential contribution to understanding what human needs are when he articulated his *Theory of Human Motivation* (1943). This theory suggests we are all driven by a desire to fulfil our potential. According to Maslow this desire is deeply entrenched in the human psyche and our behaviour is to a significant degree motivated by our striving to fulfil particular needs that are arranged in a hierarchy from the bottom up until a state of self-actualization—of fulfilling one's potential—is reached.

Starting at the most basic level, he suggests the foundations to reaching this pinnacle arise from our ability to meet our physiological needs. We require adequate air, water, sufficient nutrients, sleep and adequate shelter to maintain life. Once we have these we can focus on our second needs category: safety and security. This need is only met when our lives are not blighted by fear of assault, accident or disruption. The third needs category is 'belongingness and love', which comes from being able to experience the support of friends, a family,

Figure 2.1 Maslow's Hierarchy Suggests Meeting a Higher Order Need is Dependent on Fulfilling All the Needs Below It. Failure to Meet a Need Precludes the Possibility of Achieving Self-fulfilment.

a community, and 'having roots'. When these needs are also met it allows us to address our fourth needs category, which is esteem—an individual's sense of competence in their actions and confidence that their contribution to the world is respected. The fifth and final needs category is self-actualization. This happens when an individual or community no longer needs to worry about the needs categories lower down the hierarchy and they are therefore free to concentrate on making maximum use of his or her or their individual gifts and interests "*to become everything that one is capable of becoming*" (adapted from Hagerty 1999).

In this view failure to meet one category of needs is a barrier to going higher up the hierarchy and by extension the undermining of a basic need denies us our ability to meet a higher need (Figure 2.1). Therefore the loss of a basic physiological need such as adequate food compromises an individual's or a group's ability to function at any of the higher levels.

When this occurs, their ability to transcend self-interest and apply creativity to address the problems of the wider community is denied; a perspective that might be summed up with the traditional Burmese saying, "*a full gut supports moral precepts*".

However whilst this theory has proved influential and helpful to generations of social scientists, planners and others seeking to support people to fulfil their potential, it has only received "*moderate experimental support*" according to Hagerty (1999).

One of the experiments to test Maslow's theory was an extensive study undertaken by Gallup World Poll from 2005 to 2010 "*in each of eight sociocultural regions of the world—from Europe to Africa to Latin America. The poll included rural and poor populations that have been under-represented in past studies of subjective wellbeing.*" This poll was authored by psychologists Ed Diener and Louis Tay, who examined the association between need fulfilment and subjective well-being. They concluded that Maslow's theory was right in that there are human needs that apply regardless of culture and they all need to be met for a person to enjoy a sense of well-being (Diener and Tay 2011). However they questioned the relationship and order between the different needs categories. They suggested that rather than being arranged in a hierarchy, all the needs are important all the time. They qualified this by recognizing that although the most basic needs might get the most attention when you don't have them, you don't need to fulfil them completely in order to focus on meeting other needs and enjoying the benefits that come from these. For example people can still benefit from love and companionship even if they are hungry.

Their study also emphasized the importance of satisfying needs at the societal level, not simply at the individual level. They found that across diverse regions of the world, "*it is beneficial to live in a society with others who have their needs fulfilled. Improving one's own life is not enough; society-wide improvement is also required*" (Diener and Tay 2011).

Another helpful perspective on the nature of needs is provided by economist Ian Gough. Like Abraham Maslow, he suggests needs are universal; in other words these needs are shared by everyone, irrespective of culture. However he didn't organize them in a hierarchy nor does he share Maslow's view that human behaviour is motivated primarily by a rational desire to meet our needs. Gough suggested that the harm that derives from not meeting needs might be described "*as an impediment to successful social participation*" (2000), which is an affront to social justice in that it denies people the opportunities that arise from that participation and denies society the benefits.

Ian Gough proposed the basic needs or 'universal prerequisites' to avoid this outcome are physical health and autonomy. A degree of physical health above mere survival is necessary to give a person the ability to do the things they need to do to meet their needs. "*But that is not enough. Humans, distinct from other species, also exhibit autonomy of agency; the capacity to make informed choices about what should be done and how to go about doing it.*" He goes on to say this autonomy can be compromised by poor cognitive skills and be blocked by limits placed on an individual's opportunities to engage in social participation (Gough 2004).

Consequently he adds the need for critical autonomy. This might be seen as the ability to challenge and overcome these blocks to social participation. It is the capacity to criticize the way life is lived "*and if necessary, to act to change it. This more dynamic type of participation requires a second-order level of critical autonomy*" (2004). Critical autonomy is about going beyond the limitations of the culture of which an individual is a part and making change happen if needed.

Thus, in his view, physical health, autonomy and critical autonomy provide the foundations for needs fulfilment. If they are not present then it is not possible for an individual to sustainably meet their needs. He suggests that if people are to meet these needs for physical health and autonomy, they needed 11 'universal satisfier characteristics', irrespective of their cultural practices and values. These he described as:

- adequate nutritional food;
- adequate water;
- adequate protective housing;
- non-hazardous work;
- non-hazardous physical environments;
- appropriate healthcare;
- security in childhood;
- significant primary relationships;
- physical and economic security;
- safe birth control and childbearing; and
- appropriate basic and cross-cultural education.

He stated that these needs are not substitutable in that if a need is not being met it cannot be substituted with more of another need: "*more education is of no help to someone who is starving*" (Gough 2014). All 11 are essential to protect the health and autonomy of people and thus to enable them to participate to the maximum extent in society. When this happens Gough states that it is then possible for them to enjoy "*minimally disabled social participation"* which will in turn allow them to enjoy *"critical participation in chosen form of life"*, a state he describes as liberation (Gough 2000). He recognizes that these might be achieved in a number of ways, influenced by culture and history. What contributes to *"adequate nutritional food"* for example will be interpreted differently in different cultures.

Another insightful perspective on needs is offered by Chilean economist Manfred Max Neef. Although his framework was formulated with specific reference to Chile, its expressed focus on universal needs, his commitment to *"Human Scale Development"* and its synergies with the values that underlie this book warrant its inclusion here. He describes Human Scale Development as *"focused and based on the satisfaction of fundamental human needs"*. When any of these needs are not met, a *"human poverty"* will result which *"generates pathologies"* (1991), specifiable and largely predictable outcomes that diminish people's lives. Avoiding this requires cultivating *"self-reliance, and on the construction of organic articulations of people with nature and technology, of global processes with local activity, of the personal with the social, of planning with autonomy, and of civil society with the state"* (Max Neef 2007). He defines articulation as the *"construction of coherent and consistent relations of balanced interdependence among given elements"* (ibid).

He classifies the fundamental human needs as: subsistence; protection; affection; understanding; participation; recreation (in the sense of leisure, time to reflect or time to relax); creation; identity; and freedom. These needs can be further understood by the things and actions that satisfy those needs and the settings in which they occur. He stresses that there *"is no one-to-one correspondence between needs and satisfiers"*. An activity that satisfies a need *"may contribute simultaneously to the satisfaction of different needs, or conversely, a need may require various satisfiers in order to be met"* (1992).

Needs, Wants and Motivation

Needs are something that you have to have. A want is something you would like to have. That is not to say that our wants are somehow less noble but they are less critical. Not meeting a want may be undesirable; not meeting a need will be damaging. Unfortunately we are not always good at appreciating the distinction between the two. Instead of efficiently prioritizing behaviours that meet our needs, we are often distracted by pursuing our wants when we decide what we should do. This is not necessarily a problem in itself. However if in doing so we are distracted from meeting a need or when we deny someone else the ability to meet their needs, then there will be a diminishment of well-being and a 'human poverty' will result. *"One may desire things harmful to need-satisfaction and not desire essential need satisfiers"* according to Ian Gough (2014). He uses an example from his own life: *"I want a cigarette but I need to give up smoking"* (Gough 2000). He adds elsewhere: *"The idea that individuals are the sole authority in judging the correctness of their wants is severely compromised if there are limits to people's knowledge and/or limits to their rationality in judging the correct means to their chosen ends"* (2014). In other words sometimes we make the wrong choices.

Manfred Max Neef provides some insightful analysis about how our attempts to meet particular needs and desires affects our ability to satisfy other needs (Max Neef 1991).

Synergic satisfiers are behaviours that allow us to satisfy a particular need whilst contributing to the fulfilment of other needs. An example would be education, which assists a person's understanding but also supports them to participate, create and explore their own identity.

Singular satisfiers only meet a single need. They are largely neutral to other needs and include things such as soup kitchens that satisfy the need for subsistence but little else.

However according to Max Neef (1991) there are also many behaviours that diminish a person's ability to meet their needs. He categorizes these as:

Destroyers. These are the qualities, things, actions and settings that seek to meet a need but impair our ability to meet another need. "*These paradoxical satisfiers seem to be related particularly to the need for protection.*" Max Neef states that a defining characteristic of these violators is that they are invariably imposed on people by other people. He cites the example of the arms race that places demands on societies that inhibit people from "*meeting their needs of freedom, participation and creation*".

Pseudo-Satisfiers. These are those things that generate a false sense of satisfaction of a given need. They distract people from meeting their needs and may "*annul, in the not too long term, the possibility of satisfying the need they were originally aimed at fulfilling*". Their main attribute is that they are generally induced through propaganda, advertising or other means of persuasion. He uses the example of status symbols that seem to meet the need for identity but in fact subvert it. Caffeinated drinks that give people the illusion of quenching their thirst but in fact are diuretics would also fit into this category.

Inhibiting Satisfiers. These are those things that over-satisfy a given need and inhibit us from satisfying other needs. "*With some exceptions, they share the attribute of originating in deep-rooted customs, habits and rituals.*" He states an over-protective family would be an example of this, shielding their children from harm but limiting their ability to develop to their full potential.

These insights seem to go some way to explaining why so many needs go unmet even in wealthy societies. It seems that sometimes despite their fundamental importance to us we find needs satisfaction relatively unappealing or at least less pressing than other ways of spending our time. An example of this might be found in the number of unused gym memberships. In the UK only 27 per cent of gym members regularly go to the gym (Market Research World, 2005). Assumedly the other 73 per cent recognized the need for exercise but found that it never gets to the top of their list of priorities.

Most people would agree that good health and the ability to connect with other people are amongst those things essential to support people's well-being. However there is a wealth of evidence which suggests that despite this awareness people have been systematically making decisions that have the effect of making them less physically active (Australian Government Department of Health 2011) and fray their social connections (Putnam 1995) (Figure 2.2). This accords with the evaluation by Charles Montgomery that "*our brains are pushed and pulled by the powerful synergy of memory, culture and images*" (2013) that inform our choices about what our priorities are, sometimes in ways that are adverse to our well-being.

A Loose Framework for Understanding Human Needs in the Compassionate City

For this book I have adopted and adapted Manfred Max Neef's framework. This framework provides a very helpful pair of spectacles by which we might view cities and specific

Figure 2.2 Competing Influences and Outcomes in Our Lives, Meeting Needs May Be More Challenging in the Short Term But More Beneficial in the Long Run.

interventions and assess how well they help or hinder those affected by our work from meeting their needs. In particular:

- It helpfully links needs with the actions and settings that people require to meet these needs.
- It offers insights into the effectiveness of particular actions at meeting needs
- It offers a framework for understanding the implications of not meeting a need.

It recognizes needs as having both quantitative (e.g. nutrition, warmth) and qualitative (e.g. privacy/affection/leisure) dimensions. Thus recognizing that quality of life is something that in part has to be personally determined. We can't *tell* people they are happy, an interpretation that might be made of some of the other frameworks.

It recognizes that these needs are not bound in a hierarchy with the exception of meeting needs that are a pre-requisite for maintaining life (e.g. food, shelter, protection). These will take precedence when they are threatened. Hence it addresses the criticism of Maslow's hierarchy of needs that placed them all in a rigid and unchanging hierarchy.

In recognizing that all of these needs have to be met to avoid a diminishment of human potential, it shares one of the main strengths of Maslow's hierarchy.

Furthermore, to my eyes, Max Neef's framework best reflects the richness of human existence and the diversity of inputs that contribute to health and well-being amongst the frameworks reviewed. In particular it recognizes the importance of connecting with one another beyond the significant primary relationships suggested by Gough. On a practical level these broad connections, offering *"sturdy norms of reciprocity"* according to Robert Putnam (1995), enable us to help others, to ask for help, to co-operate and fill in the gaps of our own abilities. But perhaps most importantly they are intrinsically essential to our well-being and are a need in themselves, quite apart from what other needs they facilitate people to meet. *"Man is man's greatest joy"* to quote an Icelandic saga referenced by Jan Gehl, who added: *"which succinctly describes man's delight and interest in other people"* (Gehl 2010). Palich and Edmonds (2013) quote Kelly et al. (2012), finding *"that being socially and culturally connected is so important for health and wellbeing and that, 'for many people, improved relationships are a much more realistic path to a better life than increased income'."* Furthermore Max Neef's framework's emphasis on people and places reflects the observations (which can be made at almost any community engagement event) that this need to connect has two dimensions. These are vertical connections: the connection with one's surroundings; the roots that one puts down in a place and horizontal connections; the links between people who share that place.

His framework explicitly recognizes that there is an interplay between the different things we do to meet our needs. Some of these activities incidentally support us to meet other needs (attending school can simultaneously support needs for understanding, participation, creation and identity, for example), some activities don't really meet the need we think they do (drinking coffee to quench our thirst) and some activities meet one need at the expense of our ability to meet others (security measures that preclude the ability of people to connect with one another). Consequently it suggests we shouldn't look at a need in isolation and ideally we should consider how our choices about how we meet a particular need may help or hinder us from meeting other needs.

The next strength of Max Neef's framework over the others explored in this chapter is the emphasis it gives to the critical role of self-expression in enabling people to satisfy their needs. Self-expression allows an individual to realize their uniqueness, to explore their capacities and manifest their beliefs and values. To deny this, impose or assume a uniform set of behaviours on everyone self-evidently diminishes their ability to participate and contribute to society.

Finally Max Neef's framework emphasizes the importance of freedom and creativity. This aligns with the critical role of these factors in supporting 'community resilience' as identified by Ealy (undated). After all, it is the adaptable rather than the well adapted that survive (to paraphrase Charles Darwin). Circumstances change and will call upon us to address emerging threats (such as climate change and peak oil) that may impose change on urban communities and be socially damaging. This echoes Ian Gough's suggestion that critical autonomy is also needed and this will allow us to formulate new ways to fulfil our needs when old ways become difficult or inappropriate.

Amending the Needs Framework for Designing the Compassionate City

Whilst very useful and insightful, when viewed with specifically urban design eyes it is apparent that the description of the activities and settings that might meet these needs could be slightly refined and the framework amended.

The main additions I have suggested are the explicit inclusion of the need to be active, the need to experience beauty, the need to play/have fun and the need to experience nature.

We were designed to move. Not moving enough brings with it profound impacts that diminish the quality of our lives and expose us to many health risks (Australian Institute of Health and Welfare 2012). "*Immobility is to the human body what rust is to the classic car,*" as Charles Montgomery (2013) puts it. Max Neef's framework can be interpreted as suggesting that activity would be incidental to meeting many of his needs' categories; however in the amended framework it is suggested that it is an end in itself.

"*Man cannot live without beauty,*" according to Albert Camus (1948). It is considered self-evident that experiencing beauty is 'good for the soul' and nourishes people on a profound level. It presence inspires us and its absence diminishes us. In a report from the UK it was found that "*the appreciation of beauty is something that is much valued by the public—in one poll, 81% of those surveyed responded that everyone should be able to experience beauty regularly, with only 3% disagreeing*" (House of Lords 2016). As to what beauty is, Diessner et al. (2008) suggested it has many expressions and can be experienced in nature, in the artefacts we make and in how we interact with one another. Philosophers have argued which of these take precedence (Diessner et al. 2008) but it is not for this book to take a position on this argument, merely to acknowledge they are all important.

That beauty can be found in nature is considered to need no further explanation. For evidence of the power and importance of experiencing artistic beauty we need only look at the millions of tourists who feel drawn to invest a significant proportion of their time and income to be awed by the highest achievements of art, architecture and culture in London, Paris, New York, Prague, Venice or many other cities around the world.

For evidence of the power and importance of experiencing moral beauty we can look to personal impacts of kindnesses received or offered and the inspiration of brave and principled men and women in the news and history books. Diessner et al. (2008) quote Haidt (2003), who found that experience of moral beauty

> triggers a distinctive feeling in the chest of warmth and expansion; it causes a desire to become a better person oneself; and it seems to open one's heart, not only to the person who triggered the feeling but also to other people.

Another significant addition to the framework is 'play and fun' as an activity that is critical to meeting needs. Having fun is important at all stages in life but is of critical importance to a child's development. According to David Lloyd George (quoted in Hewes 2007): "*The right to play is the child's first claim on the community. Play is nature's training for life. No community can infringe that right without doing enduring harm to the minds and bodies of its citizens*". Play England observed, "*Play enables children to form friendships and attachments to adults and to places, allowing for the development of familiarity and intimacy with both. It can provide opportunities for independent learning and building confidence, resilience, self-esteem and self-efficacy*" (2012). Play facilitates intellectual development, such as improved creativity and imagination, and improves academic performance (Gray 2013). Einstein attributed his innovative work to the creativity born of playing (Stevens 2014).

Consequently if a child is denied a rich and active play life, their ability to thrive and develop to their fullest potential is diminished (White 2004) and with it their ability to contribute to their community. Play is innate in children and will happen whenever circumstances allow (Clements 2004; Van der Burgt and Gustafson 2013) (Figures 2.3, 2.4). However there are many pressures in urban living that act to stifle that urge (Clements 2004; Planet Ark 2011). This addition to the framework of needs requires us to design settings that release children (and adults) from these deterrents and "*let the play out*" (according to Paul Longridge, Clinical Health Planner and Mark Mitchell, Architect with Billard Leese Architects, in personal correspondence 2014).

Figure 2.3 Play Is Innate and Will Happen Anywhere Children See an Opportunity 1
Source: photograph courtesy of Gregory Dunn (www.stoneybutter.com)

Figure 2.4 Play Is Innate and Will Happen Anywhere Children See an Opportunity 2
Source: photograph courtesy of Judy Schwartz Haley

The final main amendment to the framework emphasizes the critical role of experiencing nature as a means of supporting physical and emotional health (Maas et al. 2009) and helping us to deal with many of the stressors of urban life (Khazan 2015). Richard Louv (2010) and Ray Green (pers. corr. 2015) suggest this is a core need because we are hardwired by evolution to find comfort in nature. Ray Green adds this is an echo of our hunter-gatherer forebears who needed to be near trees, water and vegetation where food and shelter could be found (ibid). Furthermore the absence of nature brings with it a range of negative

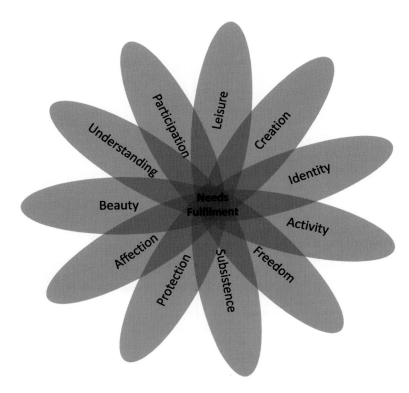

Figure 2.5 Needs Satisfaction in the Compassionate City
Source: adapted from Max Neef (2007)

consequences for children that Richard Louv (2010) described as 'nature deficit disorder'. These problems include depression and obesity and it denies children the stimulation and experience of setting and meeting challenges (and learning from when they fail to meet them) that are a critical part of learning and growing. This importance of nature in our lives reflects the sentiment of English artist Antony Gormley, reported by Tom Silverstone et al. in *The Guardian* (2015): "*human nature only makes sense in relation to nature, feeling the seasons and the elements*".

The amended framework (Figure 2.5) also:

- Recognizes that subsistence requires adequate water and air as much as food and these things are made explicit as 'needs satisfiers'. Furthermore the need for protection is taken to also mean protection from environmental contaminants and hence an action (at least part of the time) to help satisfy the need for protection is remediation/filtration.
- Assumes that many of these needs will be facilitated by people getting together which (still) requires places where this can happen. Hence the framework incorporates references to 'shared and valued places' in the list of settings where needs satisfaction occurs.
- Recognizes the importance of competence as a quality necessary to meet any of these needs, reflecting the underlying philosophy of cultivating the circumstances where people can meet their own needs.

Amended Needs Framework for the Compassionate City

Table 2.1 Needs and Needs Satisfiers

Fundamental Human Needs	Needs Satisfiers			
	Being (qualities)	*Having (things)*	*Doing (actions)*	*Interacting (settings)*
Subsistence	Physical and mental health, *competence*	Food, shelter work, *water, air, sleep*	Feed, clothe, rest, work, grow and prepare food, breast feed	Living environment, social setting, places to rest, fields, farms, gardens
Physical activity	Physical and mental health	Safety, rule of law	Walk, play, run, cycle, exercise, games	Footpaths, streets, playing fields, parks
Protection	Care, adaptability, autonomy, competence	Social and familial security, health systems, work, *safety, rule of law*	Co-operate, plan, take care of, *be active*, help, keep safe, *remediate, filter, escape/respite*	Living environment, social environment, dwelling, *nature*
Affection	Respect, sense of humour, generosity, sensuality, *belonging, competence*	Friendships, family, relationships with nature, place	Empathize, share experiences and activities, take care of, make love, express emotions	Private places intimate spaces of togetherness, *valued, shared spaces*
Understanding	Critical capacity, curiosity, intuition, competence	Literature, teachers, educational policies	Analyze, study, meditate, investigate, play/ explore, *experience, recognition/feedback*	Schools, families, universities, communities, shared spaces, *nature, places of gathering*
Participation	Receptiveness, dedication, sense of humour, competence	Responsibilities, duties, work, rights	Co-operate, *share*, dissent, express opinions, play	Associations, parties, places of gathering, neighbourhoods, *public spaces, teams/clubs*
Leisure	Imagination, tranquillity, spontaneity, competence, *respite*	Games, parties, peace of mind	Day-dream, remember, relax, *have fun*, play	Landscapes, intimate spaces, places to be alone, *places to share, nature*
Creation	Imagination, boldness, inventiveness, curiosity, competence	Abilities, skills, work, techniques	*Manifest*, invent, build, design, work, play compose, interpret, *fun/play*	Spaces for interaction and inspiration expression, workshops, audiences
Identity	Sense of belonging, self-esteem, consistency, competence	Language, religions, work, customs, values, norms,	Experience, explore, get to know oneself and surroundings, grow, commit oneself, set challenges, play	Places one belongs to, *places of ritual, landmarks and icons* everyday settings

(Continued)

Table 2.1 Continued

Fundamental Human Needs	Needs Satisfiers			
	Being (qualities)	*Having (things)*	*Doing (actions)*	*Interacting (settings)*
Freedom	Autonomy, passion, self-esteem, open-mindedness, competence, *choice*	Equal rights	Dissent, choose, run risks, develop awareness, *play, change your circumstances*	Anywhere
Beauty	Critical capacity, choice	Sense of Aesthetics	Connect with, experience, opportunity and ability to interpret surroundings	Nature, spaces of interaction and inspiration

(Adapted from www.rainforestinfo.org.au/background/maxneef.htm)
Elements amended from Max Neef's framework (2007) are italicized

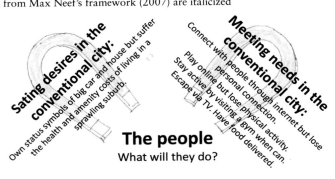

Figure 2.6 Motivational Magnets
Source: adapted from Howard (1902)

What Does This Mean for Urban Designers?

The framework in the previous section broadly relates the things we all need to be, the things we all need to have and the actions we all need to do to meet our needs. If as designers we are aware of these needs and the things that will help people meet their needs, we can look critically on emerging designs and ask ourselves how will they help or hinder people to meet their needs. If our plans fail to help people to meet their needs or hinder them then we can ask ourselves how this outcome is justified.

Furthermore, as explored in the 'Needs, Wants and Motivation' section earlier in this chapter, people are not always well equipped to judge what is best for them. Our ability to identify and act to satisfy our needs is compromised by distractions to respond to a range of desires and wants that also clamour for our attention (Figure 2.6). The messages we get from the world around us invites us to do things that may not be good for us or the people we share our surroundings with (to drive instead of walk for example). If we as designers are to avoid being accomplices in this process we must make sure the qualities we give a place make behaviours that satisfy needs relatively more attractive than behaviours that don't.

The framework also raises questions about what are good 'living environments', 'social settings' or 'places of gathering'? How do we embody beauty into our shared surroundings, etc.? Responding to these challenges calls for more than just functional responses informed by technical and quantitative standards; it requires us to delve into the qualities embodied in our urban spaces and understand the influence they hold over us. The following chapter looks at the mechanisms by which these messages are embedded in the built environment and some of the factors that influence how strongly we are swayed by what they are telling us to do.

References

Australian Government Department of Health (2011) The Health Consequences of Physical Inactivity and the Benefits of Physical Activity 2011. Accessed July 2016, www.health.gov.au/internet/publications/publishing.nsf/Content/phd-physical-rec-older-disc~chapter-3

Australian Institute of Health and Welfare (2012) *Risk Factors Contributing to Chronic Disease.* Accessed June 2016, www.aihw.gov.au/WorkArea/DownloadAsset.aspx?id=10737421546

Clements, R (2004) An investigation of the status of outdoor play. *Contemporary Issues in Early Childhood* 5(1): 68–80. Accessed July 2016, www.imaginationplayground.com/images/content/2/9/2960/An-investigation-Of-The-Status-Of-Outdoor-Play.pdf

Diener, E, and Tay, L (2011) Needs and subjective well-being around the world. *Journal of Personality and Social Psychology* 101(2): 354–65. Accessed June 2016, www.ncbi.nlm.nih.gov/pubmed/21688922

Diessner, R, Solom, R, Frost, N, Parsons, L, and Davidson, J (2008) Engagement with beauty: Appreciating natural, artistic, and moral beauty. *The Journal of Psychology* 142(3): 303–29. Accessed July 2016, www.ncbi.nlm.nih.gov/pubmed/18589939

Doyal, L, and Gough, I (1991) *A Theory of Human Need.* New York: Guilford.

Ealy, L (undated) *Co-ordinates of Resilience.* Accessed December 2011, http://localknowledge.mercatus.org/articles/coordinates-of-resilience

Gehl, J (2010) *Cities for People.* Island Press.

Gough, I (2000) *Global Capital, Human Needs and Social Policies: Selected Essays.* Palgrave.

Gough, I (2004) Human well-being and social structures: Relating the universal and the local. *Global Social Policy* 4(3): 289–311. ISSN 1468-0181

Gough, I (2014) *Climate Change and Sustainable Welfare: An Argument for the Centrality of Human Needs.* Centre for Analysis of Social Exclusion (CASE) Papers; #182. London School of Economics.

Gray, P (2013) *Free to Learn: Why Unleashing the Instinct to Play Will Make Our Children Happier, Self-Reliant, and Better Students for Life.* New York: Basic Books.

Green, R (2015) *Personal Correspondence.*

Hagerty, MR (1999) Testing Maslow's hierarchy of needs: National quality-of-life across time. *Social Indicators Research* 46(3): 249–71. www.jstor.org/stable/27522372

Haidt, J (2003) The moral emotions. In RJ Davidson, KR Scherer, and HH Goldsmith (Eds.) *Handbook of Affective Sciences* (pp. 852–70). Oxford: Oxford University Press.

Hewes, J (2007) *Back to Basics, the Right to Play.* Connections 11–2, 1–4. Accessed January 2016 http://www.cccns.org/pdf/11.2.web.pdf

House of Lords (2016) *Building Better Places, a Report of Select Committee on National Policy for the Built Environment*. HL Paper 100, House of Lords.

Howard, E (1902) *Garden Cities of Tomorrow*. London: S. Sonnenschein & Co., Ltd.

Kelly, J-F, Breadon, P, Davis, C, Hunter, A, Mares, P, Mullerworth, D, and Weidmann, B (2012) *Social Cities*. Melbourne: Grattan Institute.

Khazan, O (2015) How walking in nature prevents depression. *The Atlantic*, June 30, 2015. Accessed January 2017, www.theatlantic.com/health/archive/2015/06/how-walking-in-nature-prevents-depression/397172/

Longridge, P, and Mitchell, M (2014) *Personal Correspondence*.

Louv, R (2010) *Last Child in the Woods*. London: Atlantic Books.

Maas, J, Verheij, RA, de Vries, S, Spreeuwenberg, P, Schellevis, FG, and Groenewegen, PP (2009) Morbidity is related to a green living environment. *Journal of Epidemiology and Community Health*. 63: 967–73.

Market Research World (2005) *The Guide to Gym Memberships*. Accessed April 2016, www.marketresearchworld.net/content/view/164/

Maslow, A (July 1943) A theory of human motivation. *Psychological Review* 50(4). Accessed January 2016, http://s3.amazonaws.com/academia.edu.documents/34195256/A_Theory_of_Human_Motivation_-_Abraham_H_Maslow__Psychological_Review_Vol_50_No_4_July_1943.pdf?AWSAccessKeyId=AKIAIWOWYYGZ2Y53UL3A&Expires=1490347918&Signature=VWN3T8CxYOSYP27dPTyvaZA8VCQ%3D&response-content-disposition=inline%3B%20filename%3DA_THEORY_OF_HUMAN_MOTIVATION.pdf

Max Neef, M (1991) *Human Scale Development Conception, Application and Further Reflections*. New York: Apex Press.

Max Neef, M (1992) *Real-Life Economics: Understanding Wealth Creation*, edited by P Ekins and M Max Neef. London: Routledge, pp. 197–213.

Max Neef, M (2007) *Development and Human Needs*. www.alastairmcintosh.com/general/resources/2007-Manfred-Max-Neef-Fundamental-Human-Needs.pdf

Montgomery, C (2013) *Happy City*. London: Penguin Books.

Nuttall, D (2015) *Personal Correspondence*.

Palich, N, and Edmonds, A (2013) *Social Sustainability: Creating Places and Participatory Processes that Perform Well for People*. EDG 78, Australian Institute of Architects.

Planet Ark (2011) *Climbing Trees: Getting Aussie Kids Back Outdoors*. Accessed June 2016, http://treeday.planetark.org/documents/doc-534-climbing-trees-research-report-2011-07-13-final.pdf

Play England (2012) *A World Without Play*. www.playengland.org.uk/media/371031/a-world-withoutplay-literature-review-2012.pdf

Putnam, RD (1995) Bowling alone: America's declining social capital. *Journal of Democracy* 6(1): 65–78. Accessed July 2016, www.directory-online.com/Rotary/Accounts/6970/Downloads/4381/Bowling%20Alone%20Article.pdf

Silverstone, T, Gormley, J, Riddell, J, Michael, C, Payne-Frank' N, Gerstein, B, and theguardian.com (2015) *Antony Gormley: 'London Is Bought, Developed and Abandoned'—Video*. Accessed November 2016, www.theguardian.com/cities/video/2015/oct/22/antony-gormley-london-squatted-how-things-changed-video

Stevens, V (2014) To think without thinking: The implications of combinatory play and the creative process for Neuroaesthetics. *American Journal of Play* 7(1). Accessed January 2016, www.journalofplay.org/sites/www.journalofplay.org/files/pdf-articles/7-1-article-to-think-without-thinking.pdf

Van der Burgt, D, and Gustafson, K (2013) 'Doing time' and 'creating space': A case study of outdoor play and institutionalized leisure in an urban family. *Children, Youth and Environments*, 23(3): 24–42. http://uu.divaportal.org/smash/get/diva2:616256/FULLTEXT03.pdf

White, R (2004) *Young Children's Relationship With Nature: Its Importance to Children's Development & the Earth's Future*. White Hutchinson Leisure & Learning Group. Accessed May 2016, www.whitehutchinson.com/children/articles/childrennature.shtml

3 Embedding and Receiving the Messages in the Urban Environment

Living in villages, towns or cities, we are constantly exposed to and interpreting the messages we receive from our surroundings. These messages frame the possibilities of being in that place by suggesting to people what they can and can't do, should or shouldn't do, and hint at what other people might do (Montgomery 2013). Some of these messages are strident warnings about what might happen to people if they enter or leave that place and other messages are subtle invitations to participate in particular activities or suggest that some activities are conditional (Figure 3.1).

Effectively the people who put these messages there are conversing with other people in a language of brick, stone, steel, glass and wood that is interpreted through filters of the media, past personal experiences, values and emotions.

This language is complex and each of us interpret and use it slightly differently. Some of us may choose to ignore these messages or are impervious to the judgement they might receive by doing something unexpected (for example walking in a car-dominated area, breastfeeding in public or letting your children play outside). Others may feel compelled—at least at a subconscious level—to pay heed to what they understand their surroundings are telling or advising them to do.

Furthermore places give off mixed messages and the way we weigh up these messages will depend on many variables. For example if someone is tired or otherwise needing a seat urgently, they may find the invitation offered by the seat illustrated in Figure 3.2 to be perfectly fine. However if they are less tired or just more sensitive to their surroundings, they may find the very exposed position unappealing and choose to continue looking for a place to rest elsewhere. Consequently if the language of urbanity is to be used to communicate helpful messages that enable people to participate in and contribute to society, then we need to understand how we can converse in it and how other people interpret it.

This chapter looks at how these messages are embedded into the built and social environment, suggests the mechanisms by which they are broadcast and the strength they are received.

Embedding Messages in Our Surroundings

> *A City's environment is shaped not only by people who have an important influence, but by everyone who lives or work there.*
>
> —Robert Cowan

The players that influence the relationship between people and place can be generalized into three overlapping groups: government, civil society and industry. Those in the government

Figure 3.1 Subtly Hinted Behaviours and Conditional Invitations

grouping typically set the political context within which things happen and define the legislative and administrative landscape for interventions. This grouping includes elected or appointed office holders such as councillors and parliamentarians and the civil servants who implement their decisions and act on their authority. Civil society are the users of the space. These are the public who look to towns, cities and villages to provide them, their families and neighbours with the qualities and opportunities that enable them to meet their needs. The industry grouping comprises the professionals and others involved in producing and managing the space. The people in this grouping are the developers, architects, urban designers, planners, landscape architects and engineers of various types (to name but a few). Although these groups overlap (for example architects and planners who live in an area they work within are both producers and users of their neighbourhood), each group will see the world differently. They are likely to be subject to differing constraints, face different issues and are likely to draw different conclusions about what represents improvement (Rapoport 1982).

Figure 3.2 Mixed Messages: The Passer-by Is Invited to Sit by the Thoughtful Provision of a Seat and Discouraged From Sitting by the Surroundings of That Seat

Formal and Informal Influencers

From this perspective the governmental grouping and the industry grouping have formal status and responsibilities to make changes to the built environment. In many countries the government groupings legitimacy is derived from a democratic process (for elected representatives) or is conditional on the authority delegated of these elected representatives (in the case of their civil servants). The power of those in the industry grouping to make changes to other people's surroundings is framed by the government grouping through licencing, education and training. In most countries in the developed world both government and industry are bound by safeguards and rules that define limits to what they can do and ensure particular standards are met. Ideally both groupings have the capacity and responsibility to consider their impacts on the world around them.

However the government and industry groupings are not the only force acting on the built and social environment. All of the people who share the urban environment help to create it, deliberately or accidently moulding the settings within which other people lead their lives to varying degrees *"just as electricity is equally present in a storm with deafening thunder and blinding lightning and in the operation of a pocket flashlight"*, to draw on an unnamed Russian academic quoted in Vygotsky (2004).

Many of these interventions are made at a level untouched by the formal rules or co-ordinating capacity of most planning systems. Nonetheless these apparently small actions can make a big difference to people's quality of life and their experience of the world around them (Jay Walljasper and Project for Public Spaces 2007). By doing things such as choosing not to litter, clearing snow, planting a tree or tending a flower bed visible from a footpath and inspiring others to do likewise, we influence other people's experience of that public space. Furthermore just by walking through a street and offering the unspoken reassurance of being someone who may intervene and help if someone else needs assistance, we can make streets feel safer. In this way our presence can help to lift someone else's burden of fear. By sharing places we also create the possibility of connecting with other people and give them a boost through a kindness or the offer of support. "*An uplifting conversation that introduces hope and joy into the morning may influence physical activity, healthy food selection, or the choice to engage further in proactive social relationships later in the day or week*" (Qualls 2014).

On the other hand, other small and often unconsidered actions can create subliminal messages that accumulate to have very detrimental impacts on other people's lives. Footpath parking can force people up and down off kerbs, which might be inconvenient for some but prohibitively difficult for those in wheelchairs or pushing strollers. The understandable desire for privacy and security can lead to a response to surround private property with tall blank walls. However, in attempting to improve safety in one's personal space, the quality and utility of the surrounding public space can be diminished, as noted by Manfred Max Neef (Chapter 2). The Commission for Architecture and the Built Environment (CABE) in the UK has argued that over emphasis on security "*can result in bland and standardised places, designed for the exception or the worst-case scenario, rather than the norm*" (CABE 2008). Furthermore such security-orientated interventions can cultivate a risk-focussed mentality. As Charles Montgomery observed (2013), by creating places that aren't overlooked, we increase the chances of someone standing in such an environment as being perceived as threatening.

The equally understandable desire to facilitate our personal mobility through car travel and enjoy the benefits of living in a large-footprint house with multi-space garages contributes to the demand for low-density suburbs fractured by wide roads with fast but often congested traffic. Such places require us to drive or be driven and in doing so contribute to the demand for ever-larger roads and car parks. This increases the burden of traffic on the streets that carry all these passing vehicles. The noise, intrusion, pollution and risk this brings will (amongst other things) make it more difficult for people living on these busy roads to form friendships. A study in Bristol in the UK by Joshua Hart and Professor Graham Parkhurst (2011) found that residents on such streets have less than one-quarter the number of local friends than those living on similar streets with little traffic, reflecting the findings of the influential 1969 San Francisco study by Professor Donald Appleyard. Even though it was not the intention of any of these drivers to adversely impact on other people's quality of life, it is still the outcome.

Our Sensitivity to the Messages Embodied in Our Surroundings

The degree to which our figurative antennae are tuned to receive the messages that we get from our surroundings is influenced by a number of factors (Table 3.1) (adapted from Porteous 1990).

Table 3.1 Summary of the Factors That Influence Our Sensitivity to the Messages Embedded in Our Surroundings

Personal circumstances, experiences and values	The conclusions we draw about the messages we get from our surroundings will depend on who we are and what we are feeling at the time
The way we pass through a place	What we are influenced by will depend on whether we experience a place on foot, bicycle or by vehicle
Personal capacities	Opportunities that are prohibitively challenging are unlikely to be taken up
Distance	The further away messages are, the less they will influence us, as a rule
Physical context	What else is going on in our immediate surroundings will change our sense of whether we have to take heed of the message or not
Emotional investment	Messages in places we care more about will have a bigger impact on us
The extent to which we are present in a place	The less a place intrudes on our consciousness, the less it influences our choices
The social landscape	We are strongly influenced by the expected behaviour of others in a place and the emotional responses these expectations provoke in us

Personal Circumstances, Experiences and Values

Immediate personal circumstances play an important role in how we interpret our surroundings. For example two people may be walking through a place that they would both normally find interesting but if one of them is cold or hungry, getting warm or finding food is likely to be the focus of their attention and the attractions of their surroundings are more likely to remain unnoticed (Figure 3.3). These influences can often change quickly. A quick snack or putting on a coat can change the way they see their surroundings.

However some of the things that influence our sensitivity to our surroundings relate to more underlying characteristics that change only slowly, if at all, gradually evolving from a composite of genetics, experiences, community values, personal tastes and age, amongst other influences. To look briefly at a few of these factors:

Aging is a lifelong process that slowly changes our experience of the world around us. As we grow up and then grow older, the things that matter to us and the way we perceive our surroundings will change (Lawson 2001).

Figure 3.3 Varied Perceptions of Place

Childhood is a time of learning, exploration and play. As touched upon in Chapter 2, playing is essential for children and the desire to play is innate (Crain 2010). Children are particularly motivated by fun and look at their surroundings with a view to finding the most fun place to be and most fun thing to do. Consequently children will see anywhere they are as a potential playscape, not just parks, schools or other areas dedicated to play but also areas where it is an incidental use, such as at home, in streets, in yards and in public places such as shopping centres. Where this fun can be found is influenced by the way they process information. According to Dr Jim Stone of the University of Sheffield's Department of Psychology, *"children really do see the world differently to the way that adults do, inasmuch as their perceptions seem to be more variable."* This allows them to have a much wider range of interpretations of the things they see, hear, etc. *"No wonder they cannot look at a cloud without seeing it as a dog or a bear, whereas adults tend to see a cloud as a cloud"* (University of Sheffield 2010).

A further factor that influences children's sensitivity to the messages of their surroundings is that their range of inputs are different to adults (Rudner 2013, pers. corr.). Simply not being able to see over fences or over a crowd limits a child's visual catchment and so concentrates what they can see more in their immediate area. Likewise a child's perspective of the world as a pedestrian, from the back seat of a car or as a public transport user (Rudner et al. 2011), influences what they see and with what and whom they interact.

For most children their exposure to the influences of their surroundings is greatly influenced by the bounds established by their parents, teachers and other carers: *"Children start totally dependent. They grow towards independence only with the help of adults"* (UNICEF 2004). Rudner et al. (2011) point out the importance of accessing a wide range of experiences in moving towards this independence. However for many children opportunities to learn and explore are limited, as parents and other adults perceive the world as an increasingly dangerous place. This leads them to discourage independent and unsupervised play (Planet Ark 2011) and curtail the area within which children have permission to roam (Rudner et al. 2011).

To make matters worse, the appeal of the outdoor spaces that children can access and the physical activity these spaces invite is diminishing relative to indoor screen play (Planet Ark 2011). Although children see health benefits as important, they are more attracted by 'unhealthy' activities if they are more fun than 'healthier' activities (Hemmings 2007). As a 5th grader told Richard Louv, *"I like to play indoors better 'cause that's where all the electrical outlets are"* (Louv, 2010).

Approaching the other end of life's journey, we find the way we look on our surroundings changes as our reactions slow down, we move more slowly, our stamina reduces and our bones become less dense and more fragile. Approaching old age, we are less likely to walk from heel to toe, as is characteristic of a younger person (Ko et al. 2010), and when we get older still our gait becomes more of a shuffle (Salzamm 2010). When this happens we slide our feet along the ground and even small interruptions in the surface such as cracks, mooring points for awnings or changes in texture, unnoticed by a younger person, can become a trip hazard for an older person. When we do have accidents we find we heal more slowly and the accumulated impact of a life of too much or too little activity, accidents, poor diet or illness make themselves felt (WHO 2015).

This vulnerability is compounded as the information that we get from our senses about the world around us becomes less reliable. Our hearing, sense of smell, eyesight and field of vision may diminish (Orzech 2007), and cognitive function may decline. These factors progressively obscure our surroundings from us and diminish our ability to deal with

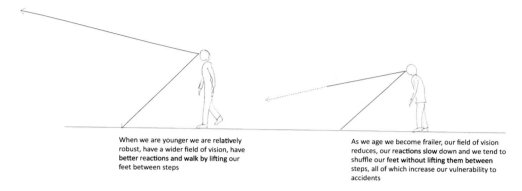

When we are younger we are relatively robust, have a wider field of vision, have **better reactions and walk by lifting** our feet between steps

As we age we become frailer, our field of vision reduces, our reactions slow down and we tend to shuffle our feet without lifting them between steps, all of which increase our vulnerability to accidents

Figure 3.4 Age and Vulnerability

Typical streetscape as interpreted by a younger person

Typical streetscape as interpreted by an older person

Figure 3.5 Changing Perceptions and Sensitivity with Age

unexpected things in our environment such as steps, dog leashes, street furniture, slopes and changes of slope or surface material (Figure 3.4).

Thus we become more susceptible to accidents at the same time as the threat posed by these things grows. Tripping over a dog lead when you are 30 is embarrassing but is unlikely to deter you from going out again. Tripping over a dog lead when you are 70 is a serious matter that is quite likely to require a hospital stay and a long recuperation. This awareness, coupled with an awareness of our diminishing abilities, tells us to be more wary about the risks and difficulties posed by our surroundings (Figure 3.5).

This may cause some—particularly older women (Martin et al. 2005)—to reduce their exposure to risk by staying at home. However by doing so they inadvertently subject themselves to greater risks that come with inactivity and isolation that hastens their physical and cognitive decline (James et al. 2011).

Another key personal factor that influences how people experience the world is their gender. Decisions are made without reference to the perspectives of either gender risk creating places that are biased to one gender over the other, potentially creating a distribution of experiences and opportunities that is unfair to one half of humanity.

Wendy Davis of the Women's Design Service in the UK (quoted in CABE 2008) eloquently sums up the differences that gender can make to the experience of our towns and cities: She states that because *women earn on average half of what men do, form the majority of carers for elderly relations and still do most of the housework and shopping, there is a whole range of issues related to planning, transport, urban design, and housing provision which will impact differently on the sexes.*

She further adds that

women continue to be victims of sexual harassment, domestic violence and rape they will have a radically different experience of what constitutes safety in homes, towns and public spaces. Women live longer than men, which has consequences for poverty in older age, disability and frailty, loneliness and isolation.

Caroline Criado-Perez (2016) offers insight into how even apparently 'non-gendered' management decisions can have a differential impact on men and women. In relation to snow-clearing priorities in the city of Karlskoga, Sweden, she noted, "*By prioritising clearing the roads, the city was prioritising the way men choose to travel, despite the fact that walking or pushing a stroller though 10cm of snow is much harder than driving a car through it.*" This awareness provoked the city to change the order of snow-clearing to focus on the pavements and cycle paths first, particularly around schools. This brought about "*an unexpected by-product, it found a marked decrease in injuries: pedestrians are three times as likely as motorists to be injured in accidents due to slippery conditions*" (ibid).

The Way We Move Through a Place

Our sensitivity to the messages broadcast by our surroundings is also a function of whether we experience a place through a car windscreen or directly: on foot, bicycle or whilst waiting for public transport. In essence driving isolates whereas active transport integrates. When we travel by car, we are enclosed in a steel carapace and travel at speed (at least sometimes) on dedicated infrastructure that is designed to simplify the stimuli to which we are exposed. This is "*the 50km hour environment*" according to Jan Gehl (2006). In such places, separation is key; bumping in to someone else is definitely not something you want to happen.

However walking and cycling (or waiting for public transport) offer an immediacy with one's surroundings and ability to interact with these surroundings that is denied to car users. Handy et al. (2002) suggest that because the pedestrian is exposed to the elements in the way that a driver is not, he or she may be more aware of the sights, sounds, smells and general environment than is the typical motorist and, consequently, is more likely to be influenced by them. For walkers (though less so for cyclists), bumping into someone is much more likely to mean the opportunity to enjoy a chance conversation with a friend or acquaintance.

Of course this immediacy isn't always a good thing. Along with feeling the sun on your face, hearing bird song, smelling the roses/coffee and enjoying interacting with people around the pedestrian or cyclist, he or she is also likely to have heightened safety concerns and a greater sense of vulnerability to extremes of weather than their car-borne neighbour.

Personal Capacities

Different people have different physical and cognitive capacities that affect their sensitivity to their surroundings and their ability to make sense of the messages they are getting from those surroundings. Some people may find their surroundings present them with challenges that would present no problems to someone else. A person who uses a wheelchair may find even the shortest flights of steps to be as insurmountable as a mountain range would be to someone else. A person with cognitive impairment such as dementia may find busy, constantly changing places or places with excessive visual stimuli are overwhelming (Mitchell et al. 2004). They may be less willing to go far from home for fear of getting lost (ibid) which would expose them to "*the sense of anxiety and even terror*" that Kevin Lynch noted (1960) is experienced by many people when they lose their way. Mitchell adds:

> *this fear can be even more debilitating for those with cognitive impairments, who are often unable to find their way home once they are lost, and for carers, who will often discourage the person from going out at all in case they come to harm.*
>
> (Mitchell et al. 2004)

Distance

Our sensitivity to the messages broadcast by our surroundings and the people with whom we share those surroundings is also influenced by distance. In general the further away we are from the source of these messages, the less they are likely to affect us: 'out of sight, out of mind', as the adage goes. However, in reality, the influence a place will have on our relationship to our surroundings will also depend on where it is, what else is distracting us, the significance of the place for us and its impact on other aspects of community life.

Reflecting the influential work of Edward Hall, J Douglas Porteous (1977) tells us each of us have a personal space, an area of vulnerability around our person. If anyone intrudes into that space unbidden, we are likely to find it stressful. Our mind automatically goes into an uncomfortable 'flight or fight' mode that provokes a strong urge to respond, usually by moving away or trying to get the intruder to leave. This desire to ensure a comfortable distance is apparent in social gatherings, queues and on public transport where people will arrange themselves to maintain a distance if at all possible. When circumstances make it impossible to create or maintain a desirable space, such as on a crowded train or in a lift, eye contact tends to be avoided to minimize intrusion and the discomfort that brings. The extent of this personal space varies according to circumstances, cultural norms, gender and age (Porteous 1977), and has been estimated to define a space that is in the range of around 1.2–1.5m from an individual (Werner et al. 1997).

Beyond this vulnerable space, interactions with strangers and acquaintances are likely to be much less stressful and potentially beneficial. This might be considered sharable space. For each of us, this zone of sharable space can be broken down into actively shared space and potentially sharable space (Figure 3.6).

An individual's zone of actively shared space encompasses all the places they are familiar with and the well-trodden paths that take them to and from these places. These are the places where they have laid down memories and have the measure of the opportunities and challenges they offer. They are those parts of their surroundings that are in 'sharp focus' (Porteous 1977). They are significant because of what happens or happened there. These important events can be personal (where they had their first kiss, where their partner proposed, a place of happy or sad memories) or have a collective significance. The latter usually has a physical manifestation, marked by the buildings or uses that are the focal points of collective feeling in any urban community. Such actively shared places are

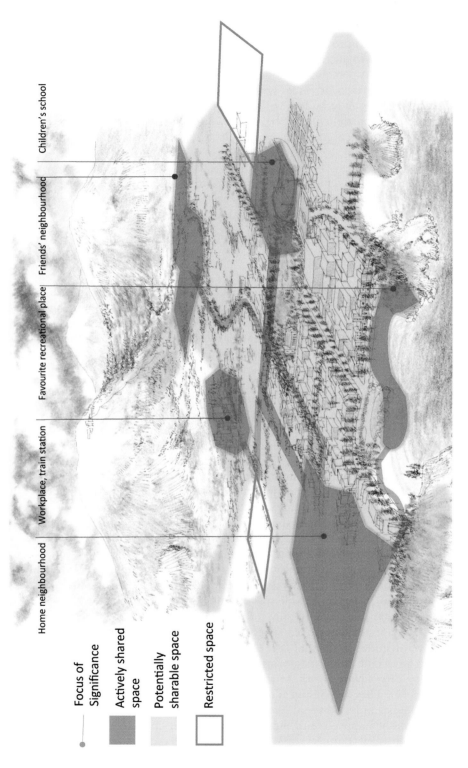

Home neighbourhood Workplace, train station Favourite recreational place Friends' neighbourhood Children's school

Focus of
Significance

Actively shared
space

Potentially
sharable space

Restricted space

Figure 3.6 Shared and Sharable Space

usually places people *know* but sometimes they are places people *know of*. For example the World War I battlefields in Gallipoli, Turkey, have a significance to far more Australians and New Zealanders than those who have actually been there.

An individual's zone of *potentially* sharable space is an amorphous area beyond and between the patchwork of actively shared spaces. This zone and its opportunities are in 'vague focus', as J Douglas Porteous (1977) puts it. They are places we are hazily aware of but haven't yet been to and/or have little interest in, places that aren't on our radar.

Amongst and beyond this collage of actively shared and potentially sharable spaces lies the restricted spaces, places we can't actually occupy. What happens in these places may be objectively significant (for example power stations, sewerage works, water works, nature reserves) but their contribution to our lives does not depend on occupying them; indeed it is usually better if we don't occupy them. Their presence is typically only felt when they fail or where they abut our actively shared space and the walls and fences that protect them visibly impact on our life and create holes in our mental maps of our city.

However, our sensitivity to our surroundings is further nuanced by the way our senses gather information. Our ability to hear sounds drops off with distance. Also our visual acuity is far from uniform. Our ability to perceive shapes, motion and colour varies across the field of view. Shape and detail recognition is concentrated in the centre of our field of vision within a range of about 20–30 degrees binocular view (Nijhuis 2013). Objects in this area are in sharp focus, whereas those on our periphery are more likely to be overlooked. This supports the evidence of experience that (stationary) objects in the centre of our field of vision will have a greater impact on our perception of our surroundings than those nearer but less central to our field of vision.

Context

The extent to which a particular message demands our attention is influenced to a large extent by the context. For example, the absence of a designated pedestrian crossing on a quiet road is unlikely to be interpreted as a deterrent to walking, as the road is not difficult to cross at any point. However the absence of a crossing on a busy road will have a significant effect on the messages received from one's surroundings that may lead someone to conclude they shouldn't walk. Likewise a car parked across a footpath is less of a problem where the road is quiet and the traffic slow (Figure 3.7), but would be a significant issue (and deterrent to walking) if passing it would require a pedestrian to enter into a busy traffic stream to continue their journey. This reflects research from the UK that found that pedestrians don't see traffic as a barrier when traffic volumes are less than 90 vehicles per hour (vph) but are reluctant to share space with traffic when volumes are over 110 vph (Quimby and Castle 2006)

Emotional Investment

Places that matter to us more will be in sharper focus than those places that don't. Emotional investment in a place bonds people to that place and can come about through the events that happened there, legal ownership or a value a place has that has a particular resonance with the people who experience it. A place of particularly notable natural beauty or important historical or personal event might attract such emotional investment. This investment can contribute to a 'sense of belonging' in that place. In some places, for some people, this sense of connection to their surroundings is almost their defining

Figure 3.7 Context Matters: Parking on the Footpath Is Less of an Issue Here Than It Would Be on a Busier Road

characteristic. In my professional experience it has not been unusual to hear people say they belong to a place as much as the place belongs to them. Yet for other people their connection to a place may be lesser and with it their interest and their sensitivity to what happens there might be correspondingly reduced.

This sense of a place mattering is an important motivating force that can express itself in many ways. It can inspire people to organize themselves, take an interest in planning matters, attend meetings and get actively involved in the design and management or protection of spaces, perhaps even involve themselves in demonstrations and protests to push for a particular outcome in that space. It can motivate people to organize and participate in events in that place or choose to visit a place more often.

Whilst powerful, emotional investment is not always a pleasant experience. It raises the stakes and can bring great distress when places are pushed and pulled by forces of history, politics and economics that can impose—sometimes violently—unwelcome changes to a place. If these forces threaten to displace people or change their surroundings in ways they consider detrimental to them, then powerful and distressing emotional responses can be provoked.

The Extent to Which We Are Present in a Place

We are increasingly leading lives mediated through the internet, smartphones and other electronic devices. According to Collin Ellard, environmental psychologist and neuroscientist at the University of Waterloo in Canada (undated), we are observing the "*hybridisation of real and virtual spaces*" as our physical environment is overlaid by a 'virtual environment' that shapes the way we think of and use our surroundings. This happens not just because of the information we access through these devices—though this is important—but also because of the demands they make on our attentional capacity. These devices *"have shifted the focus of human attention palpably downward into the upturned faces of our phones and away from our physical surroundings"* (ibid).

When our attentional capacity is fully occupied by matters other than our surroundings, we are there but not present. We are less able to take up opportunities or respond to threats presented by those surroundings. As Collin Ellard puts it, *"we are no longer there as we used to be, and our physical surroundings are no longer as real as they used to be"* (ibid).

The Social Landscape

Places acquire meaning through use and experience (Porteous 1977; Lawson 2001). Every square centimetre of our towns and cities has probably been intensely used, has been the setting of great emotion and witnessed events that have impacted people directly or indirectly. Although everyone will have a unique view of the world around them (as discussed in Chapter 1 and at the beginning of this chapter) shared experiences and community values mean that it is likely that there are significant overlaps in this accumulation of meaning and emotional capital at particular 'hotspots'. Quite often the landscape of shared values, hopes and fears can be read in the physical landscape. Usually places of meaning for the community are aligned with the landmarks, stadia, memorials, public places and community buildings where shared experience happens. Places of conflict and contested meaning are marked by defensive infrastructure of walls and gates and attract expressions of anger or disillusionment such as graffiti and vandalism. However, as noted in the section 'Our Sensitivity to the Messages Embodied in Our Surroundings' earlier in this chapter, sometimes a place may have an invisible significance for the people who experience that cannot be read by outsiders, even by an experienced designer.

If designers, no matter how well meaning, change the character, intensity or types of use of such spaces, they change the experience of that place and may inadvertently make changes that are insensitive to the landscape of shared values—the social landscape. These impacts may potentially dash hopes, realize fears and affront community values. It makes sense then that we place emphasis on understanding a place's social landscape if we want our interventions to support people's sense of what their neighbourhood is and how it contributes to their self-determined quality of life. From this perspective, the social landscape (Figure 3.8) might be seen as the context within which messages are embedded and interpreted.

Hardware, Software and Orgware

The variables in the previous section are impacted by the physical characteristics of a place, the thought process of the people who share that place and the decisions of those who manage it. Computing provides a useful analogy for looking at the way these variables interact. If a computer is to do a task, it needs to be an appropriate computer (the hardware needs to be right) with appropriate operating systems, programs or apps (the right software), and we need to have the electricity to put into it and the skills to use it (what we might call the right organizational capacity or orgware). All of these are critical. If any of these things are missing or not up to scratch, then we won't get the result we hoped for. As it is in computing, so it is in the compassionate city; the hardware, software and orgware need to be right if we want to ensure our surroundings broadcast messages that help people meet their needs, thrive and fulfil their potential.

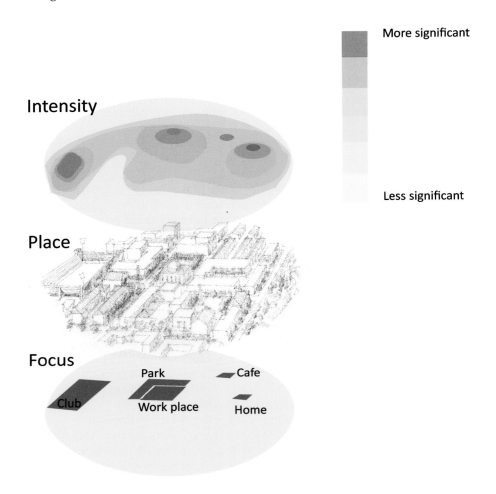

More significant

Less significant

Intensity

Place

Focus

Park

Cafe

Club

Work place

Home

Figure 3.8 Social Landscape

Hardware

The hardware of an urban community are its physical components and the relationship between these components. It consists of the things that nature put there or have been constructed such as the houses, offices, factories, shops, streets, landscape, parks, etc. and the spaces between them. They have value to us because of their utility—as places to live, learn, work, move around, relax, experience beauty, etc.—or because of their potential utility—our sense of what they might become. They can also have value because of what they mean to us, as focal points of emotion. These physical things (and perhaps their absence) are the traditional focus of the urban designer's attention. Hardware, particularly major engineering works, tend to be with us a long time and can only change relatively slowly. It is important we get it right. "*A doctor gets to bury his mistakes, an architect can only advise his clients to grow vines*", as the saying attributed to Frank Lloyd Wright goes.

Figure 3.9 The Influences on Our Software

Software

> *Cities, like dreams, are made of desires and fears.*
>
> —Italo Calvino (1972)

The impact that this hardware will have on our lives will depend not just on its physical attributes but also on the cognitive processes by which we interpret it. Our priorities, experiences and values will lead us to make choices about what that place means to us and what we can do and don't do in that place. The interplay between these things is complex, influenced by qualitative and quantitative factors, and is a function of our values, needs, wants, experiences and the anticipated behaviours of others. Each of these factors can influence the other and change the conclusions we draw about the world around us (Figure 3.9). These thought processes and the conclusions they allow us to draw might be described as our software.

Orgware (or Organizational Capability)

In addition to the hardware and software, the orgware also needs to be right. This is the framework of authority that allocates and protects resources. To paraphrase the *Web Dictionary of Cybernetics and Systems* (undated), it is a function of the vision, resources and scope of the organization(s) behind the software and hardware. As such the orgware reflects the landscape of power and the priorities of the people and agencies who make decisions. It establishes a conceptual space or envelope that strongly influences how far an idea can go towards implementation and how rigorously a value is applied.

The Relationship Between Hardware, Software and Orgware

The relationship between orgware, software and hardware can be illustrated with a hypothetical example of a footpath built to encourage people to walk in a town where travelling by car is the default mode of transport. Many things will need to happen to get the optimal result. If the footpath is to get built in the first place, it will almost definitely require the commissioning body (let's say the Local Council) to decide they want it and commit resources to make it happen. These resources are not just financial but include the time of the designer, planners and others involved. These resources all need to be coordinated and safeguarded from other competing demands. This is the orgware. If the orgware has the capacity and resolution to make it happen, then the path is built and the hardware of the town changes. If the orgware allocates resources to make sure it gets maintained, then the hardware will last into the long term. This makes walking possible but may not in itself lead to more people walking unless those people want to walk, value walking and recognize its benefits. However, if you roll health awareness measures into this suite of interventions, then people may be influenced to look differently on walking, valuing it more. When this is the case, the software is compatible with the hardware and people will walk. If the orgware commits resources for the path to be finished to a high standard and maintained well, then people can continue to walk and this healthy behaviour becomes a healthy habit. In this example, real change to the relationship between people and place happened because:

> A political landscape existed that was willing to prioritize walking (orgware)
> +
> Physical interventions were made that support walking (hardware)
> +
> People had the desire to walk (software)
> =
> Walking becomes a real option.

It is very important to note these variables aren't completely independent of each other. A place's hardware can cultivate changes in our software: experiencing places that are beautiful, fun, enlightening and moving can inspire us to see our surroundings differently. Places with such qualities may provide adequate incentive for us to walk and cycle more often, without other programmatic/promotional measures. On the other side of the coin, hardware in the form of unattractive and unpleasant public transport stops will change the way we think (our software) about using public transport by increasing our perceptions of waiting times and reducing the length of time we are happy to wait for the next bus or train (Zapata-Diomedi et al. 2015).

Our software can change our hardware when we decide we want to use a place in an inappropriate way which leads to damage. Inadequately caring about a place (a software issue) can manifest itself in physical signs of neglect (a hardware issue).

The political process can provide a translation mechanism from software to hardware via orgware. This happens when our concerns as a community (software) change and this is reflected in amended policies, priorities and design standards (orgware) that results in different built outcomes (hardware). An example of this translation mechanism was provided in The Netherlands in the 1970s. The tragic death of the child of journalist Vic Langenhoff in a traffic accident inspired him to write a moving article which "*gave the name for what was to be the most influential road safety campaign for all times—'Stop de Kindermoord' stop the child murders*" (Van der Zee 2015). The attention and the outpouring of feeling this created brought the Dutch government to reassess what streets are for and desist from their previous policy of favouring traffic over other uses (see Chapter 10).

Although hardware, software and orgware influence each other, they can also work independently, evolving along their own path and bound by their own rules and potential for change. Hence in the compassionate city we need to design in a way that is mindful of those three variables and remember change to each or any of them may impact upon the other and change the relationship between people and place. This suggests if we wish to encourage a particular outcome we should not just focus on physically building or demolishing things, nor should we assume that the orgware of the city and the software of its inhabitants are aligned with the intended outcome of our interventions. I would like to suggest that a way of considering the messages given off by a place's hardware, software and orgware is to consider the extent to which they are biased to particular outcomes.

Biases in Hardware

"*We rely upon space to create places appropriate to certain kinds of behaviour and to tell us what they are*" (Lawson 2001). Hardware biases are the physical characteristics of a person's surroundings that sway them towards or away from particular behaviours. Such biases are figuratively and sometimes literally set in stone by one or more design decisions that effectively dedicate a space to a particular activity (or activities) and deter other activities.

One of the most obvious and prevalent hardware biases in many cities is that in favour of driving.

Wide roads designed for fast speeds and high traffic volumes, with footpaths squeezed and aligned inconveniently for pedestrians, prioritize vehicle movement; as does low-density development and the corresponding large distances to shops, schools and parks, etc., which biases places for driving and against walking and cycling (Figure 3.10).

In such car-orientated places, only the most determined or those without a choice will walk, contributing to the 'retreat from the public realm' (Hart and Parkhurst 2011) and reinforcing a perception that car travel is the default transport mode. The resulting traffic from all the journeys that may otherwise have been made on foot or by bicycle adds to the influences that discourage parents from letting their children play outdoors or walk to school and diminishes the chances of all in the community receiving adequate exercise (Play England 2008). However other places are biased towards walking, cycling and playing because they embody characteristics which attract people to these activities and deter them from moving through the space fast in a car (Figure 3.11).

Rarely is this bias absolute. Many places give mixed messages that offer confusing and ambiguous or contradictory encouragements (Figure 3.12).

It is taken as self-evident that the geography of hardware biases is very uneven; in some places the overall message received by the observer is one that the area is rich in

Figure 3.10 Streetscape Biased Against Walking

Figure 3.11 Streetscape Biased in Favour of Walking

Figure 3.12 Walking Is Grudgingly Facilitated, But Is It Encouraged?

opportunities. Other places are dense with barriers and risks that deter people from benefitting from the opportunities and experiences of the public realm. If some people find their surroundings biased against the things they need to do, that only offer less healthy, more profligate opportunities that isolate them then this is profoundly unjust. Such surroundings effectively diminish the potential of their inhabitants to thrive, reducing their ability to participate in and contribute to society, and can reinforce other forms of disadvantage. When these hardware biases have the effect of enforcing car dependency in a community, it can also lock people into behaviours that are unsustainable and leave them particularly vulnerable to future challenges, such as rises in the price of oil, and make addressing problems such as climate change harder.

This bias is not usually intended but comes about as designers, clients, and other stakeholders make incremental decisions within a landscape of legislation and values that are influenced by convention and market forces. Over time these decisions can reinforce the extent to which a space is tailored to a particular use and inadvertently limits the opportunities it offers to a narrow and rigid range of activities.

Biases in Software

We may try to see things as objectively as we please. Nonetheless, we can never see them with any eyes except our own.
—American Supreme Court Judge Benjamin Cardozo, quoted in Edwards (1998)

As noted in the 'Personal Circumstances, Experiences and Values' section earlier in this chapter our gender, age, personal circumstances, values and experiences (amongst other things) interact to give us a unique perspective on the world around us and inform our views of what represents good and bad design. As a result this may be quite different from the conclusions drawn by our peers.

For example a quiet wooded path that leads between a housing estate and a town centre might be valued by some potential users as offering a secluded space to hear bird song and feel removed from the city but be avoided (at least some of the time) by other users because those secluded corners might be potential hiding places for an attacker (Figure 3.13). If this path is the only convenient way between the estate and the centre, it may be a selective barrier that dissuades some from walking but not others.

In this scenario it is worth speculating about the likely software bias of the designer of that space. No doubt he or she gave careful thought to tree selection and was diligent in establishing a maintenance regime that supported this landscape to maximize tree coverage and vegetation density, carefully aligning the path so views of buildings and urbanity were screened. The choices they made were well intentioned and faithfully reflected their view of good design. They might understandably be proud of their work. However members of the community who see the path differently and place greater emphasis on the potential risks of that place might equally understandably see the design as a bad design.

Figure 3.13 One Environment, Multiple Perceptions

Another example of the influences of personal values and priorities on software bias is provided by the different interpretations that people may have to the construction of a fast road that cuts through a residential neighbourhood. This may be interpreted by a driver who might use the road as a good design decision. However a local resident subject to the pollution, disruption, danger and inconvenience it brings might see it as a bad decision.

One environment, multiple conclusions and multiple relationships between people and place.

Exclusionary Software Bias

As the projects in Palestine (Chapter 12) and Northern Ireland (Chapter 13) reveal, the forces of history can cultivate a sense that land is either 'ours' or 'theirs', separating communities by boundaries that are physically and/or psychologically difficult to cross.

This isn't necessarily a problem if that community forges a bond with a place that had previously been unvalued, as can occur when that community reclaims abandoned space. Then it is possible that the well-being enjoyed by those people can be increased without a corresponding loss to other people (De Haan 2005). However, when creating this connection to a place brings with it the denial of that space to another community, then 'front-lines' are created that harden divisions and expose people to uncomfortable messages that they are not welcome or are seen as threats. These messages are broadcast through the physical markers left in the divided communities and/or by the way people behave (Bell et al. 2010). At its most subtle, exclusionary software bias is apparent when a community creates a feeling that outsiders are not trusted. This is a sense familiar to most people who have ever ventured down a quiet street or into a courtyard and sensed the curtains twitching. At the other extreme, the installation of walls, legal barriers and psychological barriers can aggressively deny people the ability to move between different places they may otherwise benefit from.

Within this spectrum are the symbols of belonging that are important to some but make others feel excluded, simultaneously enhancing a place for some whilst tainting it for others. An example are the murals that can be found on many walls in Northern Ireland that reflect the political aspirations of the local community and speak of victory over the other (Figures 3.14, 3.15). The uncompromising nature of many of these symbols can make them intimidating for people of the other community. These have been called 'chill factors' because of the discomfort they cause. Other sensitivities can come about by the use or absence of particular languages on official signs, the memorialization of events or the dedication of spaces such as streets or parks to a person or event. Although these places may not consciously be designed to discriminate, it is often the outcome (Bell et al. 2010), provoking emotional responses that may be as threatening for one group as it is expressive and cathartic for another.

The Resilience of Software Biases

Software biases are hard to shift. Experience suggests that familiar activities and day-to-day rituals become engrained in people's lives even though they may not always be beneficial. This tendency towards what we are used to is a function of our 'adaptive capacity', the unconscious recalibrating of our preferences in light of our situation (Elster 1982). People have a capacity to get used to something and cease to question it. In practical terms this is very helpful, allowing us to come to terms with changed surroundings and

Figure 3.14 Northern Ireland Murals
Source: Shutterstock 346211981

Figure 3.15 Northern Ireland Murals
Source: Shutterstock 178624127

circumstances, but arguably it diminishes our ability to critically assess those surroundings and circumstances. Over time these unquestioned interpretations become habits that are by their nature difficult to change, even if making that change would help us better meet our needs.

To take the example of some of the software biases that tie people to their cars and the infrastructure of existing and flawed urban areas and deter the take up of public transport:

We are more likely to believe things that do not challenge our value system. This tendency has been called confirmation bias. This is *"the unwitting selectivity in the acquisition and use of evidence"* according to Raymond Nickerson (1998) *"in ways that are partial to existing beliefs, expectations, or a hypothesis in hand"*. He suggests this is because we are likely to give preferential treatment to pleasant thoughts and memories over unpleasant ones, noting people find it *"easier to believe propositions they would like to be true than propositions they would prefer to be false"*. This may explain why scraps of evidence that seem to support a pre-conceived viewpoint are given great weight whereas a raft of evidence that challenges that viewpoint can be dismissed. A single account of an attack on a pedestrian may lead the committed driver to conclude it is unsafe to walk whilst continuing to ignore the risks posed by driving.

Our fear of stigma will influence whether we want to do something or not. Anecdotal evidence suggests that in some parts of Australia when you see an adult walking or cycling it means they are poor, have lost their licence, they are doing so because their doctor or partner has told them to do so or they can't drive (Gormann 2014, pers. corr.). These reflect poorly on the walker and cyclist and this lack of prestige seems to act as a deterrent to people choosing to walk or cycle, as it does for discretionary bus users in America (Hess 2012).

'Delay discounting' is the psychological tendency to give in to temptation. Although people know that walking and cycling have long-term benefits that might improve their quality of life, they also know getting in a car to get from A to B now offers immediate benefits of being quick and easy. When weighing up these two options, many people will place more emphasis on the immediate benefits. People can assuage their conscience by telling themselves they will walk or cycle 'tomorrow'.

Challenging Software Biases

Although stubborn, software biases can be challenged by changes to our underlying values. Change values and behaviour will follow. A report by C3 Collaborating for Health (2012) noted a study in 2011 in London that found 43 per cent of 1,000 respondents cited knowing more about the impact of walking on their carbon footprint may motivate them to walk more.

I witnessed a practical example of changing software bias when I was undertaking a project in a town in rural Victoria (Australia) and noted that despite the relative lack of cycling infrastructure at the time, there were many cyclists in the town. When I asked why that should be, I was told that the local doctor was a firm advocate of the benefits of exercising and of cycling in particular. If anyone had a health scare, their doctor often advised to take up cycling and judging from the evidence many people took his advice. In conversation with several people living in this town, it was clear that these newcomers to cycling had the zeal of the convert. Their changed understanding of their needs would often cause them to see their surroundings differently, to require different things from it. In this new light, a place is good if it enabled them to cycle but bad if it didn't.

Another example of challenging software biases is provided by nudge theory, as articulated by Richard Thaler and Cass Sunstein (2008). This suggests that making something more fun, easier or more pleasant may be more effective in encouraging a desired behaviour than strict rules and enforcement. The theory suggests that by offering these rewards, we can change the decision-making processes of groups and individuals, enabling them to see their world differently so that needs fulfilment isn't just possible but preferable.

Biases in Orgware

These can be seen as the pathways available through the landscape of authority to make change happen. Achieving some goals meets with significant resistance whilst others are facilitated. These biases make some types of change easier to achieve than others and favour those who understand this labyrinth of power. These biases are expressed through the policies and priorities of governments, the resources committed to various challenges and a preference for tried-and-tested ways of getting things done. They are reflected in what gets approved and the resources (or lack thereof) that are committed to ensuring that it is of good quality. An example of such orgware bias is the concern expressed by the UK House of Lords in their report (2016) that *"the overall emphasis on speed and quantity of housing supply appears to threaten place-making itself, along with sustainable planning for the long-term and the delivery of high quality and design standards"*. The same report further expressed concern that the deregulatory agenda that was pursued by the UK government at the time of writing progressively dilutes the capacity of local authorities to scrutinize new developments, to safeguard quality and sustainability, and to ensure that proposals contribute to an overall and beneficial sense of place.

The Balance of Influences

As touched upon in the previous section, all these biases are rarely perfectly aligned. Most of us look around our neighbourhood and find it offers us mixed and often confusing messages about what we are invited to do. In a nurturing environment, although there might be some messages we receive from our surroundings that deter a person from meeting their needs (perhaps a lack of a landscaped park), these messages can be overlooked when considered against all the other ones that invite us to meet our needs (maybe the presence of many trees in the public realm and streets that are pleasant to walk through and facilitate play). In a neglectful environment there may be isolated features that contribute to our well-being, but the overall effect is to stifle our ability to meet a need or needs. For example a neighbourhood may have a landscaped park but if that park can't be reached without crossing dangerous roads, then many are likely to be deterred from using it. Consequently for those people, meeting their needs is something that happens despite, and not because of, their surroundings. Fortunately people always have proved very resourceful in overcoming adversity to fulfil their potential and make great contributions to their community and society, irrespective of the quality of their surroundings. When the will is strong enough and personal circumstances allow, it seems people will overcome the resistance that poor surroundings place on people meeting their needs, thriving and fulfilling their potential (Figure 3.16).

Thus even in the most car-dominated suburbs of the most car-orientated cities of North America and Australia, you will still find people walking, running and cycling. For some this is because they don't have an alternative but for others their personal values and priorities provide adequate motivation for them to disregard these deterrents in their

As interpreted by the keen walker...

As interpreted by the cautious walker...

The balance of influences for walking through here...

Figure 3.16 Weighing Up the Influences of Our Surroundings

decision-making process. For these people walking or cycling is a matter of principle and they will walk or cycle unless it is aggressively and actively deterred. They need no particular design interventions to encourage them. This is all the more impressive considering all the influences act to 'tempt' people to drive. Baumeister et al. (1998) suggests that resisting repeated temptations takes a mental toll and can wear a person out. Looked at this way, choosing to walk doesn't just require a commitment of effort to walk, it requires an additional effort to decide not to drive.

This *"complicated interplay of emotions and rational thought, unconscious and conscious decision-making"* (Helliwell et al. 2012) that influence how we interpret our surroundings might be seen as a set of scales by which competing options might be considered and weighed up against each other. Although represented here as a weighing scales balancing two options, in reality there might be many options to be weighed up, either together or in sequence: go to the park or not? If so walk, cycle or drive there? For any of these decisions, both sides of the balance are likely to contain a mix of physical environmental attributes and personal values that we weigh up to draw conclusions about what we do. For example, a 10-minute walk to the shops might be too far for most people if the walk is perceived as dangerous and unpleasant. However a walk of over 20 minutes may not be too far if the environment is pleasant (physical characteristics), they enjoy walking and appreciate the health benefits (personal values). Thus changing any of these personal values or physical characteristics may help shift the overall balance and with it the conclusions people draw about what they want to do and don't want to do.

What Does This Mean for Urban Designers?

Everyone, professional urban designers included, will look at their surroundings through a set of personal lenses and filters that enables them to see something unique. These filters and lens include our circumstances at the time, past experiences, personal and cultural values, and our abilities and tastes. These lenses put different parts or aspects of those surroundings into sharp focus whilst leaving others unknown and unconsidered. This creates a lumpy environment of significance, with some places and issues being particularly meaningful to each of us but other places and issues less so. If we are to create settings that many people find rich in relevant opportunities to do the things they need to do to enjoy a good quality of life, we need to be aware of the diversity of perceptions and their fluidity. We need to be guided as much by the social landscape as the physical landscape. *"Experience shows that interventions concerning the physical environment alone hardly constitute best practice: to become successful they have to incorporate the social dimension"* (Kjellstrom et al. 2007).

This suggests that some of the core challenges of ensuring our interventions contribute to creating the compassionate city are:

- to give due weight to the perspectives of those for whom that space matters and those for whom it will matter, as best we can;
- to ensure as far as practical the places we help create are responsive to these diverse views;
- to ensure that the physical landscape can evolve to respond to changes in the social landscape; and,
- to create spaces that can be seen and interpreted as inviting multiple needs-fulfilling activities with minimal conflict.

When we force people into interacting in spaces that impose intrusion into another's personal space, then we will risk making people uncomfortable. Equipping the public realm to facilitate interactions in sharable space rather than personal space will improve the chances of those interactions being seen as pleasant.

When the aspirations, skills, insights and needs of the people who live in a city (its software) are poorly served by their surroundings (the hardware) there will be a social cost, a mismatch between what the city facilitates and what its citizenry need. Furthermore when those who have influence and know-how to affect change in their city or municipality (the orgware) lack commitment to address this problem, then the problem becomes ingrained.

Urban design can help address these problems in several ways; by directly influencing the hardware we can change its biases so it favours needs-fulfilling activities. We can influence software when we encourage people to focus on the positive experiences of a needs-fulfilling activity. We also have the ability to influence a community's orgware by creating inspiring places that provide evidence of the differences that can be made by thoughtful design. We can use our voice and insights to prepare design guidelines, briefing notes (and books!) that raise awareness and help inform decision-makers about how they can address inequity in the way that civic assets are distributed.

The next chapter considers the impact that the messages we get from a place may have on the people who receive them and whether or not they contribute to making a place either nurturing or neglectful.

References

Baumeister, R, Bratslavsky, E, Muraven, M, and Tice, M (1998) *Ego Depletion: Is the Active Self a Limited Resource?* Accessed June 2016, https://faculty.washington.edu/jdb/345/345%20Articles/Baumeister%20et%20al.%20(1998).pdf

Bell, J, Jarman, N, and Harvey, B (2010) *Beyond Belfast, Community Relations Council and Rural Community Network.* Accessed December 2011, www.conflictresearch.org.uk/Resources/Documents/CRC%20Beyond%20Belfast%20(Web).pdf

C3: Collaborating for Health (2012) *The Benefits of Regular Walking for Health, Well-being and the Environment.* London: C3 Collaborating for Health. Accessed December 2011, www.c3health.org/wpcontent/uploads/2009/09/C3-report-on-walking-v-1-20120911.pdf

Calvino, I (1972) *Invisible Cities.* Torino: Giulio Einaudi.

Commission for Architecture and the Built Environment (2008) *Inclusion By Design: Equality, Diversity and the Built Environment.* London: CABE.

Crain, W (2010) Is childrens play innate? *Encounter: Education for Meaning and Social Justice* 23(2). Accessed February 2016, www.fairplayforchildren.org/pdf/1290046915.pdf

Criado-Perez, C (2016) *What-Works-for Men Doesn't Work for Everyone, Why Cities Need to Start Planning for Women.* City Metric. Accessed February 2016, www.citymetric.com/politics/what-works-men-doesn-t-work-everyone-why-cities-need-start-planning-women-mind-2123

De Haan, H (October 2005) *Social and Material Appropriation of Neighborhood Space: Collective Space and Resistance in a Dutch Urban Community.* Paper for the international conference 'Doing, Thinking, Feeling Home: The Mental Geography of Residential Environments', Delft University of Technology, Delft Wageningen University, The Netherlands. Accessed September 2011, www.tudelft.nl/live/binaries/2e2a5b07-3f77-4d71-b1d1-33a897e794aa/doc/Conference%20paper%20Haan.pdf

Edwards, C (1998) *Responsibilities and Dispensations: Behavior, Science, & American Justice.* Four Oaks Press.

Ellard, C (undated) *Streets With No Game.* Aeon. Accessed February 2016, https://aeon.co/essays/why-boring-streets-make-pedestrians-stressed-and-unhappy

Elster, J (1982) Belief, bias, and ideology. In M Hollis and S Lukes (Eds.) *Rationality and Relativism* (pp. 123–148). Cambridge, MA: MIT Press.

Gehl, J (2006) *Life Between Buildings*. Hørsholm: The Danish Architectural Press.

Gormann, F (2014) *Personal Correspondence*.

Handy, S, Boarnet, M, Ewing, R, and Killingsworth, R (August 2002) How the built environment affects physical activity: Views from urban planning. *American Journal of Preventive Medicine* 23(2) (supplement). Accessed January 2016, www.ajpmonline.org/article/S0749-3797(02)00475-0/abstract

Hart, J, and Parkhurst, G (2011) *Driven to Excess: Impacts of Motor Vehicles on the Quality of Life of Residents of Three Streets in Bristol UK*. University of Western England. http://eprints.uwe.ac.uk/15513/1/WTPP_Hart_ParkhurstJan2011prepub.pdf

Helliwell, J, Layard, R, and Sachs, J (Eds.) (2012) *World Happiness Report*. The Earth Institute. Accessed May 2016, www.earth.columbia.edu/sitefiles/file/Sachs%20Writing/2012/World%20Happiness%20Report.pdf

Hemmings, P (2007) Renegotiating the primary school: Children's emotional geographies of sport, exercise and active play. *Children and Geographies* 5: 353–71. Accessed June 2015, www.tandfonline.com/doi/abs/10.1080/14733280701631817

Hess, A (2012) *Race, Class, and the Stigma of Riding the Bus in America*. The Atlantic Citylab. Accessed June 2016, www.citylab.com/cityfixer/2012/07/race-class-and-stigma-riding-bus-america/2510/

House of Lords (2016) *Building Better Places, a Report of Select Committee on National Policy for the Built Environment*. HL Paper 100, House of Lords.

James, BD, Wilson, RS, Barnes, LL, and Bennett, DA (2011) Late-life social activity and cognitive decline in old age. *Journal of the International Neuropsychological Society* 17(6): 998–1005. Accessed June 2016, www.ncbi.nlm.nih.gov/pubmed/22040898

Kjellstrom, T., Mercado, S., Barten, F., WHO Commission on Social Determinants of Health, Knowledge Network on Urban Settings, Centre for Health Development, World Health Organization, & Ompad, D. (2007). *Our cities, our health, our future: acting on social determinants for health equity in urban settings : report to the WHO Commission on Social Determinants of Health from the Knowledge Network on Urban Settings*. Kobe, Japan: WHO Kobe Centre.

Ko, S, Hausdorff, JM, and Ferrucci, L (November 2010) Age-associated differences in the gait pattern changes of older adults during fast-speed and fatigue conditions: Results from the Baltimore longitudinal study of ageing. *British Geriatrics Society, Age and Ageing* 39(6): 688–94. doi:10.1093/ageing/afq113. Epub September 10, 2010. Accessed June 2016, http://ageing.oxfordjournals.org/content/39/6/688.full#cited-by

Lawson, B (2001) *The Language of Space*. Oxford: Architectural Press.

Louv, R (2010) *Last Child in the Woods*. London: Atlantic Books.

Lynch, K (1960) *The Image of the City*. Cambridge, MA: MIT Press.

Martin, FC, Hart, D, Spector, T, Doyle, DV, and Harari, D (2005) Fear of falling limiting activity in young-old women is associated with reduced functional mobility rather than psychological factors. *Age and Ageing* 34: 281–7. [PubMed]. Accessed January 2016, www.ncbi.nlm.nih.gov/pubmed/15863412

Mitchell, L, Burton, E, and Raman, S (2004) Dementia-friendly cities: Designing intelligible neighbourhoods for life. *Journal of Urban Design* 9(1). Accessed January 2016, www.tandfonline.com/doi/abs/10.1080/1357480042000187721

Montgomery, C (2013) *Happy City*. London: Penguin Books.

Nickerson, R (1998) Confirmation bias: A ubiquitous phenomenon in many guises. *Review of General Psychology* 2(2): 175–220. Accessed January 2016, psy.ucsd.edu/~mckenzie/nickerson ConfirmationBias.pdf

Nijhuis, S (2013) *Visual Research in Landscape Architecture*. TU Delft. Accessed March 2017, http://rius.tudelft.nl/article/view/209/264

Orzech, D (2007) Betrayed by our bodies—sensory loss. *Aging Social Work Today* 7(1): 20. Accessed January 2016, www.socialworktoday.com/archive/janfeb2007p20.shtml

Planet Ark (2011) *Climbing Trees: Getting Aussie Kids Back Outdoors*. Accessed July 2016, http://treeday.planetark.org/documents/doc-534-climbing-trees-research-report-2011-07-13-final.pdf.

Play England (2008) *Play for a Change*. Accessed June 2015, www.playengland.org.uk/media/120438/play-for-a-change-low-res.pdf

Porteous, JD (1977) *Environment & Behavior: Planning and Everyday Urban Life*. Addison-Wesley.

Porteous, JD (1990) *Landscapes of the Mind: Worlds of Sense and Metaphor*. Toronto, Canada: University of Toronto Press.

Qualls, S (2014) *What Social Relationships Can Do for Health*. American Society of Ageing. Accessed July 2016, www.asaging.org/blog/what-social-relationships-can-do-health

Quimby, J, and Castle, J (2006) *A Review of Simplified Streetscape Schemes*. TRL Limited. Accessed July 2011, http://content.tfl.gov.uk/review-of-simplified-streetscape-schemes.pdf

Rapoport, A (1982) *The Meaning of the Built Environment: A Nonverbal Communication Approach*. University of Arizona Press.

Rudner, J (2013) *Personal Correspondence*.

Rudner, J, Kennedy, M, Holland, W, Wilks, J, Donovan, J, Neville, D, Shaw, M, Budge, T, and Butt, A (2011) *The Place of Our Children in Community Building: Turning Theory Into Practice. Children's and Young People's Engagement Report*. Volume 2. Bendigo: La Trobe University.

Salzamm, B (2010) *Gait and Balance Disorders in Older Adults*. American Academy of Family Physicians. Accessed June 2016, www.aafp.org/afp/2010/0701/p61.html

Thaler, R, and Sunstein, C (2008) *Nudge: Improving Decisions About Health, Wealth, and Happiness*. Yale University Press.

UNICEF (2004) *Building Child Friendly Cities a Framework for Action*. Accessed July 2016, www.unicef-irc.org/publications/pdf/cfc-framework-eng.pdf

University of Sheffield 2010, 'Researchers shed light on children's perception', 14 October 2010, accessed June 2015 https://www.sheffield.ac.uk/news/nr/1767-1.174108

Van der Zee, R (2015) How Amsterdam became the bicycle capital of the world. *The Guardian*, May 2015. Accessed June 2016, www.theguardian.com/cities/2015/may/05/amsterdam-bicycle-capital-world-transport-cycling-kindermoord

Vygotsky, L (January–February 2004) Imagination and creativity in childhood. *Journal of Russian and East European Psychology* 42(1): 7–97. Accessed June 2016, http://lchc.ucsd.edu/mca/Mail/xmcamail.2008_03.dir/att-0189/Vygotsky__Imag___Creat_in_Childhood.pdf

Walljasper, J (2007) *The Great Neighborhood Book: A Do-It-Yourself Guide to Placemaking*. New Society.

Web Dictionary of Cybernetics and Systems (undated) *Orgware*. Accessed May 2016, http://pespmc1.vub.ac.be/ASC/INDEXASC.html

Werner, CM, Brown, BB, and Altman, I (1997) Environmental psychology. In JW Berry, MH Segall, and C Kagitcibasi (Eds.) *Handbook of Cross-cultural Psychology: Volume 3. Social Behavior and Applications* (2nd ed., pp. 255–290). Needham Heights, MA: Allyn and Bacon. Published.

World Health Organisation (2015) *World Report on Ageing and Health*. Accessed June 2016, http://apps.who.int/iris/bitstream/10665/186463/1/9789240694811_eng.pdf?ua=1

Worpole, K, and Knox, K (2007) *The Social Value of Public Spaces*. Joseph Rowntree Foundation. Accessed January 2016, www.jrf.org.uk/report/social-value-public-spaces

Zapata-Diomedi, B, Brown, V, and Veerman, L (2015) *An Evidence Review and Modelling Exercise: The Effects of Urban Form on Health: Cost and Benefits*. Centre for Population Health, NSW Ministry of Health, and Brokered by the Sax Institute for the Australian Prevention Partnership Centre. Accessed June 2016, http://preventioncentre.org.au/wp-content/uploads/2015/12/1511-built-environment-exec-summary_final_PDF_revFinal2.pdf

4   What Makes a Place Nurturing or Neglectful?

As observed in the last chapter, our lives are influenced in many different ways by the messages we receive from our surroundings. This chapter maps my understanding of the key variables that determine whether these messages point people towards needs-fulfilling behaviours or away from them. The list is not exhaustive nor is it suggested that each of these factors will exert an equal and consistent influence in all circumstances. In a system as complex as a city, which is part organic and part mechanical and has so many linked and reciprocating 'moving parts', the relationship between these factors is one of constant change. In different circumstances they can work in concert or act independently. All the variables influence the relationship that people have with their surroundings but some act more on the hardware, some more on the software and others on the orgware (Figure 4.1).

Our Choices of Ways to Move Around

A place is nurturing when it makes it easy for people to get to all the places they need to go in ways that are intrinsically beneficial to their well-being and do not diminish other people's well-being. A place is neglectful when it traps people in a particular location and/or demands that nearly all trips incur significant environmental, social and economic costs.

Unless we are determined to live a hermit-like existence of monastic austerity, it is very unlikely that we will be content to stay in the one place forever, no matter how well designed it is. However, as Charles Montgomery observes in *Happy City*: "*we all live in systems that shape our travel behaviour. And most of us live in systems that give us almost no choice in how to live or get around*" (2013a).

Our surroundings nurture us when they facilitate us to access the places where we can meet our different needs as they rise to the top of our priorities. However it is not just the ability to move that is important in making a place nurturing, it is also the way we move. As noted in Chapter 2, we need to have physical activity. Without it we become more vulnerable to a wide range of illnesses including Ischaemic heart disease, stroke, type 2 diabetes, kidney disease, osteoporosis, coleo-rectal cancer and depression (Australian Institute of Health and Welfare 2012). These risks should not be underestimated. Inactivity is as important as unhealthy diets and tobacco use as a modifiable risk factor for chronic diseases (WHO undated). Across the world inactivity accounts for 9 per cent of premature mortality or 5.3 million deaths annually (Min Lee et al. 2012) and in 2013 was estimated to cost INT$67.5 billion through healthcare expenditure and productivity losses (Ding et al. 2016).

This cost is easy to avoid. A study in New York found "*investments in bicycle lanes come with an exceptionally good value because they simultaneously address multiple public health problems. Investments in bike lanes are more cost-effective than the majority of*

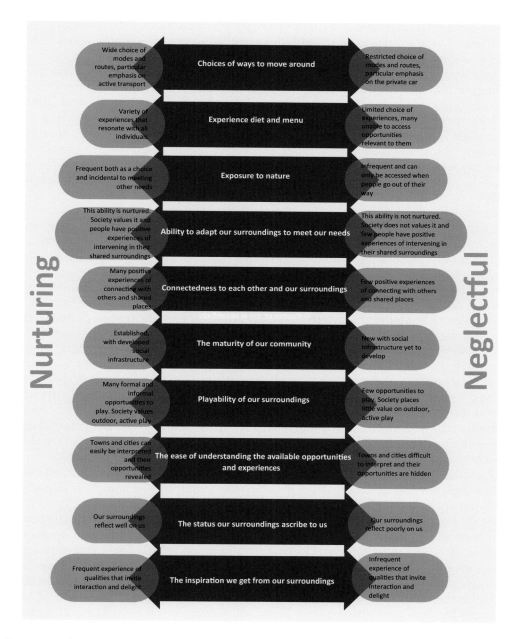

Figure 4.1 The Variables That Influence Whether a Place is Nurturing or Neglectful

preventive approaches used today and are many times more cost effective than treating the diseases that arise from inadequate activity" (Gu et al. 2016).

Physical inactivity is induced by lifestyles that present few demands for physical exertion (International Obesity TaskForce 2002). Active transport (trips that have a significant component of walking and cycling) and by extension public transport (which also typically involves a walk or a cycle at either end of the journey) can help address this issue. Active transport is also more accessible—more people can walk than drive—and, as noted in Chapter 3, it integrates us better with our surroundings and the people with whom we share those surroundings.

There is also much to be said for active transport apart from its benefits to the person walking or cycling. It is less resource intensive than travelling by private motor vehicle, demanding much less space and requiring much lower inputs of energy (Mason 2000). It results in much fewer contaminants than would occur if these trips were made in a car (Australian Government Department of Environment and Heritage 2005). Consequently replacing vehicle movements with active and public transport can be intrinsically beneficial to society at large as well as the walker or cyclist. As a result places that facilitate people to get to and between the diverse settings they have to get to in order to meet their needs by active transport are much more nurturing than places that don't.

The characteristics that encourage or discourage active transport have been explored by many authorities. Although the research findings are not entirely aligned, there seems to be broad agreement that rates of active transport are influenced by both qualitative and quantitative factors. Sallis et al. (2016) found that the "*design of urban environments has the potential to contribute substantially to physical activity*". The Department for Transport (UK) found that "*high quality design of townscapes and rural transport infrastructure can help to encourage walking and cycling*" (DfT 2004). Safety is important and its absence can be a powerful deterrent (Bhalla 2014). In terms of specific characteristics, most authorities agree that active transport-friendly places are typically compact, built at high(er) densities and diverse in land uses, and so offer correspondingly short distances to destinations such as shops, parks, etc. They are places with direct walking and cycling routes, places with good infrastructure on the journey (good paths, seats, lighting, etc.) and at the journey's end (showers, lockers, bike racks). They are places which offer walkers and cyclists legible and pleasant surroundings which feel safe.

Unfortunately, the mono-use, car-dominated suburbs that are surrounding many cities in an ever-thickening band create communities with unsafe, unattractive public realms, dominated by busy roads and fast traffic. Cars, whilst offering the promise of liberation for their users, entrap non-users, who are often hemmed in by barriers of busy roads and isolated by the low densities that car usage makes possible. This low density of housing is echoed in a low density of destinations such as shops, parks and other shared facilities which are spread thinly throughout (sub)urban areas, putting most of them a considerable distance away from most of the people they serve. The combination of long distances and unpleasant, unsafe walking and cycling journeys leaves their inhabitants in little doubt that active transport is not just less appealing but often prohibitively difficult and unwise. In the face of such messages, the walker or cyclist will need to be determined to ignore what their surroundings are telling them and walk or cycle anyway. The rest of us will weigh the balance of influences and decide to drive or do without. Those who live in such places and can't drive (either because of age, medical condition or poverty) and those who won't drive are effectively trapped where they are and denied access to the opportunities available to more mobile peers. Either way, people living in places where their fundamental choice is either travel by car or don't travel are less likely to be adequately active. This is an outcome observed in both developed and developing countries (Kjellstrom et al. 2007).

The higher rates of accidents and pollution that car dependency brings are also having a significant and growing impact on the well-being of urban communities: "*over the last two decades, deaths due to road crashes grew by 46%. Deaths attributable to air pollution, to which motor vehicles are an important contributor, grew by 11%*" (Bhalla et al. 2014).

Accidents, injuries and pollution from vehicles contribute to six of the top 10 causes of death (ibid). The same report found that the burden of disease attributable to both road injury and air pollution from vehicles exceed those from HIV, tuberculosis or malaria (ibid).

Globally Haagsma et al. (2016) found that there were over 11 million road traffic accidents worldwide in 2013 that required in-patient hospital care and 1,396,000 people died from their injuries. This is over 16 times more deaths than any other type of transport accidents. Charles Montgomery notes, *"The WHO estimate that the cost of auto crashes in injuries, medical care and property damages exceeds $518 billion worldwide"* (Montgomery 2013a).

In relation to pollution:

> *It is well known that congestion and heavy levels of traffic have negative health implications; Public Health England, in a 2014 report, estimated that 5.6% of all deaths in over-25s in England were linked to air pollution, although the figures vary considerably by region. Heavy levels of traffic also contribute to noise pollution; about 10% of the UK population is thought to live in areas where daytime sound levels exceed those which the World Health Organisation considers detrimental to health, and 34% in areas where night-time sound levels exceed 50 decibels. It is known that continuous internal noise of over 30 decibels disturbs sleep.*
>
> (House of Lords 2016)

An extensive study by Chen et al. (2017) in Canada found that living close to heavy traffic was associated with a higher incidence of dementia.

The costs of living in places exposed to traffic are borne particularly by the most vulnerable in the community. Poorer people have less ability to compete for quieter, less congested and more salubrious places to live (Cucurachi 2013). The same study also found that children who lived in noisier neighbourhoods did less well at school and noted *"excessive noise runs like a loud thread through many of the UK's most broken communities."* Older people feel the perceptions of danger from accidents more keenly than other sections of the community and this contributes greatly to the deterrents to venturing outside. However the resulting sedentary life and lack of physical and cognitive stimulation speeds up the aging processes and contributes to cognitive decline, loss of bone density and muscle tone (Mechling and Netz 2009). These in turn make older people more susceptible to injury and increase the sense of risk posed by their surroundings, and hence add to the reluctance to go out, fuelling a vicious cycle of decline.

Furthermore, even for those who can drive, if they live in low-density suburbs they may find they have to bear the personal and social costs that come from being bound to a time-consuming, sedentary and often stressful lifestyle; Charles Montgomery quotes a Swedish study that found *"that people who endure more than a 45-minute commute were 40% more likely to divorce"*. He also noted other research that found that a

> *person with a one-hour commute has to earn 40% more money to be as satisfied with life as someone who walks to the office. On the other hand, for a single person, exchanging a long commute for a short walk to work has the same effect on happiness as finding a new love.*
>
> (Montgomery 2013a)

Concerns about traffic risks contribute to parents setting increasingly tight bounds for their children's independent mobility, reducing it significantly from the range enjoyed by children of the same age in years past (VicHealth 2015). Children who are driven around more by their parents are less active and have less opportunity for free time and self-directed play (Gibbs et al. 2012; VicHealth 2015). Their relationship with their surroundings is highly mediated. Many potential learning and playing opportunities are compromised, as they are inadvertently trapped by fearful parents whose eyes and ears are attuned to seeing their surroundings as a threat, as observed by Rudner (pers. corr. 2013).

To relate this back to the framework of fundamental needs identified in Chapter 2, if we have only limited transport options, our ability to get to the settings where any of these needs can be met may be compromised. If active transport is not a realistic option for most of the trips we have to make or choose to make, our ability to meet our fundamental needs for physical activity, leisure and protection may be adversely affected. Table 4.1 shows some of the key factors that will influence whether the hardware, software and orgware of a place makes it harder or easier for these needs to be met.

Table 4.1 The hardware, software and orgware factors that influence how we choose to move around

Hardware factors that influence how we move . . .		Software factors that influence how we move . . .		Orgware factors that influence how we move . . .	
. . . in the compassionate city	*. . . in the neglectful city*	*. . . in the compassionate city*	*. . . in the neglectful city*	*. . . in the compassionate city*	*. . . in the neglectful city*
Quality active transport infrastructure offering attractive, interesting, legible, direct routes that feel safe	Low-quality/ absent active transport infrastructure offering routes that are indirect, disconnected, illegible and feel unsafe	Walking, cycling valued	Walking, cycling, public transport not seen as realistic choices	Investment and promotion of active transport	Investment in private vehicle infrastructure
Quality public transport infrastructure	Low-quality or absent public transport	Public transport (and the people who use it) considered important	Public transport (and the people who use it) considered unimportant	Investment and promotion of public transport	Investment in private vehicle infrastructure
High-density, mixed-use environments that minimize distances to a range of uses and make active and public transport viable	Low-density areas of single uses that separate out activities and increase the average distances between activities	Walking and cycling seen as contributing to quality of life	Walking and cycling seen as chore	Political will to move away from primacy of private motor vehicle and look at changes in the way cities are designed and planned	No political will to move away from primacy of private motor vehicle or look at changes in the way cities are designed and planned

Our Experience Diet and Menu

A place is nurturing when it offers a wide range of relevant opportunities that support diverse appropriate and appealing experiences. A place is neglectful when it offers only scant or irrelevant opportunities and thus offers limited experiences or an excess of negative experiences.

Each of us have an 'experience diet'. This is the sum of the things we see, hear, smell, feel or do in our day-to-day lives. We select these experiences from the breadth of possibilities open to us, which is framed (partly) by the availability of appropriate settings to undertake different activities. The extent of all these possibilities is our experience menu. This idea is derived from Simeon Packard's concept of a 'play diet' (Play England 2008a). This is his way of describing the mix of play activities in which a child participates. Exposure to this idea—drawing a parallel with our food diets to emphasize the importance of getting quantity, variety and quality right—inspired me to observe that this was a useful way of explaining the importance of quality and quantity of experience in other aspects of our lives.

Just like a food diet, our experience diet can be good or bad. Also like a food diet, a good experience diet requires many different inputs and balance. Just like a food diet, the way you combine things is important and a little bit of what you enjoy has its place. Emily Ballantyne Brodie, an insightful friend, was telling me of her choices of cafés to visits with her young daughter. Her choice was *"the café that was all white bread, pasties and sugar with warm smiles from the staff and a child friendly attitude or the café that was organic but [where] the staff were rude/standoffish. We went to the 'white bread' café because it was more 'nourishing'"* (pers. corr. 2015).

Some people are fortunate to enjoy surroundings that offer a wide choice of pleasant and nurturing 'people' and 'place' experiences that they can move to and from as they wish. These people have no difficulty finding and enjoying a healthy experience diet from the extensive and well-presented experience menu offered by their surroundings. Others though may look around their surroundings and find they offer only limited, unappealing or unhealthy experiences. This paucity of opportunity and corresponding lack of choice diminishes the ability of the people who live there to exercise autonomy and live happy, fulfilled lives. Such places offer only a poor experience diet, lacking in the equivalent of variety, taste or nutritional value.

When our surroundings offer us too little stimuli, our experience diet is bland and limited. We become bored and over time our cognitive functions atrophy (Porteous 1977). Collin Ellard (undated) suggests that inadequate stimulation brings with it profound health impacts, stating that *"even brief boring episodes increased levels of cortisol, which fits well with other recent suggestions that there could actually be a relationship between boredom and mortality rates"*. This is particularly the case for the vulnerable in our community.

A place with an experience menu that offers children little choice in their 'play diet' (Simeon Packard in Play England 2008a) denies them many potential developmental benefits that come from the diverse nature of play activities: *"Play is the way that children learn about themselves and the world they live in. In the process of mastering familiar situations and learning to cope with new ones, their intelligence and personality grow, as well as their bodies"* (Wheway and Millward 1997).

If older people find their (often quite limited) sharable surroundings lacking in relevant opportunities, then these places are unlikely to have sufficient appeal to justify the effort and time needed to make the journey. If they choose instead to stay at home, they are less likely to get the mental and physical stimulation they need to counter the ravages of age (WHO 2007).

Collin Ellard noted:

> *boredom or inadequate stimulation can also lead to risky behaviour. Surveys among people with addictions, including substance and gambling addictions, suggest that their levels of boredom are generally higher, and that episodes of boredom are one of the most common predictors of relapse or risky behaviour.*

(undated)

However it is not simply a matter of the more experiences a place offers, the better it is. We function best at the 'Goldilocks' amount of stimulation: not too much nor too little—and as in a food diet, what is too little or too much will be different for each of us, for the reasons outlined in the previous chapter. When our ability to process and respond to these experiences is exceeded, we risk being overwhelmed, triggering a stress response that brings with it a range of mental and physical health issues. Adli Mazda elaborates:

> *Living in an urban environment is long known to be a risk factor for psychiatric diseases such as major depression or schizophrenia. This is true even though infrastructure, socioeconomic conditions, nutrition and health care services are clearly better in cities than in rural areas. Higher stress exposure and higher stress vulnerability seem to play a crucial role. Social stress may be the most important factor for the increased risk of mental disorders in urban areas. It may be experienced as social evaluative threat, or as chronic social stress, both of which are likely to occur as a direct consequence of high population densities in cities. As for the impact on mental health, social stress seems to outweigh other urban stressors such as pollution or noise. Living in crowded areas is associated with increased social stress, since the environment becomes less controllable for the individual. Social disparities also become much more prominent in cities and can impose stress on the individual. . . . A recent meta-analysis showed that urban dwellers have a 20 per cent higher risk of developing anxiety disorders, and a 40 per cent higher risk of developing mood disorders. For schizophrenia, double the risk has been shown, with a 'dose-response' relationship for urban exposure and disease risk. Longitudinal studies on patients with schizophrenia indicate that it is urban living and upbringing per se, rather than other epidemiological variables that increase the risk for mental disorders.*

(Mazda 2011)

The threshold of what represents too much exposure will vary depending on what we are exposed to. Many environmental contaminants such as lead, tobacco smoke or Radon gas (Wigle and Lanphear 2005) are so toxic that there is no safe level. However traffic, noise, light at night and danger amongst other largely unescapable facts of urban living can add to our stress once certain thresholds are reached. Over exposure to these stimuli and under exposure to experiences that can mitigate these negative impacts can add to our allostatic load—the cumulative physiological impacts on our bodies of dealing with stress over prolonged periods. This can result in *"poor subjective health, disability, cognitive decline, cellular aging, diseases, death"* (Read and Grundy 2012). Research commissioned by the EU suggests that the social cost of noise and air pollution, including death and disease, could be nearly €1 trillion (University of Western England 2016).

Unfortunately the contaminants that form part of a person's experience diet are inequitably distributed: *"it is often society's poorest who live and work in the most polluted environments. Furthermore, these same people may be more impacted by pollution's damaging effects than more advantaged groups of society"* (ibid).

Assuming that some exposure is inevitable, *"the question is therefore how to mediate the bad and the excessive"* (Daly 2016). Mediating the bad and excessive stimuli requires enabling people to escape these stressful environments, minimizing exposure to them and/or enabling them to experience places that allow them to counter their detrimental effects. Experience and a wealth of research suggests that enabling people to enjoy nature offers a relief to the demanding and detrimental immediacy of many urban stimuli (Berman et al. 2008; Green 2015 pers. corr.) as well as being a positive contribution to a person's experience diet in its own right (explored in more detail in the 'Our Exposure to Nature' section later in this chapter).

To turn back to the experience menu, theoretically it is very extensive; with enough will and determination anyone can go almost anywhere and enjoy the opportunities that can be found there. In practice though our experience menu is limited to those experiences and opportunities that we consider to be practically accessible and worth the effort. Katherine Shaver (2005) observed that there are limits to how far people will go out of their way to enjoy a rewarding experience.

A way to look at it is to consider every item on our experience menu as having a price tag. Evidently opportunities on our doorstep are easier to take up; they need little investment of time and are likely to be in a place you feel comfortable within—you might say they have a lower price—than opportunities in an unfamiliar place, with unfamiliar people an hour and two bus rides away. When the 'price tag' of walking, running, participating in community events or other nurturing activities makes them uncompetitive against less healthy, unfulfilling behaviours, then they are less likely to be taken up.

Other key factors that influence this price tag are our ability to compete economically for proximity to these desirable experiences, the impacts of others on our ability to enjoy these experiences and the density of experiences.

Places we enjoy, places that enrich us or places that offer convenience to important destinations do not only nurture people but also often attract a market premium as people compete economically to access these qualities. For example UK Environmental Development Agency Groundwork found that houses close to parks are on average 8 per cent more expensive than similar properties further away (Dobson 2012). As a result poorer people with less buying power end up in less supportive environments, 'priced out' of more nurturing places. Poorer people *"are getting pushed out of working class neighbourhoods that are 'good enough' to attract people and investment, while the poorest and most vulnerable neighbourhoods remain mired in persistent poverty and concentrated disadvantage"* (Florida 2015).

Equally, places that may potentially benefit and nurture a section of the community may be denied to them in practice when another section of the community dominates that space, effectively appropriating that place because of the way they act or are just perceived to act. When this happens, a positive experience for one group becomes a negative for another group, as young children may conclude if they find a playground dominated by older children (Rudner et al. 2011).

The value to cost equation is also sensitive to the saturation of experiences and opportunities. Experience and research (such as Leyden 2003) suggests that mixed-use, high(er) density environments are more likely to offer a rich variety of opportunities and experiences within walking distance.

Table 4.2 The hardware, software and orgware that influence our experience menu and diet

Hardware factors that influence our experience menu and diet		*Software factors that influence our experience menu and diet*		*Orgware factors that influence our experience menu and diet*	
. . . in the compassionate city	*. . . in the neglectful city*	*. . . in the compassionate city*	*. . . in the neglectful city*	*. . . in the compassionate city*	*. . . in the neglectful city*
Diverse spaces, capable of multiple, valid interpretations and uses that can happen without conflict. Active transport investment to facilitate ease of movement to, from and between diverse places	Few spaces, each one dedicated exclusively to a narrow range of uses. Mono-use, low-density development that 'create a "50km/hour environment" and isolate people behind a wheel' (Jan Gehl)	Imagination and adaptability to see the potential in a range of different places. Respect for other users. Acceptance that space may be shared with people who may use it differently	Space seen in zero-sum terms, ours or theirs	Investment and management of space to accommodate multiple activities	Lack of investment in design to make places robust enough to accommodate multiple uses. Investment in security to keep out uses and activities that don't conform to narrow management expectations

To relate this back to the framework of fundamental needs identified in Chapter 2, our experience diet and menu influence our ability to meet all our needs, as they describe the range of opportunities available to us. Table 4.2 shows some of the key factors that will influence whether the hardware, software and orgware of a place make it harder or easier for these needs to be met.

Our Exposure to Nature

A place is nurturing when it allows us to interact with nature and neglectful when it separates us from nature.

Just as 'greens' are important in a food diet, green space and features are important in the experience diet. As noted in Chapters 2 and 3, it can help us deal with the stresses of city living. Marc Berman et al. (2008) suggested this happens because nature 'modestly' attracts people's attention, inviting us to enjoy it and giving us relief from other urban stimuli that 'dramatically' demand our attention. They noted that one doesn't have to be immersed in nature for nature to be restorative; simply looking at a natural scene can help. The beneficial impacts of exposure to nature impact upon many aspects of people's lives. People who can experience immersion in nature find it easier to be more caring and are better able to cultivate relationships (Weinstein et al. 2009). In 2015 Weinstein et al. also noted that exposure to nature is linked to improved community cohesion and reduces crime. Wolf (2010) suggested that "*public housing residents with nearby trees and natural landscapes reported 25% fewer acts of domestic aggression and violence*". A WHO report (2016) noted that there is also evidence that suggests the provision of new green spaces in disadvantaged neighbourhoods (e.g. greening of vacant lots) can reduce crime. It also referred to Japanese studies that have demonstrated associations between visiting forests and beneficial immune responses, including expression of anti-cancer proteins (ibid).

Prospective passengers waiting at transit stations where they can see mature trees will perceive waiting time as less than those who can't (Lagune-Reutler et al. 2016). Wolf (2010) notes studies that found drivers who see natural roadside views show lower levels of stress and frustration compared to those in urban settings. A study by Naderi et al. (2008) found street-side trees significantly increased driver perception of the spatial edge and with it their perception of safety regardless of contextual environment. They found this leads to *"a reduction in driving speed in suburban landscapes for both faster and slower drivers"*.

Several authorities note that exposure to nature is of greater benefit to those disadvantaged in urban communities. A paper by Jenny Roe and Peter Aspinall (2011) found that the restorative effects of a walk in nature was greater for people who had poor mental health than it would be for those who already enjoyed good mental health. Likewise a study by Jolanda Maas et al. (2006) found that people from less well-off sections of the community got a greater boost to their well-being from open space than those from better-off areas.

On the other side of the coin, the adverse effects of an experience diet deficient in nature was also borne out in a large epidemiological study (Mitchell and Popham 2008) that found that people who lived further away from natural places tended to have worse health outcomes than those who lived nearer them.

To relate this back to the framework of fundamental needs identified in Chapter 2, exposure to nature influences our ability to meet our needs for protection, understanding, leisure, participation and beauty. Table 4.3 shows some of the key factors that will influence whether the hardware, software and orgware of a place make it harder or easier for these needs to be met.

Table 4.3 The hardware, software and orgware factors that influence our exposure to nature

Hardware factors that influence our exposure to nature		Software factors that influence our exposure to nature		Orgware factors that influence our exposure to nature	
. . . in the compassionate city	. . . in the neglectful city	. . . in the compassionate city	. . . in the neglectful city	. . . in the compassionate city	. . . in the neglectful city
Presence of nature green space easily found, nature emphasized and celebrated, natural processes revealed	No nature visible. Lights, noise, other sources of stress compete with nature for our attention and dominate, green space not easily found	Awareness of the benefits of experiencing nature	Poor awareness of the benefits of experiencing nature, emphasis on the difficulties of experiencing nature	Investment in design and long-term planning necessary for nature to survive, reach maturity and achieve its optimal contribution Clear and strictly applied laws to protect nature and ecological health	Emphasis on the quantitative aspects of creating the built environment to the exclusion of the qualitative Ambiguous, weak or poorly applied laws to protect nature

Our Ability to Adapt Our Surroundings to Meet Our Needs

A place is nurturing when it can respond to people's changing needs; either over time where the needs of the users change or concurrently where different users seek to use that space for different purposes. A place is neglectful when it offers experiences that are rigidly dedicated to a particular use and can't or won't change to accommodate people's needs.

Unfortunately, *"the dominant situation for modern life is individuals living in a setting which was not built for them,"* according to Serge Bouleurline, quoted in Porteous (1977). If our experience diet is inadequate and we cannot find the experiences and opportunities that support our well-being in our experience menu, we need to change that menu. As explored in Chapter 2, the abilities to make things happen, feel a sense of control over one's life and take satisfaction from contributing to others' lives are intrinsically rewarding. Evidently, facilitating people to exercise a degree of control to meet their needs and contribute to their community could result in many different outcomes, depending on their needs, values and the resources available to make the changes. At one end of the spectrum (of all this may entail) are things such as being able to cast a careful eye over what goes on in a place; being able to move a chair to find a more comfortable or self-determined place to sit (Whyte 1980); painting a front door a particular colour; or planting a flower bed that expresses horticultural skill and brightens up the surrounding streetscape. At this smaller, fine-grained end of the scale, these interventions are self-evidently best undertaken by local people. At the other end of the spectrum are major infrastructure projects that require wholesale demolition and rebuilding. These larger, more capital-intensive interventions aren't those that you would want to leave to local non-professionals to just 'have a go at'.

Somewhere on this spectrum is a point at which responsibility to intervene goes from being best undertaken by civil society to being best undertaken by industry and government. In nurturing places, that point is higher than it is in neglectful places and people individually and collectively have more power and ability to self-organize to adapt their personal and shared surroundings should they wish to exercise this power.

However it should be noted that there will always be a point at which outside experts will need to exercise increasing control. Although the resources and insights held within a motivated and organized community can be significant, it is unlikely that they will encompass a strategic overview of the impacts of their interventions. There is also always the potential that a community might unknowingly appropriate resources that may best be shared or protected for future generations.

Furthermore, as Graham Duxbury of Groundwork (a federation of independent charities that seek to improve social and development outcomes in disadvantaged communities) told me (pers. corr. 2015): even if a community is given the right to make changes it may not have the ability. *"People have got used to dumbed-down design and poor quality engagement, sometimes people need help to imagine how things could be better"* (Duxbury, pers. corr. 2015). Consequently there will always be a need for respectful collaboration between professional outsiders, designers, planners, etc. and the community within which changes occur.

An inspiring example of this is found in the work of organizations such as Gap Filler that sprang up in Christchurch after the earthquakes of 2010–2011. Gap Filler is a *"creative urban regeneration initiative that aims to innovate, lead, and nurture people and ideas—contributing to conversations about city-making and urbanism in the 21st century"* (Gap Filler, undated-a). As well as creating their own unique projects, they provide advice, education and practical help for a range of installations, events, artworks and the

Figure 4.2 Dance-O-Mat
Source: courtesy of Gap Filler

creation of community spaces and temporary architecture. Their approach has cultivated a flowering of inexpensive, easily relocatable, quirky, innovative and delightful interventions to fill Christchurch's tragically vacated spaces.

One such project is the Dance-O-Mat (Figure 4.2). In 2012, in response to the lack of spaces to dance in the city post-quake and in an attempt to bring people, life and energy back to the central city, Gap Filler created an open-air dance floor that anyone can use. It features a coin-operated ex-laundromat washing machine that powers four speakers surrounding a custom-made dance floor. "*To use the Dance-O-Mat, people bring any device with a headphone jack such as an Ipod, phone or Mp3 player and plug it into the converted washing machine, insert $2 to activate the power and get dancing!*" (Gap Filler, undated-b). They go on to add,

> *The Dance-O-Mat was first located on a vacant site in 2012 and has occupied three different gaps in the city since then. This project in its first iteration was extremely successful, getting 600 hours of use at our best guess (based on the $2 coins collected) across 3 months.*

> (ibid)

Another is the *Think Differently Book Exchange* (Figure 4.3), a public book exchange located inside a recycled fridge on a cleared lot on the fringes of the city centre. It was created with minimal works from a discarded glass-doored fridge adapted for safety and with some minor landscaping works. It has been running since Sunday 17 July 2011 (Rachel Welfare, pers. corr.). Acknowledging its inspiration from a similar project in the UK, the

Figure 4.3 Think Differently 'Fridge Library'
Source: courtesy of Gap Filler

website states that "*the 'Think Differently' moniker was intended to attract books which readers/exchangers have found life-changing and challenging*" (undated).

> *The Book Exchange has shown its resilience through a number of setbacks. It was pushed over and one panel of glass broken in October, 2011, and suffered two further push-overs in its first year. The fridge was adapted with a stake at its back to stabilise it, and the glass doors were replaced with perspex. Nearly all of the books were stolen from the fridge twice, but the exchange continued with new books replacing the stolen ones. The local community responded to all acts of violence and theft quickly, showing how important the fridge has become, and continues to be.*
>
> (Gap-Filler undated c)

Our Ability to Influence the Design Agenda

Better-off communities tend to be better educated, more articulate and have greater experience of accessing decision-makers. Furthermore the professionals who make planning and design decisions will probably be better attuned to these voices. These people are after all from a similar social strata as the professional designers and planners. As a result these designers, etc. are more likely to share their interpretations of what is important and be swayed by their arguments. Thus people who live in wealthier areas are more likely to have experience of getting things done and of their views being taken into account. Unfortunately people who live in less well-off areas and are of different backgrounds may find they cannot attract the attention of those with power or skills to get things fixed, or if they do they are misunderstood and their priorities misinterpreted. They may also find they are not permitted to contribute themselves or are indeed able to do so. "*Designers are educated and articulate: many user clients are less educated and often inarticulate. This exacerbates the already immense social gap between them,*" according to J Douglas Porteous (1977). This is a viewpoint backed up by the UK social policy think tank Demos, which found that those people in the worst socio-economic status communities get left out of the decision-making process or when they do receive attention it is not as wholehearted or appropriately applied as it would be for wealthier, 'more helpful/co-operative' communities. For people in disadvantaged communities, "*the social distance between planner and planned for is further widened by administrative distance*" (Porteous 1977). Furthermore, "*caught in a web of economic, social and political constraints, planners find themselves unable to respond to the needs of the users*" (ibid).

I saw this myself when I worked in a London borough and noticed that the worst-maintained park with the lowest level of provision was in the poorest part of the borough. I asked a colleague who led the open space design program and whom I knew to be a competent and caring landscape architect why this was so. He said with genuine hurt: "*we did that park up twice and it was vandalised, f**k 'em. They will only vandalise it again if we do it up. Better to spend the money where it can make a difference.*" Already disadvantaged, this sense of distance between designers and 'designed-for' meant that the local neighbourhood had to make do with a less inviting or inspiring park than those enjoyed in more salubrious areas.

Experience suggests that for most people their ability to adapt their surroundings and set the agenda is influenced by the default positions of the people doing the design for them. This is informed by personal values, experience and the day-to-day realities of life of the professional designer or the people who have our ear. We know what we know and often, if no one draws our attention to an issue outside our familiar world, we might miss it. Even if we know of an issue (for example the need for play or to cater for disabled access), if we haven't children or don't personally need universal access, we can overlook it or ascribe it only with attention needed to meet the guidelines. This means that some issues are more likely to be at the forefront of our attention to the detriment of others that subconsciously get put down the list of priorities. In relation to play, Beunderman et al. (2007) observed, "*over the past decades, two other uses of the public realm have been consistently privileged above play: cars and commerce*".

To relate this back to the framework of fundamental needs identified in Chapter 2, the degree to which we are able to tailor our surroundings influences our ability to meet any or all our needs. Furthermore, the action of tailoring our surroundings (if our designers help us!) may in itself contribute to meeting our needs for understanding, creation, freedom and the expression of our identity, our ability to give and receive affection, to participate in society and to protect ourselves. Table 4.4 shows some of the key factors that will influence whether the hardware, software and orgware of a place make it harder or easier for these needs to be met.

Our Connectedness to Each Other and Our Surroundings

A place is nurturing when it provides people with ample, low-risk opportunities to form a bond with each other and their surroundings. A place is neglectful when it offers few or irrelevant opportunities for these connections to form and grow.

These connections are of profound importance, *"a healthy built environment is one which connects citizens together to create a sense of community"* (Thompson and Kent 2014). In the compassionate city, people can choose and modify the types and depths of the connections they make with each other and with their environment to create the networks they need. Without these connections, people become cut adrift from society and cannot contribute to nor benefit from their community's social capital. Unfortunately, *"we have created human societies where it is easier for people to become cut off from all human connections than ever before,"* according to George Monbiot writing in *The Guardian* (Oct 2014). This isolation can have profound effects on people's mental and physical well-being and has been linked to a compromised immune system, high blood pressure, heart disease, stroke risk and ultimately premature death (Valtorta et al. 2016).

Charles Montgomery states that

> *Simple friendships with other people in one's neighbourhood are some of the best salves for stress during hard economic times—in fact, sociologists have found that when adults keep these friendships, their kids are better insulated from the effects of their parents' stress.*
>
> (2013a)

He adds that friendships enhance not just the quality of life but its quantity: people who enjoy connections with those around them sleep better, consistently report being happier, are better equipped to tackle adversity and live longer (ibid). Qualls (2014) reported a meta-analysis of 148 studies that found *"a 50 percent increase in survival of people with robust social relationships, regardless of age, gender, country of origin, or how such relationships were defined"*.

These benefits accrue at many different levels. A review of international evidence undertaken to prepare Melbourne's Metropolitan Plan in 2011 found that broad and inclusive community networks have a significant impact on social and economic outcomes, including:

- Individuals benefitted from better physical and mental health; positive parenting and improved child development; success at school; better employment outcomes; and more positive aging (less institutionalization and better cognitive functioning);
- Communities benefit from the spread of information and innovation; greater social cohesion; effective control of negative behaviours; resilience to disasters and improved ability to turn assets into outcomes.

(Pope and Zhang 2011)

This research found that networks are built through participation. It noted that participation, and opportunities for participation, are not evenly distributed across Melbourne, with the lowest rates in lower socio-economic areas and areas of recent urban expansion.

Table 4.4 The hardware, software and orgware factors that influence our ability to adapt our surroundings

Hardware factors that influence responsivity...		Software factors that influence responsivity...		Orgware factors that influence responsivity...	
...in the compassionate city	...in the neglectful city	...in the compassionate city	...in the neglectful city	...in the compassionate city	...in the neglectful city
Evidence of positive change	No evidence of positive change	Confident and articulate community members Positive experience of having made a difference somewhere within the community Co-operation	Unconfident and inarticulate community members Absent or bad experience of trying to make a difference Conflict, disillusionment and cynicism	Role of community enshrined in planning framework	No role for community in planning framework
Easy to adapt places	Places with every characteristic locked in and unchangeable without outside expert help	Technical and design skills held within the community to make some changes happen (subject to consideration of official views and the needs of other communities) Designers with an ability and inclination to understand the community's design agenda	Community hold few technical or design skills Designers with little ability or inclination to understand the community's design agenda	Community empowered and their contribution is respected and celebrated	Community not empowered and/or are unable to gain the necessary permissions.
Diverse spaces, capable of multiple, valid interpretations and uses that can happen without conflict	Few spaces, each one dedicated exclusively to a narrow range of uses	Imagination and adaptability to see the potential in a range of different places Respect for other users	Space seen in zero-sum terms, ours or theirs	Investment, promotion and management of space to accommodate multiple activities	Lack of investment in design to make places robust enough to accommodate multiple uses Investment in security to keep out uses and activities that don't conform to narrow management expectations

Yet it is not simply a matter of the more connections the better. Unwanted connections are distressing. Nicola Bacon (2010), writing for the UK Social Issues Think Tank the Young Foundation, found that *"experiments to force people to interact with their neighbours have not been a success. Choice is key. A massive study of the 1970's British 'good neighbours' schemes ended with a simple conclusion that 'good fences make good neighbours'."* The New Zealand Ministry for the Environment quotes research by Shehayeb that found that people interact more when they have the choice to avoid it (NZ Ministry for the Environment 2005). As such the compassionate city is about giving people agency to determine their preferred form and amount of interaction, who they interact with and what role they play in their community.

Another dimension of connectedness comes from the bonds that people have with their surroundings. As noted in Chapter 3 many people invest great emotional capital in their surroundings, valuing them for what they represent, their utility or their intrinsic beauty. Nurturing places are informed by processes that respect and consider the value of this bond when making decisions about how to meet emerging challenges and evolving expectations. Neglectful places ignore the nature of this bond and allow things to be built that give no consideration of the emotional connections that people have to a place. This is a view reflected by Ken Worpole and Katharine Knox in their insightful study for the Joseph Rowntree Foundation of the social value of public spaces. Regeneration strategies that *"override or fail to take into account local attachments to existing spaces and places may undermine local communities in the longer term"* (2007).

Jane Frances Kelly et al. (2012) stressed the importance of the streets outside our homes as settings for these bonds to form, noting it is *"on the street that we are most likely to meet those who live closest to us—our neighbours"*.

However, although important, for most people the street outside their house will inevitably not be able to meet all their social needs. For example it is unlikely that any street, no matter how well designed, will meet the requirements of most organized team sports. Given the diversity of any community, the diversity of preferences within a community and the varied specifications of places to facilitate different activities, this suggests that nurturing places should provide a wide variety of accessible and adaptable spaces and facilities.

The Importance of Trust

Trust is a precondition to connecting, it provides reassurance that the people around us add to our experience of the public realm and are potential helpers rather than a potential threat. It helps us satisfy our need to be around other people and makes chance encounters something to be welcomed rather than feared. These interactions provide the basic foundations upon which social connections can flourish; as Jane Jacobs put it, *"the small change from which a city's wealth of public life may grow"* (quoted in Kelly et al. 2012). Trust is influenced by social processes (Wilkinson and Pickett 2010) and city form: *"People who live in mono-functional, car-dependent neighbourhoods outside urban centres are much less trusting of other people than people who live in walkable neighbourhoods where housing is mixed with shops, services and places to work,"* according to Charles Montgomery, writing in *The Guardian* (2013b). Charles Montgomery also noted that people were more trusting in environments that were more open and where passive surveillance from surrounding properties was possible (2013a).

In the neglectful city, trust is less well embedded in the social fabric and fear of what other people will do weighs heavily on the balance of influences and cultivates a sense of 'stranger danger'. This contributes to some people and particularly women choosing not to pass through some areas and only visit other places during daylight hours, isolating them from the opportunities they may otherwise enjoy. It also contributes to the pressures that reduce children's independent range (Kepper et al. 2016), which brings with it many and significant attendant health and developmental issues (Rudner et al. 2011). People in places lacking in trust may understandably seek to protect themselves from others and retreat into secure environments. Once there they look around their homes and workplaces and incrementally make design decisions that end up defining the public realm by the security infrastructure of walls, fences, shutters and surveillance equipment. In doing so they can blight their surroundings and deny themselves a significant area of opportunity to connect with other people.

Blight

Intentionally or unintentionally, some uses and activities blight the space around it, negating its potential to meet people's needs. Perhaps the most significant blighting of space arises from the speed, volume, danger and intrusion of vehicles on many streets. Their dominance forces life indoors or to the peripheries of shared space, diminishing the setting for community life and with it people's ability to form and nurture friendships (Hart and Parkhurst 2011). Another significant type of blight comes from a fear of what other people might do in a place (Montgomery 2013b). In their insightful study for The Joseph Rowntree Foundation, Holland et al. found that *"places acquire reputations (fairly or unfairly) that persist and affect whether and how people use them"* (2007). Nurturing cities seek to allow places to be shared by diverse users without any group or use inadvertently tainting that place for other users. Neglectful cities do little to stop this blight and allow people or uses to deny the enjoyment of places to other people or uses. This might be seen as a 'zero-sum game' situation in which the benefits gained by one person or group are only achieved by a loss to another.

It should be noted though that taking effective control of a place by a group need not always be a negative thing. As Holland et al. noted in their study of Aylesbury in the UK, *"in addition to the social function of public spaces, some people use them for privacy or to support a sense of territorial ownership—this particularly applies to groups of young people and marginalised groups"* (2007). The study goes on to note they observed the tendency of people to yield this control to other people or groups at different times, so that places were shared, just not at exactly the same time. The report then suggests that policy-makers can support this by encouraging diversity and harnessing people's tendency to 'self-regulate' to avoid conflict. They further add that over-regulated environments are not conducive to vibrancy and integration (ibid).

To relate this back to the framework of fundamental needs identified in Chapter 2, our connectedness to each other and to our surroundings influences our ability to become settled in a place and enjoy a sense of belonging. Specifically this may help us meet our needs to develop a unique identity, participate in society, and earn and offer affection to others; this also offers us a sense of protection from belonging to something bigger. Table 4.5 shows some of the key factors that will influence whether the hardware, software and orgware of a place makes it harder or easier for these needs to be met.

Our Confidence in Our Community

A place is nurturing when its occupants feel assured they are being well looked after and can conclude that their investment of emotional capital in the area is shared and justified. In such places, people feel that they are not exposed to unnecessary risks, everyone will be

Table 4.5 The hardware, software and orgware factors that influence our ability to connect with one another

Hardware factors that influence connectedness		Software factors that influence connectedness		Orgware factors that influence connectedness	
. . . in the compassionate city	*. . . in the neglectful city*	*. . . in the compassionate city*	*. . . in the neglectful city*	*. . . in the compassionate city*	*. . . in the neglectful city*
Community life isn't forced out of the public realm by traffic Passive surveillance of shared space to ensure it feels adequately safe Comfortable and appealing shared environments that increase the chances of people staying in a place long enough to bump into someone they know	Traffic-dominated streets No passive surveillance of shared space Places that don't support incidental social interaction	Risk and fear put in context Positive experiences of interactions on balance	Risk and fear not put in context, given great and disproportionate significance Negative experiences of interactions on balance	Risk and fear put in context Security measures discrete	Risk and fear not put in context, allowed to dominate Security measures dominant and a priority
Changes retain and enhance the qualities broadly valued in the community that influence place attachment Diverse spaces, capable of being shared for multiple, valid interpretations and uses that can happen without conflict	Changes retain and enhance the qualities broadly valued in the community that influence place attachment Few spaces, each one dedicated exclusively to a narrow range of uses and users			Emotional attachment to a place considered in design decisions Investment and management of space to accommodate multiple activities in spaces	Emotional attachment to a place considered in design decisions Lack of investment in design and management to make places robust enough to accommodate multiple uses without conflict Investment in security to keep out uses and activities that don't conform to narrow management expectations

treated fairly, that their rights will be respected and that they collectively have the capacity to respond to existing and emerging challenges. A place is neglectful when it gives people little reason to invest emotionally in the people around them or the place they share.

We don't experience our surroundings as a snapshot in time. Places have momentum. Our towns and cities and the communities that occupy them are dynamic systems, always responding to changing environmental circumstances, expectations, demographics, political and economic pressures, technological possibilities and fashions. The legacy of observed change in the past and the promise of more in the future will draw people to a conclusion about whether this change is good or bad and will bring with it a perception that things are getting better or worse.

This awareness provokes a response. For example in many countries the perceived risk from traffic accidents is increasingly compelling more and more parents to drive their children to school in bigger vehicles. This further increases the number of vehicles on the road in the morning peak and so increases the risk of accidents, leading to a vicious circle in which the obvious solution (to drive) only makes the problem worse. Parents grow more concerned, more time pressures are added to their lives and children are denied the health and social benefits of making their own way to school (Basbas et al. 2011).

Furthermore, as noted previously, people become used to the way their surroundings are and even positive changes, if poorly considered, explained or executed, can erode people's comfortable and familiar sense of their community and leave them with a sense of *'solistalgia'*—a *"homesickness felt at home"* (Glenn Albricht, quoted in Seed 2008), separated by time rather than distance from a place that resonated with them and to which they can never return.

Experience suggests that places that are felt to be in decline produce a sense of *'why bother?'* and foster a reluctance to invest capital, emotional or financial, in their community. Denied the motivation that comes from hope, decline is hastened and the sense that investing in that community will be unrewarded is reinforced.

However, this downward momentum can be challenged. The inventive responses to the NZ Canterbury earthquakes of 2010 and 2011 provide some inspiring examples of how urban design can be used to re-instil confidence that a better future isn't just possible but is being actively achieved.

One of the features of the tragedy was its selective destructiveness. *"Churches, pubs and chimneys"* bore the brunt of the earthquake (Councillor Claudia Read of Christchurch City Council pers. comm.), denying the region many of the typically older, grander, often brick buildings that had been the traditional centres of community life. Christchurch city centre was particularly badly affected; it was the scene of most deaths and for 28 months all, and then parts of it, were a 'red zone' considered too dangerous to re-occupy. During this time, 80 per cent of its buildings were cleared or demolished (Re:Start website, undated). The denial of the city centre for such a long period threatened to unravel the fabric of the city's shared identity and its social infrastructure as people began to go to a variety of suburban centres to meet the needs they had previously looked to the city to meet.

The city responded to this challenge with a number of innovative and thought-provoking design responses. Perhaps the flagship project was Re:Start, a retail and open space development deep within the abandoned CBD constructed of shipping containers (Figure 4.4). This sought to reverse this drift to the suburbs and growing sense that the city centre's abandonment was permanent with a powerful built statement that captured the community's imagination. Paul Lonsdale, manager of the trust that developed the centre (The

Figure 4.4 Re:Start

Re:Start the Heart Trust) told me how the development was intended to represent a big vote of confidence in the city centre. It sought to enable people to overlay new and positive memories of the CBD over the sad ones of the past and rekindle the sense that the CBD was a source of civic pride and the natural place to shop and socialize. Although at the time of writing the development was approaching the end of its lease (February 2017), it has proved effective and popular. Tim Hunter, chief executive of Christchurch and Canterbury Tourism noted that the complex had soon become *"an essential part of the city's international image and reputation"* (reported by Tess McClure and Cecile Meier 2013).

Paul Lonsdale told me that critical to achieving this was the commitment, hard work and vision of the city's Property and Building Owners group and the developers, the way it was built and its design features. The developers demonstrated a mastery of the theatrical to capture the public's imagination: all the containers arrived on one ship as if relieving a besieged city to create a media-friendly, identifiable 'start point' for the project. From that day to opening the construction took only 61 days, creating a sense of rapid and positive change. The design (by the Brisbane office of Buchan Architects) uses bright colours and cantilevered stacked containers, as well as incorporates new and existing landscaping to create a 'wow' factor and provide a focus for renewed civic pride. The use of shipping containers allows the development to morph easily to accommodate the rebuilding process. Furthermore the size of the development, offering over 50 retailers and facilitating the return of the iconic Ballantynes department store as an anchor, created a critical mass of activity that has drawn people back into their city centre. As such the project provided an impressive symbol of Kiwi resilience, a welcome boost to the community and an

Figure 4.5 Albion Square

important symbol of recovery. It has also provided an icon for a new Christchurch that has allowed it to challenge its staid, conservative reputation, or throw off its 'conservative veil', as eloquently put by Paul Lonsdale (pers. corr. 2015).

The nearby port township of Lyttleton had also been severely damaged in the earthquakes, losing much of its historic centre and challenging people's sense of confidence in the future of their community. The development of Albion Square (named after the pub that had stood on the site) offers another example of creating a symbolic and practical statement that said the decline had stopped and a more hopeful future was a possibility. The project did this by adding an urban square to the range of spaces the township offers, filling in a long-identified gap in provision and reconciling diverse civic and recreational uses. It is finished to a very high standard to make a strong contribution to the streetscape and creates a memorable image for the township with the towering Port Hills as a backdrop to the activity and visual interest of the square (Figure 4.5).

The Importance of Safety

A sense of safety or its absence is a powerful motivator on our behaviour (Bhalla et al. 2014) and has a major impact on the confidence people have in their community. As noted in Chapter 3 an absence of safety is felt most keenly amongst the more vulnerable sections of the community. It can be a significant deterrent to doing things such as walking, cycling, interacting with others or even just leaving the house. This brings with it a range of health impacts. A study by Putrik et al. (2015) that explored associations between certain features of neighbourhood environment and self-rated health and depressive symptoms in

The Netherlands found that residents of unsafe communities were less likely to report good health and had a higher incidence of depressive symptoms.

In a report commissioned by the World Bank to investigate the burden of disease from motorized transport, Kavi Bhalla pointed to research that found the provision of safety infrastructure for walking and cycling is amongst the most important ways to encourage active modes of transport (Bhalla et al. 2014). The same report noted the growing body of literature that suggests that reassuring people that active transport wasn't prohibitively risky had both physical and psychological components, requiring *"an integrated approach that includes providing safe infrastructure such as sidewalks and bike lanes, supportive land use planning, and advocacy and education".*

The Importance of Social Capital

An important contributor to a sense of confidence in one's community is social capital. A study by Weel and Akçomak (2008) of the relationship between social capital and crime in The Netherlands found *"that higher levels of social capital are associated with lower crime rates".* They suggest this is because

> *an individual is less likely to commit crime if his peers and the community he belongs to punish deviant behaviour. If one individual decides not to commit crime, it is less likely that others will do so, which creates an external effect of one person's behaviour on the others.*

> (Weel and Akçomak 2008)

The Importance of the Rule of Law

Good urban design will take time to maximize its social returns and justify its cost to the community. This can be one week for a pop-up park, one season for a community garden or many generations in the case of significant street trees, and somewhere in between for the buildings and infrastructure that need time to cover their construction costs, find acceptance and support, and weave themselves into the social fabric. If people and communities are to feel comfortable making an investment that will only pay a dividend far into the future they need the reassurance that it enjoys and will continue to enjoy the reliable protection of fair and consistently applied laws. As Richard Horton (2016) puts it, the rule of law is not just about respecting statutes passed by a legislature, it is far more important than that. It is a quality of the political culture that places great significance on good governance, independent accountability and respect for certain rights. He goes on to reflect that

> *The greater the attention societies gave to ideas of liberty, justice, and respect for persons—in other words, to the intrinsic value of individual human beings—the more those societies created the conditions, incentives, and obligations for governments to invest in the value of individual human beings.*

> (Horton 2016)

He adds that this commitment finds expression through investments in health, education and social protection (Horton 2016).

Resilience and Vulnerability

Resilience is *"the ability of a system, community or society exposed to hazards to resist, absorb, accommodate and recover from the effects of a hazard in a timely and efficient manner"* (UN Office for Disaster Risk Reduction 2007). Places lacking resilience will be less able to cope with the disruptions brought about by existing and emerging challenges. Awareness that there will be risks—some that can be foreseen and some that can't—will create uncertainty. This can weigh heavily on people's minds and act to deter people from investing emotional and physical capital in their community or re-invest it after disruptive events for which they were unprepared (Parkinson 2000).

Resilience comes from the ability to adapt to changing circumstances. This requires that people can access the resources of materials, wealth, innovation and skills to make any necessary adjustments to the way they live, how they derive a sense of self-worth and the rules that govern their lives. Vulnerable communities are those that are exposed to a high risk that the foundations of their well-being and valued assets could be lost to them. This can happen through disasters, conflict, economic or social change that might make a community's familiar and valued ways of living obsolete or otherwise inadequate.

Resilience is strongly influenced by social factors. There is a weight of evidence that suggests that the more equitable a community is the more resilient it is (Wilkinson and Pickett (2010). Communities with higher levels of social capital tend to recover more effectively, efficiently and quickly after disasters (Dash 2009; Vedantam 2011; Aldrich undated). According to Aldricht (undated): *"Three mechanisms allow these tightly knit communities to bounce back: information, collective action, and connections."*

Furthermore, communities with strong social capital enjoy an enhanced sense of assurance that conflicts can be overcome: *"Strong attachment and involvement in community matters also leads to strong social bonds by which conflicts are resolved in a more peaceful way compared to communities with weak social bonds"* (Weel and Akçomak 2008).

To relate this back to the framework of fundamental needs identified in Chapter 2, the reassurances offered by a place influence our ability to be able to predict with reasonable confidence what a place will be like in the future. This will allow us to make self-determined, well-informed plans about how to invest in our surroundings and protect what is important to achieve life's goals. Thus it can influence our ability to meet needs relating to protection and identity. Table 4.6 summarizes some of the key factors that will influence whether the hardware, software and orgware of a place make it harder or easier for these needs to be met.

The Maturity of Our Community

A place is nurturing when it has developed a rich network of formal and informal networks and people have been able to forge connections with each other and with the place. A place is neglectful when it has not adequately matured enough to provide these things.

The bonds that connect us to each other and our surroundings take time to grow. As put most eloquently by American author Wallace Stegner:

> *A place is not a place until people have been born in it, have grown up in it, lived in it, known it, died in it—have both experienced and shaped it, as individuals, families, neighborhoods, and communities, over more than one generation.*
>
> (undated)

Table 4.6 The hardware, software and orgware factors that influence the confidence people have in their community

Hardware factors that influence our confidence in our community		Software factors that influence our confidence in our community		Orgware factors that influence our confidence in our community	
. . . in the compassionate city	. . . in the neglectful city	. . . in the compassionate city	. . . in the neglectful city	. . . in the compassionate city	. . . in the neglectful city
All built form demonstrably accords with key planning requirements (e.g. heights and setbacks) for that area to create a built landscape that reflects even-handedness and equality before the law	Exceptions to key planning requirements for particular developments that give that development a particular economic or other advantage	Understanding of relevant planning provisions and their rationale / Integrity of the planning and development process valued and protected	Lack of understanding of relevant planning provisions or their rationale / Corruption in the development and planning process	Transparency in development decisions / Recognition of the importance of natural justice / Planning rules balance flexibility and certainty / Clear rules about what gets built and what doesn't / Clear rules about the circumstances that justify departing from the planning and development rules	Opacity in development decisions / No recognition of the importance of natural justice / Planning rules too rigid or too vague / Poorly articulated rules about what gets built and what doesn't / Vagueness about the circumstances that justify departing from the planning and development rules
Significant investment in education and a wide range of social facilities for people to develop their skills, resources and social capital	Little investment in education and a limited range of social facilities for people to develop their skills, resources and social capital	Experience addressing many challenges in life directly or within a community (rather than through outside help) / Significant social capital, personally held skills and resources and awareness of others' skills and resources	All challenges met through outside help / Little social capital, personally held skills and resources or awareness of others' skills and resources in the community	Investment in responding to emerging challenges such as climate change / Cultivation of resourcefulness in the community and support for the development of a wide range of social networks	Little investment in responding to emerging challenges such as climate change / Poor cultivation of resourcefulness in the community and little support for the development of a wide range of social networks
Observed enhancement of physical and social qualities that are considered important to the community / Change is explained in a way that is accessible to members of the community affected	Observed erosion of physical and social qualities that are considered important to the community / The community are not engaged in the design process and changes are not explained in a way that is accessible to members of the community affected	Sense that planners have integrity and can be trusted / Widely held perceptions that participating in community engagement sessions is worthwhile / Widely held perception that people are listened to and the reasons for changes are understood	Sense that planners have little integrity and cannot be trusted / Widely held perceptions that people are not listened to and the reasons for changes are not understood.	Sincere efforts made to engage the community in the design process and decisions explained	The community are not engaged in the design process in any meaningful way

New communities are often blighted by the inadequacy of such connections. In the UK, '*new town blues*' was the term coined to describe the "*loose grouping of mental health vulnerabilities experienced by New Town residents*" (Goh and Bailey 2007). Many of them experienced disruption, loneliness and dashed hopes, where the familiarities of past connections were well known but no longer available and the connections of the future had yet to emerge and possibly would never emerge. This is both a hardware issue and a software issue: the hardware is difficult to provide when the population numbers just don't exist to support the necessary services, clubs, shops and facilities needed to catalyse connections; and it is a software issue as people don't have enough experience of their new neighbours or knowledge of the opportunities of their surroundings to make the necessary connections.

An example of the cost of inadequate and unformed connections in a community's software comes from a study that sought to examine why the residents of Cambourne, a new settlement of 3300 dwellings in Cambridgeshire in the UK, suffered a disproportionate amount of mental health issues. The study by the Cambridgeshire Primary Care Partnerships attributed this to social links that had been frayed when people moved and had not yet been re-established in their new community. The report found: "*Planning for the hard infrastructure alone would never build a community and that it would only be done by a matrix of formal and informal opportunities or supported activities*" (Goh and Bailey 2007).

To relate this back to the framework of fundamental needs identified in Chapter 2, the more mature a community is, the more developed the settings and opportunities for needs satisfaction are likely to be. This may be neighbours who know one another and look out for each other or parks with established landscapes or a variety of services, community groups and societies. The more deeply embedded this social infrastructure is and the greater the experience of people benefitting from it, the more that community is likely to

Table 4.7 The hardware, software and orgware factors that influence the maturity of a community

Hardware factors that influence the maturity of the community		Software factors that influence the maturity of the community		Orgware factors that influence the maturity of the community	
. . . in the compassionate city	*. . . in the neglectful city*	*. . . in the compassionate city*	*. . . in the neglectful city*	*. . . in the compassionate city*	*. . . in the neglectful city*
Social infrastructure well established	Social infrastructure not established or only established after a considerable period	Strong sense of community	Weak sense of community.	Policies and tenure favour stable populations and low turnover of inhabitants High priority for social infrastructure	Policies and tenure favour high turnover of inhabitants Low priority for social infrastructure
Physical infrastructure to cater for all ages and allows people to age in place	Physical infrastructure to cater for only one age group	Experience and familiarity with opportunities of the place	Little awareness of the opportunities of the place	Age and family-friendly policies allowing multiple generations to share the community	Little support for families and the elderly

offer a wealth of '*well-worn paths*' to beneficial outcomes. As such this variable may influence our ability to meet our identity, participation and protection needs. Table 4.7 shows some of the key factors that will influence whether the hardware, software and orgware of a place make it harder or easier for these needs to be met.

The Playability of Our Surroundings

A place is nurturing when it offers children *and* adults opportunities to have fun, either as an end in itself or as an added bonus to doing needs-fulfilling things. A neglectful place offers few opportunities to do things for fun and makes meeting needs unnecessarily tiresome.

Playing is an essential part of a balanced experience diet. Fun and play are an end in themselves and a means to an end, supporting many different aspects of emotional, cognitive and physical development (Play England 2008b). The term 'play' encompasses a very wide range of activities that children and young people do when adults aren't telling them what to do. Play can happen in a wide variety of different settings and take many forms, far more than the activities that most adults will consider when they think about play. It can be entirely in one's head or have an obvious external expression. Play can be individual (observing, sitting, daydreaming, imagining). It can be social (for example team games, role-playing, problem-solving and imitation). It can be active (ball games, running, sliding, jumping, swinging, skipping, hopping, bouncing). It can be cognitive and creative (making or destroying things, planning things, problem-solving, exploring, discovering and other related activities) (adapted from City of Marion 2008). It can be more than one of these things at any time and can move between different types of play in a single session.

The compassionate city is intrinsically playable and offers us all plentiful opportunities to have fun whilst engaging with the world around us. It provides catalysts to "*let the play out*" (Paul Longridge and Mark Mitchell, pers. corr.). This can happen in a range of ways; it might be by creating a sense of reassurance so carers are happier to let children out to find their own opportunities, or it may be by providing features that invite active interaction with the place or other people or fire an individual's imagination.

The compassionate city embeds playability into otherwise mundane (but needs-fulfilling) activities and offers fun as a reward for undertaking activities that may benefit us but may otherwise not be so appealing. For example getting adequate exercise can be a chore when it is monotonous and repetitive, but when it is achieved as part of a game or sport, the balance of influences may change and the hard work may become a less significant factor, counteracted by the fun. The *Fun Factory* provides an expression of this idea. Although an attempt at 'stealth' advertising by a car manufacturer, it has a very powerful underlying message that "*something as simple as fun is the easiest way to change people's behaviour for the better*" (Fun Theory website, undated). An example of the Fun Theory is the experiment conducted in 2009 where steps in a metro station in Stockholm were adapted to become working piano keys in an attempt to encourage people not to use the escalator. The promise of fun (offering the 'hidden' health benefits of exercise) proved effective in changing people's behaviour "*Turning a set of subway stairs into a real-life piano make people 66% more likely to use them*" according to Herchmer (2012). The idea inspired many other similar interventions (Figure 4.6).

Another example of emphasizing fun is found in the work of Edi Rama, former mayor of Tirana in Albania from 2000–2003. Seeking a way to regenerate the capital and shake off both its communist-era drabness and avaricious capitalist excesses, he initiated a program of reclaiming public space from illegal commercial construction and painting buildings in

Figure 4.6 Piano Staircase
Source: courtesy of istock

bright colours (Figure 4.7). The program was a distinctive and striking rejection of both excess and repression at a profound emotional level, effectively seeking to change the DNA of the city. Sophie Arie writing in *The Guardian* (2003) reported Edi Rama as saying that *"cheering Albania up is the key to its social, economic and political renaissance and to changing the country's international image as the 'land of prostitutes and illegal immigrants'"*. She goes on to add that polls found that *"around 80% of Albanians approve of the facelift Rama has given their capital city"* (ibid).

On my visit in 2016 I noted these civic interventions had been maintained (Figure 4.7a) and the idea adopted by individuals (Figure 4.7b). Reflecting on the legacy of the time, Edi Rama observed that the colours cultivated a new and deeper connection between people and place: *"Once the buildings were coloured, people started to get rid of the heavy fences of their shops. In the painted roads, we had 100% tax collection from the people, while tax collection was normally 4%"* (Jason Farago, in *The Guardian* 2016).

Another good example of incorporating playability into the built environment can be found in Warin (wombat), a sculpture in Melbourne's City Square (Figure 4.8). Warin is one of Melbourne's best-loved works of public art. Constructed of river red gum (*Eucalyptus camaldulensis*) wood, it is of a colour, shape, size and material that invites people to find delight in it. For children this comes from the subconscious invitation it gives them to clamber all over it, adorning it with their presence. For adults who would typically be more reluctant to climb on it, the sculpture offers delight in its texture and beautiful form. According to the artist Des McKenna his design reflected his desire that it would be *"just the right height for children and young at heart to sit on and feel"* (pers. corr. 2015).

In the neglectful city fun is not valued and play—in particular active, outdoor play—happens less, frozen out by an inadequacy of inviting, safe opportunities. Not so much because of children's reluctance to play—children will play almost anywhere, inspired by their imaginations (see Chapter 2)—but because their parents or guardians increasingly interpret places as threatening (Clements 2004; Planet Ark 2011) or prioritize other activities and actively deter children from playing.

To relate this back to the framework of fundamental needs identified in Chapter 2, the promise of fun may tip the balance and influence us to participate in a range of activities we may otherwise not do. This may allow us to benefit from the protective advantages of exercise, learn about ourselves and the world around us, test and develop our skills, benefit from the satisfaction of little achievements and provide opportunities to interact with other people. It can provide an outlet for us to express ourselves. Thus it can influence our ability to meet our needs for physical activity, leisure, understanding, creation, identity, freedom and protection. Table 4.8 shows some of the key factors that will influence whether the hardware, software and orgware of a place make it harder or easier for these needs to be met.

The Ease of Understanding the Available Opportunities and Experiences

A place is nurturing when it is legible and clearly communicates to the people who share it the options available to them. A neglectful city obscures its assets and opportunities and fails to share its stories.

An individual's ability to take up opportunities available to them is to a large extent dependent on their ability to read their surroundings and understand what those opportunities are. Kevin Lynch's influential and insightful book *The Image of the City* (1960) sheds a light on the processes by which the visible city becomes embedded in people's

Figure 4.7 Examples of the Repainting of Buildings in Tirana (top) and an Example of the Private Colouring It Inspired (bottom)

Source: Shutterstock 585399503 and author

Figure 4.8 Warin
Source: courtesy of Belinda Strickland

awareness, helps people orientate themselves and help people get a sense of where they should go or avoid. Although *The Image of the City* has been criticized for relating only to the visible expression of the physical city, ignoring the messages of our other senses (de Lange 2009), it is useful in the way it spans and links the hardware and software of the city and provides a helpful language by which we might articulate the social landscape.

Kevin Lynch suggests that people make sense of the city with

> *a generalized mental picture of the exterior physical world that is held by an individual. This image is the product both of immediate sensation and of the memory of past experience, and it is used to interpret information and to guide action.*
>
> (1960)

He suggests that clear cerebral maps of the urban environment protect a person against the fear of disorientation and bring with them a sense of emotional security, allowing a person to experience the city at ease.

He categorizes the components of a city (Figure 4.9) that form this mental map as: (1) Paths: these are routes along which people move throughout the city and from which they experience it; (2) Edges: these are boundaries that create discontinuities in the urban fabric; (3) Districts: areas that share a common set of characteristics; (4) Nodes: these are strategic focus points such as squares and junctions that provide points of orientation and that can be occupied and passed through; and (5) Landmarks: these are distinctive points in the landscape that allow people to orientate themselves, usually experienced externally.

Experience suggests that when these elements are clearly articulated in the urban fabric, the city becomes intrinsically legible and requires less additional interventions such as signs to give people the reassurance that they are heading in the right direction as they move through the city. This reassurance enables people to interpolate the gaps in their mind maps and explore, turning potentially sharable space into actively shared space, to relate it to some of the concepts introduced in the last chapter.

Table 4.8 The hardware, software and orgware factors that influence the playability of a community

Hardware factors that influence the playability of the community		Software factors that influence the playability of the community		Orgware factors that influence the playability of the community	
. . . in the compassionate city	*. . . in the neglectful city*	*. . . in the compassionate city*	*. . . in the neglectful city*	*. . . in the compassionate city*	*. . . in the neglectful city*
Frequently accessible, high-profile, attractive, dedicated play areas	Few, unattractive play areas	Belief in the importance of children's independent play and reassurance that the public realm is safe enough to warrant it	Little belief in the importance of children's independent play or little assurance that the public realm is safe enough to warrant it	Play seen as a priority and encouraged in adults and children	Play not seen as a priority and only tolerated or even discouraged
Variety of 'loose-fit' open spaces to accommodate a range of activities at the same time or consecutively	Dangerous informal play opportunities Heavily trafficked streets	Experience of others playing safely and happily in the public realm	Little experience of others playing in the public realm or advice that it is dangerous or 'not for nice kids'		
Frequent informal play opportunities such as street furniture and public art compatible with playing, by virtue of its material, location, form (wherever appropriate)	No consideration of the comfort of attending carers and non-playing child				
Streets/lanes with low traffic volumes and slow traffic to accommodate street play					
Grid network allowing for streets to be closed for play events					
Trees, seats and other street furniture to allow comfort for the carer and non-playing child					

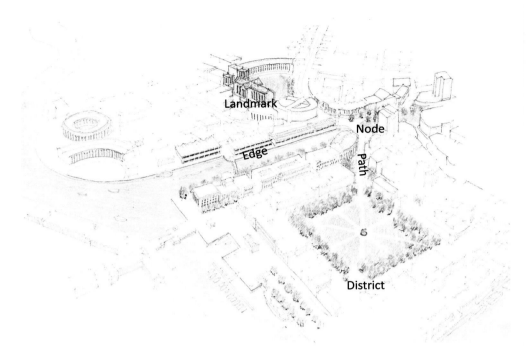

Figure 4.9 Examples of Lynch's Five Elements Based on Bristol, UK

Kevin Lynch's work was built upon by Ian Bentley et al. (1985) with their influential *Responsive Environments*. This book suggests that "*people can only take advantage of the choices which those qualities offer if they can grasp the place's layout, and what goes on there.*" Based on their experience and interpretation of the research, they suggested a series of design techniques that reinforce the effectiveness of Lynch's five elements, making nodes more obviously node-like and landmarks more distinctive, for example. Their recommendations stressed the importance of design that was grounded on an understanding of how local people saw their surroundings and the visual conventions that allowed people to draw conclusions about the activities that take place in a building or area from its external characteristics.

However there is more to understanding a town or city than being able to place yourself geographically and locate activities within it. Any place is likely to have a wealth of historical layers (which may or may not have a physical expression) which may create emotional hotspots. The compassionate city nurtures its inhabitants by revealing those layers and allowing us all to look upon our surroundings in a way informed by this understanding. When we can place these layers in chronological order and understand the evolution of a place, we can interpret its momentum, giving us a sense of where it has come from and perhaps where it is going to go.

In the neglectful city these structuring elements are lacking or are obscured by poor, homogenous urban form or drowned out by an overload of information from such things as advertising or the demands of moving through congested cities. In such places mental maps fail to come into focus. People get lost, provoking "*the sense of anxiety and even terror*" that many people experience when they lose their way (Lynch 1960). Their occupants find that past beneficial experiences of places they have enjoyed cannot be 'topped

Table 4.9 The hardware, software and orgware factors that influence the ease of understanding a place

Hardware factors that influence how easy it is to understand an area		Software factors that influence how easy it is to understand an area		Orgware factors that influence how easy it is to understand an area	
... in the compassionate city	*... in the neglectful city*	*... in the compassionate city*	*... in the neglectful city*	*... in the compassionate city*	*... in the neglectful city*
Buildings designed to reflect easy-to-understand conventions about the activities they offer	Buildings designed with no regard to conventions about the activities they offer	Design processes give weight to understanding how people interpret their surroundings and the conventions about what particular building types and uses look like	Design processes give little consideration to understanding how people interpret their surroundings and the conventions about what particular building types and uses look like	Design guidelines stress importance of legible street network, good signage, conventions about the appearance of particular land uses and the responsibilities of high-profile locations in assisting wayfinding	Design guidelines define what is acceptable with no reference to legibility.
Legible, easy-to-understand street network and signage	Illegible, difficult-to-understand street network and poor signage				
Presence of distinguishing features (landmark buildings or spaces) visible at decision points such as intersections	No distinguishing features at decision points such as intersections				
Physical markers for historical events	No physical markers for historical events	Significant historical awareness	Little historical awareness	History and heritage valued, researched and funded	History and heritage not valued, researched or funded

up' with further visits as the effort needed to find these places again remains stubbornly high, even after multiple visits.

To relate this back to the framework of fundamental needs identified in Chapter 2, The ease with which we can understand our surroundings influences our ability to take up the opportunities it offers and gain a sense of what it means to us. As such it may help meet our needs of understanding, participation and identity. Table 4.9 shows some of the key factors that will influence whether the hardware, software and orgware of a place make it harder or easier for these needs to be met.

The Status Our Surroundings Ascribe to Us

A place is nurturing when all of its inhabitants enjoy surroundings that reflect well on them and there is little that invites others to negatively stereotype them. A place is neglectful when it reflects badly on the people who share it.

How people are perceived matters. Wilkinson and Pickett (2010) suggest a characteristic of humanity is that we often have difficulty differentiating esteem and self-esteem and tend to take on board the judgements that others make of us: we are a failure if people think we are. Unfortunately the built environment that surrounds us and the activities it accommodates can give other people many messages that they will interpret as saying something about who we are. Where we live can make people form the view of whether we are likely to be trustworthy or not, rich, poor, working or unemployed, educated or not educated, locally born or an immigrant.

Josephine Parsons, writing in *The Guardian*, suggested such 'postcode prejudice' (Parsons 2016) creates an uneven landscape of opportunity and makes it harder for people in some areas to access the opportunities or benefit from other people's trust and acceptance than they would if they lived elsewhere. Speaking of the negative perceptions of Sydney's western suburbs, she notes that this *"postcode problem has created a class divide so great that it threatens to determine our potential"*.

Similarly, in the UK, the inhabitants of many urban renewal projects found the strong association that these places had with crime and unemployment meant that an address in many of these places stigmatized their inhabitants (CABE 2008). Other people thought less of an inhabitant of these areas not because of what they had done but because of what they perceived people from these places to be like.

Table 4.10 The hardware, software and orgware factors that influence the status our surroundings attribute to us

Hardware factors that influence what our surroundings say about us		Software factors that influence what our surroundings say about us		Orgware factors that influence what our surroundings say about us	
. . . in the compassionate city	*. . . in the neglectful city*	*. . . in the compassionate city*	*. . . in the neglectful city*	*. . . in the compassionate city*	*. . . in the neglectful city*
Well-maintained and attractive surroundings	Poorly maintained and unattractive surroundings	Outsiders have positive experience of the people who live there	Outsiders have negative experience of the people who live there	Promotional campaigns to address stereotypes	Stereotypes left unchallenged
Proximity to centre of power or symbol of refinement (square, park, beautiful landmark building)	Distant from centres of power or symbols of refinement	Hope that a positive reflection can be maintained or a negative one will be improved	A sense that things are getting worse	Investment in developing a community	Investment in controlling a community
'Higher order' aesthetics, social or ecological objectives prominent in building design	'Lower order' security objectives dominant in building design	Perception that the people who live here are successful	Perception that the people who live here are failures	Well-maintained public infrastructure	Poorly maintained public infrastructure

To relate this back to the framework of fundamental needs identified in Chapter 2, the status our surroundings ascribes to us can impact our ability to self-determine our identity by influencing the faith other people are prepared to place in us. It does this when an association with a place brings with it pre-conceived ideas about what people from that place are like. It can close doors to people and deny them opportunities that they may have had if they came from elsewhere. In doing so it influences our ability to meet our needs to participate in society and forge our own identity. Table 4.10 shows some of the key factors that will influence whether the hardware, software and orgware of a place make it harder or easier for these needs to be met.

The Inspiration We Get From Our Surroundings

A place is nurturing when it incorporates design qualities that inspire and invite people to do things that support their well-being, not because they have to do them but because the quality of their surroundings provokes the desire to do so. A place is neglectful when it offers them little invitation to do these things.

What we do is to an extent defined by what our surroundings invite and inspire us to do. Play England (2008b) reported that "*animal research indicates that environmental enrichment (the provision of attractive stimuli in an environment) will increase play behaviours and thus enhance brain plasticity, reduce anxiety-like behaviour, promote physical activity and enhance immune systems.*"

As explored in Chapter 2, our needs have a qualitative component. It is not enough to merely have quantitative access to the opportunities to meet needs if these opportunities are utilitarian and do nothing to provoke an emotional response in the visitor or invite them to make the effort to participate in the opportunities the place offers. This invitation happens when places provoke a sense of delight, awe, insight or sense of communion with other people—or the place—and in doing so provoke a desire to explore and share that place. Such places captivate us, lift our spirits, recharge our emotional batteries and move us, literally and figuratively, to do things we wouldn't have done and feel things we wouldn't have felt.

This strong motivational force can come most dramatically from experiencing places of sublime beauty, built and natural majesty, significant activities or events, and/or the company of interesting, fun, engaging people. When this inspiration is present and it fires us up to improve the way we look after the places we are responsible for, or makes people want to visit the local park, or play, interact with others and learn about the world, then it has helped people meet their needs. What gives a place such appeal is beyond breaking down into component qualities but it is important to stress it rarely (if ever) happens by accident. It can be created, enhanced or diminished by the way we design. Perhaps one of the most obvious examples of using the constructed environment to inspire people comes from the cathedrals, mosques, shrines and temples that have for millennia sought to use scale, drama, craftsmanship and a commitment to architectural beauty to set them aside from their surroundings and amplify a sense of spirituality and awe in those who visit them (Figure 4.10).

Although not an exact match, there is considerable evidence that the motivational effect of design inspiration to enhance lives can be found in the broader factor of design quality and in particular quality landscape design: "*In a recent study in the Netherlands, de Vries et al. (2013) found an association between the quantity and, even more strongly, the quality of streetscape greenery and perceived social cohesion at the neighbourhood scale*" (WHO 2016). A study in Western Australia confirmed the differential attraction

Figure 4.10 Westminster Cathedral

of high-quality open space over mundane spaces, noting that people will walk farther to access attractive, well-designed and large public open spaces (Giles-Corti et al. 2005).

This reflects research from Australia by Veitch et al. (2007), who found that the aesthetics of a park would influence children's desire to play there. Their study also states that "*one of the most common issues, especially for the children aged 8–12 years, was that they found the playground equipment uninteresting, not challenging enough, and primarily designed for younger children.*" They also found some children also commented that there was a lack of variety between playgrounds, with the same equipment often found in different parks. They noted that "*these concerns regarding the play equipment seemed to discourage some children visiting parks and resulted in the children preferring alternative activities*" (ibid).

To relate this back to the framework of fundamental needs identified in Chapter 2, the inspiration might be seen as a magnet that can be used to attract people to undertake any of the activities from which they can meet their needs. Table 4.11 shows some of the key

Table 4.11 The hardware, software and orgware factors that influence how inspiring our surroundings are

Hardware factors that influence the inspiration we get from our surroundings		Software factors that influence the inspiration we get from our surroundings		Orgware factors that influence the inspiration we get from our surroundings	
. . . in the compassionate city	*. . . in the neglectful city*	*. . . in the compassionate city*	*. . . in the neglectful city*	*. . . in the compassionate city*	*. . . in the neglectful city*
High quality of materials, craftsmanship and maintenance High standard of architectural design applied to social places	Low quality of materials, craftsmanship and maintenance Low standard of architectural design applied to social places	High standard of design effort demanded and given	Indifferent effort applied and generic design responses offered	Design processes, budgets and timelines reflect a commitment to design excellence, particularly at identified places of significance	Design processes, budgets and timelines reflect an acceptance and expectation of low-quality design

factors that will influence whether the hardware, software and orgware of a place make it harder or easier for these needs to be met.

The Social Gradient of Invitation

Simply put, the idea of 'the social gradient of invitation' is that a person's well-being, wealth and the design quality invested in their surroundings tend to be bound together, influence one another and are directly proportional. For the poorest and most vulnerable in society, these factors, or rather their absence, marked out by the variables noted in this chapter, typically work together to deny people an invitation to take up opportunities, which compounds disadvantage, locks people into diminished lives and denies them opportunities enjoyed by others.

According to Graham Duxbury, chief executive of Groundwork UK, economic disadvantage is echoed and amplified in a poorer quality public realm. Access to quality green space—"*for leisure, for exercise, for social contact—is one of the many things that mark out the haves and the have nots in society*" (Duxbury 2015). Another UK report found that "*at present, the distribution of areas with high levels of social exclusion typically coincides with areas of sparse green space which is of limited quality*" (House of Lords 2016). This inequity reflects research from the UK undertaken for the "*Urban Green Nation*" study by the Commission for Architecture in the Built Environment (CABE) in the UK in 2010 that confirmed that the quality of green space is worse in deprived areas than in affluent areas. This is despite the fact that other studies have found that whilst everyone benefited from equal exposure to green space, the lowest income groups benefited the most (Maas et al. 2006).

There is also a robust evidence base that suggests that the higher the quality of open space, the more likely it is to be used (CABE 2010). This report noted over 70 other studies that found that levels of physical activity were highest in those wealthier areas that enjoy a high level of quality and quantity of open space. Although it is not suggested that poorer design in poorer places is the only factor influencing activity, the alignment between poverty and (in)activity is striking: "*The most deprived wards have only 40 percent of adults doing moderate physical activity regularly, while this rises steadily across the bands to nearly 60 percent in the most affluent wards*" (ibid).

Hence I would like to suggest there is a social gradient of invitation, echoing and perhaps amplifying the social gradient of health (Marmot and Stafford 2010). Communities of lower socio-economic status find their relative disadvantage compounded by surroundings that offer a lesser level of encouragement to do the things they need to do to nurture themselves. The spaces these poorer communities experience are more likely to be mundane and utilitarian, as well as lacking in the power to inspire genuine delight and to invite people to do things such as stay and play in these places. This is not to deny or ignore the very many noble initiatives by many agencies and individuals that seek to address this inequity; it merely notes that it is an issue.

This inequitable distribution of quality has huge health implications. Natural England has estimated that if each household in England was provided with equitable access to quality green space, then savings of £2.1bn could be achieved every year in averted health costs (quoted in the House of Lords 2016).

What Does This Mean for Urban Designers?

This inequity of inspiration and invitation offered by our surroundings is an important matter that should demand our attention. The importance of design quality suggests a line can be drawn between the investment of emotional capital by the designers and those who care for a place and the emotional response of the people who experience it. When a place is poorly invested with the care of these decision-makers, as explored in the section 'The Social Gradient of Invitation' earlier in this chapter, it is unlikely to inspire its potential users to engage with it. In such generic, poorly thought through, inadequately managed or 'designed by box ticking' places, the emotional responses of their users are likely to be indifference or avoidance. Many will be seduced by 'easier' (but not needs-fulfilling) ways to spend their time, as they are likely to look out their windows and conclude that it's preferable to stay indoors or only venture out in a car to further afield, more-appealing places. Furthermore, without other people sharing an activity in a neighbourhood, there is a lack of evidence that it is 'the done thing' in that community. For example, if you never see someone run or cycle or (for new mothers) see other mothers breast feed in public in your neighbourhood, you are less likely to consider it part of your experience menu. In such places if someone does choose to walk, cycle or play, breast feed in public or indeed participate in any of the activities that support health and well-being, they are doing so because they really want to do so rather than because their surroundings inspire the desire to do so.

Consequently places lacking in 'inspiration of place' are uncompetitive in attracting people's attention and the needs that they were designed to meet are more likely to go unmet unless an individual can summon up a great deal of personal motivation (Figure 4.11). Whilst some people will overcome these disadvantages and meet their needs by sheer will power, focus and dedication, others will give up, unwilling or unaware of the imperative to make different choices. These people are disadvantaged by their surroundings and the threshold of effort to achieve well-being is more difficult for them to reach (perhaps prohibitively difficult) than it would be for someone in an area offering more invitation.

Place embodying little inspiration   **Place embodying significant inspiration**

In this situation the place offers very little
invitation to walk.
Unless people have a strong motivation to walk
they are likely to be deterred from walking.

In this situation the place offers a strong invitation
to walk and so makes walking relatively easy.

Figure 4.11 Places Offering Inspiration of Place Make Lesser Demands on Personal Motivation to Meet Needs

Repeated over a neighbourhood or even a city, this denies its occupants many opportunities and can reflect and reinforce other forms of division. Distance and inconvenience to access better designed, more inspired places create arbitrary barriers within and between communities, making winners and losers of their inhabitants.

Unfortunately disadvantaged communities lack the resources, power, skills and experience to demand things or make these things happen themselves or protect what they value (Duxbury, pers. corr. 2015). Urban designers can help by seeking to see the world through the eyes of those who experience that place, now and in the future. Given the diversity of needs and perspectives, urban designers should also seek to design places to meet multiple needs and deter activities that preclude needs satisfaction. This requires a design process that is informed by all potential users of the space, including those traditionally disadvantaged and marginalized as well as those not yet born. Realizing change in communities with limited access to resources also requires that designs can be implemented and maintained without big investments of money or expensive expertise and so are less dependent on big capital or technical skills that are normally in the control of power elites.

This plea for greater local control comes with an important caveat: it will always be necessary to consider broader issues rather than just a list of priorities established by a single community. In an interconnected world, we will always need to ensure that development to serve one community does not happen in a way that is unfair to other communities, now or in the future. Balancing the needs of the client community with those not yet born or who can't participate will always present a challenge that will call on all our creative and communication skills, particularly when it requires tempering the aspirations of the people who share a place in the here and now.

References

Aldrich, D (undated) *The Power of People: Social Capital and Post-Disaster Recovery.* Accessed June 2011, www.purdue.edu/research/gpri/docs/papers/society/disaster-recovery.pdf

Arie, S (2003) Regeneration man. *The Guardian.* Accessed June 2011, www.theguardian.com/world/2003/oct/22/worlddispatch.sophiearie

Australian Government Department of Environment and Heritage (2005) *Air Quality.* Accessed June 2011, www.deh.gov.au/index/atmosphere.html

Australian Institute of Health and Welfare (2012) *Risk Factors Contributing to Chronic Disease.* Cat No. PHE 157. AIHW, Canberra. www.aihw.gov.au/WorkArea/DownloadAsset.aspx?id=10737421546 2012

Bacon, N (2010) *Never Again Avoiding the Mistakes of the Past.* London: The Young Foundation,

Basbas, S, Konstantinidou, Giorgou, A in Pratelli, C. A. Brebbia (eds) (2011) *Urban Transport XVII: Urban Transport and the Environment in the 21st Century.*Southampton, UK: WIT Press.

Ballantyne Brodie, E (2015) *Personal Correspondence.*

Bentley, I, Alcock, A Murrain, P Mcglynn, S Smith, P (1985) *Responsive Environments.* Oxford: Architectural Press.

Berman, M, Jonides, J, and Kaplan, S (2008) The cognitive benefits of interacting with nature. *Psychological Science* 19(12): 1207–12. Accessed August 2016, http://journals.sagepub.com/doi/abs/10.1111/j.1467-9280.2008.02225.x

Beunderman, J, Hannon, C, and Bradwel, P (2007) *Seen and Heard: Reclaiming the Public Realm With Children and Young People.* London: Demos.

Bhalla, K, Shotten, M, Cohen, A, Brauer, M, Shahraz, S, Burnett, R, Leach-Kemon, K, Freedman, G, and Murray, C (2014) *Transport for Health: The Global Burden of Disease From Motorized Road Transport.* Washington, DC: World Bank Group. Accessed June 2016, http://documents.worldbank.org/curated/en/984261468327002120/Transport-for-health-the-global-burden-of-disease-from-motorized-road-transport

Chen, H, Kwong, JC, Copes, R, Tu, K, Villeneuve, PJ, van Donkelaar, A, Hystad, P, Martin, RV, Murray, BJ, Jessiman, B, Wilton, AS, Kopp, A, and Burnett, RT (2017) Living near major roads and the incidence of dementia, Parkinson's disease, and multiple sclerosis: A population-based cohort study. *The Lancet* 389(10070): 718–26.

City of Marion (2008) *Play Strategy.* Accessed June 2016, www.marion.sa.gov.au/play-space-strategy

Clements, R (2004) An investigation of the status of outdoor play. *Contemporary Issues in Early Childhood* 5(1): 68–80. Accessed June 2016, www.imaginationplayground.com/images/content/2/9/2960/An-investigation-Of-The-Status-Of-Outdoor-Play.pdf.

Commission for Architecture and the Built Environment (2008) *Inclusion By Design: Equality, Diversity and the Built Environment.* London: CABE.

Commission for Architecture and the Built Environment (2010) *Community Green.* London: CABE.

Cucurachi, S (2013) Book Review *Why Noise Matters: A Worldwide Perspective on the Problems, Policies and Solutions,* by John Stewart with Francis McManus, Nigel Rodgers, Val Weedon, and Arline Bronzaft, Abington, Oxon, UK: Routledge, 2011, 174 pp., ISBN 978-1-84971-257-6, *Journal of Industrial Ecology* 17: 336. doi:10.1111/j.1530-9290.2012.00544.x. Accessed June 2016.

Daly, J (2016) Why we need 'enriching' cities (but not too enriching). *Architecture News,* January 18th, 2016. Accessed May 2016, https://sourceable.net/why-we-need-enriching-cities-but-not-too-enriching/

Dash, S (2009) *Post-Disaster Psychosocial Support: A Framework From Lessons Learnt Through Programmes in South-Asia 2009.* Massey University. Accessed July 2011 www.massey.ac.nz/~trauma/issues/2009-1/dash.htm

De Lange M, (2009) *review: Kevin Lynch – The Image of the City* Accessed January 2017 http://themobilecity.nl/2009/05/08/review-kevin-lynch-the-image-of-the-city/

Department for Transport (UK) (2004) *LTN 1/04—Policy, Planning and Design for Walking and Cycling.* Accessed June 2016, www.ukroads.org/webfiles/LTN%201-04%20Policy,%20Planning%20and%20Design%20for%20Walking%20and%20Cycling.pdf

de Vries S, van Dillen SM, Groenewegen PP, Spreeuwenberg P. (2003) Streetscape greenery and health: stress, social cohesion and physical activity as mediators. *Social Science & Medicine*, 94(October 2013): 26–33.

Ding, D, Lawson, K, Kolbe-Alexander, T, Finkelstein, E, Katzmarzyk, P, van Mechelen, W, Pratt, M for the Lancet Physical Activity Series 2 Executive Committee (2016) The economic burden of physical inactivity: A global analysis of major non-communicable diseases. *The Lancet*, The Lancet, 388(10051): 1311–24. Dobson, J (2012) *Grey Places Need Green Spaces.* Groundwork.

Duxbury, G (2015) People don't just need social housing, they need green spaces close by. *The Guardian*, www.theguardian.com/society/2015/jun/23/social-housing-green-spaces-health-benefits

Ellard, C (undated) *Streets With No Game.* Aeon. Accessed February 2016, https://aeon.co/essays/why-boring-streets-make-pedestrians-stressed-and-unhappy

Farago, J (2016) Meet Edi Rama, Albania's artist prime minister. *The Guardian*, Tuesday November 15th, 2016. Accessed December 2016, www.theguardian.com/artanddesign/2016/nov/15/meet-edi-rama-albanias-artist-prime-minister-exhibition

Florida, R (2015) *The Complicated Link Between Gentrification and Displacement.* Accessed November 2016, www.citylab.com/housing/2015/09/the-complicated-link-between-gentrification-and-displacement/404161/

Fun Theory (undated) www.thefuntheory.com/

Gap Filler (undated-a) *About Gap filler.* http://gapfiller.org.nz/about/

Gap Filler (undated-b) *The Dance-O-Mat* http://gapfiller.org.nz/news/2013/dance-o-mat/

Gap Filler (undated-c) *Think Differently.* https://gapfiller.org.nz/project/think-differently-book-exchange/

Gibbs, L, MacDougall, C, Nansen, B, Vetere, F, Ross, N, Danic, I, and McKendrick, J (2012) *Stepping Out: Children Negotiating Independent Travel.* VicHealth Report, Jack Brockhoff Child Health and Wellbeing Program, McCaughey VicHealth Centre for Community Wellbeing, University of Melbourne.

Giles-Corti, B, Broomhall, MH, Knuiman, M, Collins, C, Douglas, K, Ng, K, Lange, A, Donovan, RJ (2005) Increasing walking: How important is distance to, attractiveness, and size of public open space? *American Journal of Preventive Medicine* 28(2) (supplement 2): 169–76. Accessed January 2016, www.ncbi.nlm.nih.gov/pubmed/15694525

Goh, S, and Bailey, P (2007) *The Effect of the Social Environment on Mental Health: Implications for Service Provision in New Communities.* Cambridgeshire Primary Care Trust. Accessed June 2016, www.social-life.co/media/files/Never_Again.pdf

Graham Duxbury (2015) *Personal Correspondence.*

Green, R (2015) *Personal Correspondence.*

Gu, J, Mohit, B, and Muennig, P (2016) The cost-effectiveness of bike lanes in New York City. Columbia University Academic Commons. Accessed June 2016. doi:10.7916/D8HD7VWG

Haagsma, JA, Graetz, N, Bolliger, I et al. (2016) The global burden of injury: Incidence, mortality, disability-adjusted life years and time trends from the Global Burden of Disease study 2013. *Injury Prevention* 22: 3–18. Accessed November 2016, http://injuryprevention.bmj.com/content/early/2015/10/20/injuryprev-2015-041616

Hart, J, and Parkhurst, G (2011) *Driven to Excess: Impacts of Motor Vehicles on the Quality of Life of Residents of Three Streets in Bristol UK.* University of Western England. http://eprints.uwe.ac.uk/15513/1/WTPP_Hart_ParkhurstJan2011prepub.pdf

Herchmer, B (January 12th, 2012) *Leadership: For Active Creative Engaged Communities.* iUniverse.

Holland, C, Clark, A, Katz, J, and Peace, S (2007) *Social Interactions in Urban Public Places.* York, UK: Joseph Rowntree Foundation.

Horton, R (2016) Offline: The rule of law—An invisible determinant of health. *The Lancet* 387(10025): 1260. Accessed May 2016, www.thelancet.com/journals/lancet/article/PIIS0140-6736(16)30061-7/fulltext?rss%3Dyes

House of Lords (2016) *Building Better Places, a Report of Select Committee on National Policy for the Built Environment.* HL Paper 100, House of Lords.

International Obesity TaskForce (2002) *Obesity in Europe.* www.worldobesity.org/site_media/uploads/Sep_2002_Obesity_in_Europe_Case_for_Action_2002.pdf

Joseph Rowntree Foundation (2007) *The Social Value of Shared Space.* www.jrf.org.uk/sites/default/files/jrf/migrated/files/2050-public-space-community.pdf

Kelly, J-F, Breadon, P, Davis, C, Hunter, A, Mares, P, Mullerworth, D, and Weidmann, B (2012) *Social Cities.* Melbourne: Grattan Institute.

Kepper, M, Broyles, S, Scribner, R, Tseng, T, Zabaleta, J, Griffiths, L, and Sothern, M (December 21st, 2016) Parental perceptions of the social environment are inversely related to constraint of adolescents' neighborhood physical activity. *International Journal of Environmental Research and Public Health.* Accessed January 2017, www.ncbi.nlm.nih.gov/pmc/articles/PMC5201407/

Kjellstrom, T, Barten, F, Bartram, J, Becker, D, Burns, C, Burris, S et al. (2007) *Our Cities, Our Health, Our Future: Acting on Social Determinants for Health Equity in Urban. Settings Report to the WHO Commission on Social Determinants of Health From the Knowledge Network on Urban Settings.* WHO Kobe Centre, Kobe, Japan. Accessed June 2016, www.who.int/social_determinants/resources/knus_final_report_052008.pdf

Lagune-Reutler, M, Guthrie, Y, Fan, Y, and Levinson, D (2016) Transit Riders' perception of waiting time and stops' surrounding environments. *Journal of the Transportation Research Board.* Accessed June 2016, http://conservancy.umn.edu/handle/11299/180075

Leyden, KM (2003) Social capital and the built environment: The importance of walkable neighborhoods. *American Journal of Public Health*, 93(9): 1546–51. Accessed January 2015, http://ajph.aphapublications.org/doi/abs/10.2105/AJPH.93.9.1546

Longridge, P, and Mitchell, M (2014) *Personal Correspondence.*

Lynch, K (1960) *The Image of the City.* Cambridge, MA: MIT Press.

Maas, J, Verheij, RA, Groenewegen, P, de Vries, S, and Spreeuwenberg, P (2006) Green space, urbanity, and health: How strong is the relation? *Epidemiol Community Health* 60: 587–92. doi:10.1136/jech.2005.043125. Accessed June 2016, http://jech.bmj.com/content/60/7/587

Marmot, M, and Stafford, M (2010) *Fair Society, Healthy Lives: The Marmot Review.* Executive Summary, Strategic Review of Health Inequalities in England Post-2010. London: University College.

Mason, C (March 6th, 2000) Transport and health: En route to a healthier Australia? *Medical Journal of Australia* 172(5): 230–2. Accessed June 2016, www.ncbi.nlm.nih.gov/pubmed/10776396

Mazda, A (2011) *Urban Stress and Mental Health, Cities Health and Well-being.* Urban Age Conference Newspaper. Accessed November 2014, https://LSECiti.es/u246d12b2

McClure, T, and Meier, C (2013) Re:Start mall may close in April. *The Press.* Accessed May 2016, www.stuff.co.nz/the-press/business/9537670/Re-Start-mall-may-close-in-April (updated 20/12/2013).

McKenna, D (2015) *Personal Correspondence.*

Mechling, H, and Netz, Y (2009) Aging and inactivity—capitalizing on the protective effect of planned physical activity in old age. *European Review of Aging and Physical Activity* 6: 89. doi:10.1007/s11556-009-0052-y. Accessed May 2016, http://link.springer.com/article/10.1007/s11556-009-0052-y

Ministry for the Environment (2005) *The Value of Urban Design, The Economic, Environmental and Social Benefits of Urban Design.* Ministry for the Environment, NZ. Accessed May 2016, www.mfe.govt.nz/publications/towns-and-cities/value-urban-design-economic-environmental-and-social-benefits-urban

Min Lee, I, Shiroma, E, Lobelo, F, Puska, P, Blair, S, and Katzmarzyk, P (2012) Effect of physical inactivity on major non-communicable diseases worldwide: An analysis of burden of disease and life expectancy. *The Lancet* 380(9838): 219–29, 21. Accessed May 2016, www.thelancet.com/journals/lancet/article/PIIS0140-6736(12)61031-9/fulltext

Mitchell, R, and Popham, F (2008) Effect of exposure to natural environment on health inequalities: An observational population study. *The Lancet* 372(9650): 1655–60. Accessed January 2016, www.thelancet.com/journals/lancet/article/PIIS0140-6736(08)61689-X/fulltext

Monbiot, G (2014) The age of loneliness is killing us. *The Guardian*, October 15th, 2014. Accessed January 2017, www.theguardian.com/commentisfree/2014/oct/14/age-of-loneliness-killing-us.

Montgomery, C (2013a) *Happy City*. London: Penguin Books.

Montgomery, C (2013b) The secrets of the world's happiest cities. *The Guardian*, November 2nd, 2013. www.theguardian.com/society/2013/nov/01/secrets-worlds-happiest-cities-commute-property-prices

Naderi, J, Rosenblatt, K, Byoung, S, and Maghelal, P (2008) The street tree effect and driver safety. *ITE Journal on The Web/February*. www.naturewithin.info/Roadside/Tree&Driver_ITE.pdf

Parkinson, F (2000) *Post Trauma Stress*. Cambridge, MA: De Capo Long Life.

Parsons, J (2016) Sydney: We need to talk about our postcode prejudice. *The Guardian*. www.theguardian.com/culture/2016/aug/23/sydney-we-need-to-talk-about-our-postcode-prejudice

Planet Ark (2011) *Climbing Trees: Getting Aussie Kids Back Outdoors*. Accessed July 2016, http://treeday.planetark.org/documents/doc-534-climbing-trees-research-report-2011-07-13-final.pdf

Play England (2008a) *Design for Play*. Accessed May 2016, www.playengland.org.uk/media/70684/design-for-play.pdf

Play England (2008b) *Play for a Change*. Accessed May 2016, www.playengland.org.uk/media/120438/play-for-a-change-low-res.pdf

Pope, J, and Zhang, W (2011) *Indicators of Community Strength in Victoria: Framework and Evidence*. Mebourne: Policy and Strategy, Department of Planning and Community Development.

Porteous, JD (1977) *Environment & Behavior: Planning and Everyday Urban Life*. Addison-Wesley.

Putrik, P, de Vries, NK, Mujakovic, S, van Amelsvoort, L, Kant, I, Kunst, AE, van Oers, H, and Jansen, M (2015) Living environment matters: Relationships between neighborhood characteristics and health of the residents in a Dutch municipality. *Journal of Community Health*. Accessed June 2016, www.ncbi.nlm.nih.gov/pubmed/24917124

Qualls, S (2014) What social relationships can do for health. *American Society of Ageing*. Accessed July 2016, www.asaging.org/blog/what-social-relationships-can-do-health

Read, S, and Grundy, E (September 2012) *Allostatic Load—A Challenge to Measure Multisystem Physiological Dysregulation*. London School of Hygiene and Tropical Medicine and University of Cambridge. Accessed June 2016, http://eprints.ncrm.ac.uk/2879/1/NCRM_workingpaper_0412.pdf

Re:Start (undated) *About Us*. http://restart.org.nz/contact-about

Roe, J, and Aspinall, P (January 2011) The restorative benefits of walking in urban and rural settings in adults with good and poor mental health. *Health & Place* 17(1): 103–13. Health Geographies of Voluntarism. Accessed January 2016, www.sciencedirect.com/science/article/pii/S1353829210001322

Rudner, J, Kennedy, M, Holland, W, Wilks, J, Donovan, J, Neville, D, Shaw, M, Budge, T, and Butt, A (2011) *The Place of Our Children in Community Building: Turning Theory Into Practice*. Children's and Young People's Engagement Report, Volume 2, La Trobe University, Bendigo.

Rudner J, (2013) *Personal Correspondence*.

Sallis, J, Cerin, E, Conway, T, Adams, M, Frank, L, Pratt, M, Salvo, D, Schipperijn, J, Smith, G, Cain, K, Davey, R, Kerr, J, Lai, P et al. (April 1st, 2016) Physical activity in relation to urban environments in 14 cities worldwide: A cross-sectional study. *The Lancet*. Accessed April 2016, www.thelancet.com/journals/lancet/article/PIIS0140-6736(15)01284-2/fulltext

Seed (2008) What is solistalgia? *Seed Magazine*, July 31st, 2008. Accessed July 2011, http://seed-magazine.com/content/article/what_is_solistalgia/

Shaver, K (2005) The Starbucks effect. *The Washington Post*. Accessed July 2011, www.washingtonpost.com/wp-dyn/articles/A61460-2005Apr17.html.

Stegner, W (undated) *A Place Is Formed by Slow Accrual*. www.importanceofplace.com/2011/06/place-is-not-place-until-people-have.html

Thompson, S, and Kent, J (2014) Connecting and strengthening communities in places for health and well-being. *Australian Planner* 51(3): 260–71. Accessed May 2015. doi:10.1080/07293682.2013.837832

UN Office for Disaster Risk Reduction (2007) *Resilience*. Accessed May 2015, www.unisdr.org/we/inform/terminology

University of Western England, Science Communication Unit, Science for Environment Policy (2016) *Links Between Noise and Air Pollution and Socioeconomic Status*. Indepth Report 13 Produced for the European Commission, DG Environment by the Science Communication Unit, UWE, Bristol. Accessed May 2016, http://ec.europa.eu/environment/integration/research/newsalert/pdf/air_noise_pollution_socioeconomic_status_links_IR13_en.pdf

Valtorta, N, Kanaan, M, Gilbody, S, Ronzi, S, and Hanratty, B (2016) Loneliness and social isolation as risk factors for coronary heart disease and stroke: Systematic review and meta-analysis of longitudinal observational studies. *Heart*. doi:10.1136/heartjnl-2015-308790. Accessed November 2016, http://heart.bmj.com/content/102/13/1009

Vedantam, S (2011) *The Key to Disaster Survival? Friends and Neighbors*. Accessed January 2012, www.npr.org/2011/07/04/137526401/the-key-to-disaster-survival-friends-and-neighbors

Veitch, J, Salmon, J, and Ball, K (2007) Children's perceptions of the use of public open spaces for active free-play. *Children's Geographies* 5(4): 409–22. Accessed September 2016, www.tandfonline.com/doi/abs/10.1080/14733280701631874

VicHealth (2015) *Beyond the Bubble Wrap*. Melbourne: Victorian Health Promotion Foundation.

Weel, B, and Akçomak, S (2008) *The Impact of Social Capital on Crime: Evidence From the Netherlands*. Institute for the Study of Labor. Accessed September 2016, http://ftp.iza.org/dp3603.pdf

Weinstein, N, Balmford, A, Dehaan, C, Gladwell, V, Bradbury, R, and Amano, T (December 2015) Seeing community for the trees. *BioScience* 65(12): 1141–53. Accessed May 2016, https://academic.oup.com/bioscience/article/65/12/1141/223866/Seeing-Community-for-the-Trees-The-Links-among

Weinstein, N, Przybylski, A, and Ryan, R (2009) Can nature make us more caring? Effects of immersion in nature on intrinsic aspirations and generosity. *Personality and Social Psychology Bulletin* 35(10): 1315–29. First published date: August 5th, 2009. Accessed June 2015, http://selfdeterminationtheory.org/SDT/documents/2009_WeinsteinPrzybylskiRyan_Nature.pdf

Wheway, R, and Millward, A (1997) *Child's Play: Facilitating Play on Housing Estates*. York, UK: Chartered Institute of Housing and the Joseph Rowntree Foundation.

Whyte, W (1980) *The Social Life of Small Urban Spaces*. New York: Project for Public Space.

Wigle, DT, and Lanphear, B (2005) Human health risks from low-level environmental exposures: No apparent safety thresholds. Accessed May 2016, www.ncbi.nlm.nih.gov/pmc/articles/PMC1255761/

Wilkinson, R, and Pickett, K (2010) *The Spirit Level: Why More Equal Societies Almost Always Do Better*. London: Penguin Books.

Wolf, KL (2010) Crime and fear—a literature review. In *Green Cities: Good Health College of the Environment*. University of Washington. Accessed May 2016, http://depts.washington.edu/hhwb/

World Health Organisation (undated) *Chronic Diseases and Health Promotion*. WHO.

World Health Organization (2007) *Global Age-Friendly Cities: A Guide*. WHO.

World Health Organization (2016) *Urban Green Spaces and Health*. Copenhagen: WHO Regional Office for Europe.

5 Living in the Compassionate City

It's about the realization of talent and potential, and the feeling that you are able to make the most of your abilities in life.

(Montgomery 2013)

This chapter looks to what it might be like to live somewhere where the messages that a person receives from their surroundings support the nurturing outcomes outlined in the previous chapter. I would like to suggest that living in such a place creates many metaphorical pathways that can help us develop our capacities and in doing so enjoy well-being rewards that help us get closer to fulfilling our potential in life. These well-being rewards are belonging, health, hope, empowerment and ultimately happiness.

Like Abraham Maslow I have expressed these steps to self-fulfilment as a progression, with each well-being reward a stepping stone that helps to create the circumstances where the next well-being reward can be enjoyed. However most of the time this relationship will be far more complex than this simple model suggests. In reality rather than this consistent linear sequence, each person's pathway is in fact a modular system and the actual order that the well-being rewards are achieved will be different for different people in different circumstances. This supports Ed Diener's and Louis Tay's (2011) critique of Maslow's hierarchy that

> the needs tend be achieved in a certain order but that the order in which they are achieved does not strongly influence their effects on SWB (Subjective Well Being). Motivational prepotency does not mean that fulfilling needs 'out of order' is necessarily less fulfilling.

To paraphrase Ed Diener, these well-being rewards are like vitamins—without them the realization of one's potential becomes impossible but the order you have them and the way you take them is your own concern. Or to put it another way, although the ingredients of happiness are broadly the same for everyone, each of us will have our own preferred recipe for achieving it (Figure 5.1).

It is also recognized that these well-being rewards are also very broadly defined concepts with blurred edges. The relationships between elements—such as between health and hope (Scioli et al. 1997)—is evidently far more complex than one well-being reward acting solely on one other well-being reward in a consistent and one-directional way, as might be inferred from these pages.

Figure 5.1 The Diverse Recipes for Happiness

The route to happiness outlined here is a different route to happiness than that marked out by the pursuit of materialism (Kasser and Ahuvia 2002), perhaps the assumed route to happiness for many city dwellers. The materialist path is well illuminated, appears direct and well trodden, is the focus of attention of massive industries and is the brain power of many very clever people who will seek to hurry us along that road. Although the path has appeal, it may ultimately not arrive at happiness. In the language of the second chapter of this book, it is a philosophy of wants, rather than needs. In a single-minded pursuit of more, better and bigger things to own or assert our social standing, we may overlook many of our fundamental needs. As Tim Kasser and Aaron Ahuvia found, *"the American dream has a dark side and the pursuit of wealth and ambitions may be undermining our wellbeing"* (2002), although they could to an extent have been writing about the Australian dream or indeed the aspirations commonly shared by many other nationalities. That is not to say that this book suggests that private ownership is wrong. It just suggests that responsibilities come with private ownership (of buildings and spaces in particular) if we want to make sure that material success for some isn't realized as a loss of their and others' potential happiness.

Of course, as noted in Chapter 1, a person's or community's progress down the path to self-fulfilment is influenced by far more than the design of their surroundings. In reality if the hypothetical and idealized model of the relationship between people and place described in this chapter is ever to happen, it would probably owe a great deal more to things such as enlightened health, education and housing policy and the enforcement of environmental protection standards than it will to urban design. However, although urban design may not always be the *most* significant determinant shaping our lives, it is still an important one that can help all these other aspects of supporting human well-being to achieve their optimal benefit.

Belonging

As mentioned in Chapter 2, *"the human need for connectedness"* outweighs *"almost everything else"* (Kelly et al. 2012). Consequently the hierarchy of well-being rewards places 'belonging' and a sense of resonance with one's surroundings as the foundations upon which people might move towards achieving self-fulfilment. The compassionate city supports people to grow comfortable in their surroundings, gather positive experiences from those surroundings and the people they share them with, and so encourage them to put down roots there, increasing the amount and significance of their actively shared space (Chapter 3). The compassionate city reassures people these connections are protected. In cultivating a sense of connectedness between people and place and offering a variety of choices about how people might use and share their surroundings, a varied 'experience menu' can be enjoyed. By seeking to enable people to tailor their surroundings to better meet their needs and the needs of others in their community, they are more likely to have 'skin in the game' and invest emotional capital in their shared surroundings (Groundwork undated), thus enhancing their sense of connection to those surroundings and of belonging to a community (Toker 2012). By providing diverse opportunities for people to contribute to their community, people have the ability to care for others and be cared for by others. This may help provide the interpersonal connections, such as love and respect, that Ed Diener and Louis Tay found were most linked with everyday life satisfaction (2011).

The compassionate city seeks to encourage people out of their houses on foot or by bike and offer a rich choice of shared experiences of the public realm. Of course, shared experiences could be good or bad, but it is suggested that the emphasis on design quality, comfort, cultivating the magic of a place, reconciling conflicts, enhancing safety and minimizing the intrusion of vehicles will make these experiences *more likely* to be positive. Thus the effort to move through the public realm on foot or by bicycle is rewarded by the promise of a pleasant journey through valued surroundings and uplifting interactions with others, planned or unplanned, within a welcoming space. Furthermore, the sense of belonging outlined in this section may provide a protective cloak of a sense of community that can diminish the adverse effects of loneliness (Kelly et al. 2012).

Health

The compassionate city is a place where there are many opportunities to enjoy healthy experiences, the inescapable causes of ill health are at a low concentration and these causes are not dumped on those already disadvantaged. It seeks to make health-supporting activities intrinsic to living in the city rather than an industrialized commodity and a problem that has to be fixed. To this end the compassionate city and the nurturing places within them aim to provide people of diverse abilities with the opportunity to stretch themselves, metaphorically and literally. By presenting (and favouring) realistic alternatives to the 'drive or don't go anywhere' binary choice offered by generic suburbia and offering a wide variety of self-chosen social interactions, it can help support physical and psychological health. Facilitating social interactions, providing opportunities to experience nature and diminishing the impact of private vehicles can help people reduce their allostatic load—the wear and tear on their bodies that comes from an accumulation of stress.

Hope

The compassionate city seeks to provide fertile ground for hope to flourish. As noted in Chapter 1, hope is an inspiring force and helps people to make plans. Hope encourages people to challenge the prevalent momentum of the community if it is going down and encourages them to act to safeguard it if it is going up.

I would like to suggest that people who are physically and emotionally healthy and are invested in their community are in a better position to make plans for themselves, inspire others to develop their plans and co-operate in the realization of shared plans. When the powers that be offer the reassurance of a commitment to transparent and equitably applied rules that reflect the community's aspirations and are respectful of diversity, then a philosophical space is created within which people can envisage an (even) better future. This will make it easier for people to *dare to care* and invest emotional capital in their surroundings as well as (hopefully) cultivating trust and respect between different parties.

Empowerment

The compassionate city facilitates people to turn this hope into reality. As psychologist Sharon Toker noted, *"it is pragmatically and psychologically beneficial for people to shape their environment to benefit their individual and community life"* (2012). Enabling people to make self-determined things happen is satisfying (Thin 2012) and can help people develop a sense of being in control of their own lives (Gough 2000; Max Neef 2007). It also offers people practical evidence and reassurance that they can adapt around future problems and make changes to their circumstances if needed (Ealy undated). It enables its inhabitants to invest financial, social, emotional and human capital into their surroundings and it gives them more reason to contribute to improvement by making them stakeholders in their collective futures.

The compassionate city is designed to offer places that provide people with challenges that can be overcome and is a rich source of experiences, inspirations and opportunities that offers them satisfaction. This provides those people with opportunities to build up an ever-clearer picture of what their skills are and allows 'islands of competence' (Brooks 2003) to form, grow and coalesce. The orgware of such a city incorporates safeguards that ensure appropriate physical interventions or investments of other capital (emotional, social) are respected and enthusiasm can find many different outlets. Thus the inhabitants are empowered to act on their choices, take responsibility for them, learn from their actions and be acknowledged for their contributions.

In the compassionate city, people are empowered to follow a path through life that enables them to invest in their own and others' well-being. For example, by encouraging play, the compassionate city can improve the chances of healthy childhood development and the development of fine and gross motor skills and social skills. Encouraging activity when a person is an adult will help keep them healthy and robust when they are older (WHO 2015). Walking and cycling and inviting people to share the street adds to the sense of safety felt by others and encourages them to walk or cycle as well.

Happiness

Happiness, as defined in Chapter 1, is a state of the best possible psychological health that will help those experiencing it to thrive. I would like to contend that when people feel a sense of connection to one another and their surroundings, are healthy, can identify their goals in life and can chart a course to achieving them, then they are in a position to flourish and strive towards happiness. What this means exactly will be different for everyone and consequently one of the key characteristics of the compassionate city is the diversity of life experiences it can offer its inhabitants.

Not every opportunity will suit everyone. In going through the doors that have been unlocked by living in a nurturing place and exploring one's potential, there will no doubt be many dead ends and unrewarding and disappointing experiences. However at least some of the experiences on this extensive experience menu will lead to the discoveries and enhancements of talents, lead to the development of friendships and cultivate a sense of self-determination. The personal lessons made available to us from these diverse experiences may not make life easy but they do make it more likely that it will be fulfilling. This book suggests that people living in such a place will enjoy: the *"Aristotelian ideals of belonging and benefiting others, flourishing, thriving and exercising excellence"* (C. D. Ryff 1989). These ideals are: (1) autonomy; (2) personal growth; (3) self-acceptance; (4) purpose in life; (5) environmental mastery; (6) positive relations with others.

What Does This Mean for Urban Designers?

Ed Diener and Louis Tay (2011) assert that optimal subjective well-being requires that people need to fulfil a variety of needs and engage in a mix of daily activities. One way to cater for everyone to meet their diverse needs would be to design dedicated spaces for each of those needs. However accommodating such a long list of needs would probably require very big cities with many occasionally used spaces. Much better, it would seem, would be to design sharable spaces that could be used and seen by many different people to meet many different needs at the same time. Self-evidently creating places that enable people to fulfil these diverse aspirations in a necessarily limited number of spaces will present a myriad of design challenges. This is particularly the case given that the people most disadvantaged by their surroundings are those with the least resources to do anything about it, as explored in Chapter 4. Table 5.1 seeks to identify these challenges in order to build up a picture of how well or otherwise our design interventions meet the needs of the people who experience them. It does this by relating the framework of fundamental needs identified in Chapter 2 with the three dimensions of an urban community identified in Chapter 3 to create a matrix of challenges.

Addressing and reconciling all these diverse challenges (or at least resolving as many as possible) will co-ordinate the messages a place broadcasts to the people who share it. So aligned, these messages will be consistent in inviting people to do all the things they need to do to meet their needs, their influence uncompromised by contra messages that might otherwise tip the balance of influences against meeting needs. Evidently, 'threading the needle' and meeting all these challenges and reconciling their diverse demands will be difficult. For example designing for protection points to design solutions of high walls, minimizing risk and prioritizing security infrastructure. However as the Joseph Rowntree Foundation noted (2007), *"Regeneration strategies or policing approaches intended to 'design out crime' can end up 'designing out' people. Approaches that strip public spaces of all features vulnerable to vandalism or misuse actively discourage local distinctiveness and public amenity."*

The next section of the book seeks to tell the stories of some projects that can shed some light on how these and other qualities may be reconciled and challenges might be overcome. For each of these stories, it explains the context within which particular projects were undertaken, the challenges they sought to address in physical and human terms, the design techniques used to meet these challenges and the outcome. Most provide us with a mix of both successful and less-successful features. All projects provide us with important insights. The stories themselves cover a variety of different contexts and locations. They were not selected through scientific sieving; rather they are all projects I have worked on or studied. Like all personal stories, they are selective and bound by personal circumstances and opportunity at the time. However all the projects share an explicit intention to address existing or emerging social problems and enable people to reform their

Table 5.1 The hardware, software and orgware challenges of meeting needs

Needs	Challenge		
	Hardware	Software	Orgware
Subsistence	Range of places to grow food, distribute it, prepare it, consume it and manage the waste Consideration of supporting green infrastructure to ensure the broader ecological health of the context within which food can be grown, consumed and waste managed Implementation of WSUD principles Public realm facilitates breastfeeding	Recognition of the value in ecological, aesthetic, social or urban agriculture Desire to participate in it and contribute to urban agriculture Food-growing and preparation skills Awareness of nutrition and diet Community facilitates breastfeeding mothers/does not discourage breastfeeding	Protection and promotion of a 'right to farm' Promotion of urban agriculture through promotional-design guidance such as City of Vancouver's urban agricultural guide Promotion of greater awareness of issues surrounding nutrition
Activity	Comprehensive and continuous network of footpaths, cycle paths, traffic calming measures, parks, open spaces, sports facilities, high-quality landscape, high-quality and well-located street furniture	Awareness of importance and pleasure of being active	Promotion of greater awareness of benefits of activity Investment and management priorities to allow landscape interventions to reach maturity and optimal contribution
Protection	Streets that minimize traffic speed Built form that cultivates a sense of safety, such as territorial enhancement, passive surveillance, access control, investment in image and maintenance, activity support and target hardening (Moffat 1983)	Sense of peace of mind, reassurance about the behaviour of others Awareness of other users of shared spaces such as roads	Commitment to the rule of law, personal protection, provision of safeguards and enforcement of design standards that achieve the hardware described to the left Dedication of adequate funding for maintenance
Affection	Variety of places of gathering, or retreat Variety of experiences Spaces that can be personalized Spaces to undertake shared challenges such as sports clubs and facilities, men's sheds, cafés, parks	Sense of freedom of expression, movement, education, minimally restricted awareness of personal values and few distractions Ability to connect with a place and other people	Rule of law Recognition of valued places in property and planning rules Dedication of adequate funding for maintenance
Understanding	Interpretation material Legible surroundings (Bentley et al. 1985)	Education, minimally restricted awareness of personal values and few distractions	Provision of adequate resources for education, promotion, awareness building Dedication of adequate funding for maintenance

Participation	Places of gathering or retreat Accessibility for all	Confidence in own ability Ability to make informed choices Education, minimally restricted awareness of personal values and few distractions	Democratic value system Provision of adequate resources for education, promotion Recognition of diversity of perspective and contribution in communities
Leisure	Parks, other open spaces, cafés, restaurants, sports centres, galleries museums, places of gathering or retreat Accessibility for all	Sense of freedom of movement, education, minimally restricted awareness of personal values and few distractions	Labour laws and standards that safeguard non-working time Emphasis on importance of leisure to well-being
Creation	Inspirational public spaces, places of gathering or retreat Historical, cultural, ecological insights about the community revealed to the passer-by	Education highly valued, minimally restricted awareness of personal values and few distractions, ability to express oneself	Education recognized as an important priority
Identity	Distinctive places, respect of an area's genus anmi Historical, cultural, ecological insights about the community revealed to the passer-by	Education, opportunities to explore personal values and few distractions	Recognition of diversity of perspective and contribution in communities
Freedom	Variety of accessible experiences, accessibility	Education, minimally restricted awareness of personal values and few distractions	Reassurance of the rule of law
Beauty	Access to nature, architectural/urban design quality, galleries, places of gathering and performances, places of privacy	Education, minimally restricted awareness of personal values and few distractions	Education, recognition and protection of natural values

relationship with their surroundings and each other in a way that enhances their chances of thriving and fulfilling their potential.

Reflecting Collin Ellard's observation about the "*hybridisation of real and virtual space*" (Ellard undated), the projects covered have sought to adjust this relationship through changing the hardware of a place, the orgware of those who administer it and web-based projects that have sought to change the software of the community that share it.

References

Bentley, I, Alcock, A, Murrain, P, McGlynn, S, and Smith, G (1985) *Responsive Environments*. Oxford: Architectural Press.

Brooks Robert (2003) *Self-Worth, Resilience and Hope: The Search for Islands of Competence*. Accessed June 2014, www.cdl.org/articles/self-worth-resilience-and-hope-the-search-for-islands-of-competence/

Diener, E, and Tay, L (2011) Needs and subjective well-being around the world. *Journal of Personality and Social Psychology* 101(2): 354–65. Accessed May 2016, http://academic.udayton.edu/jackbauer/Readings%20595/Tay%20Diener%2011%20needs%20WB%20world%20copy.pdf

Ealy, L (undated) *Co-ordinates of Resilience*. Accessed December 2011, http://localknowledge.mercatus.org/articles/coordinates-of-resilience

Ellard, C (undated) *Streets With No Game*. Aeon. Accessed February 2016, https://aeon.co/essays/why-boring-streets-make-pedestrians-stressed-and-unhappy

Gough, I (2000) *Global Capital, Human Needs and Social Policies: Selected Essays*. Palgrave.

Groundwork (undated) *Community Spaces Evaluation End of Programme Evaluation*. Groundwork, UK. https://www.groundwork.org.uk/community-spaces

Joseph Rowntree Foundation (2007) *The Social Value of Shared Space*. Accessed May 2016, www.jrf.org.uk/sites/default/files/jrf/migrated/files/2050-public-space-community.pdf

Kasser, T, and Ahuvia, A (2002) Materialistic values and well-being in business students. *European Journal of Social Psychology* 32: 137–46. Accessed May 2016, http://onlinelibrary.wiley.com/doi/10.1002/ejsp.85/abstract

Kelly, J-F, Breadon, P, Davis, C, Hunter, A, Mares, P, Mullerworth, D, and Weidmann, B (2012) *Social Cities*. Melbourne: Grattan Institute.

Max Neef, M (2007) *Development and Human Needs*. www.alastairmcintosh.com/general/resources/2007-Manfred-Max-Neef-Fundamental-Human-Needs.pdf

Moffat, R (1983) Crime prevention through environmental design—a management perspective. *Canadian Journal of Criminology* 25(4): 19–31. Accessed May 2016, www.ncjrs.gov/App/Publications/abstract.aspx?ID=86835

Montgomery, C (2013) *Happy City*. London: Penguin Books.

Ryff, CD (1989) Happiness is everything, or is it? Explorations on the meaning of psychological well-being. *Journal of Personality and Social Psychology*, 57: 1069–81. Accessed May 2016, http://ggsc-web02.ist.berkeley.edu/images/uploads/Post-AltruismHappinessHealth.pdf

Scioli, A, Chamberlin, CM, Samor, CM, Lapointe, AB, Campbell, TL, MacLeod, AR, and McLenon, J (1997) A prospective study of hope, optimism, and health. *Psychological Reports* 81: 723–33. Accessed June 2016, www.ncbi.nlm.nih.gov/pubmed/9400065

Thin, N (2012) *Social Happiness: Research Into Policy and Practice*. Bristol: Policy Press.

Toker, U (2012) *Making Community Design Work: A Guide for Planners*. Chicago and Washington, DC: American Planning Association.

World Health Organisation (2015) *World Report on Ageing and Health*. Accessed February 2016, www.who.int/ageing/events/world-report-2015-launch/en/

6 Play Quarters, London

Breaking down the barriers to playing out on the streets of London

Communal life has ebbed from many streets as they have become increasingly dedicated to the single purpose of moving cars through them. Prominent amongst the casualties of this withdrawal from shared space has been a reduction in children playing outside. This chapter looks at 'play quarters', an initiative of London Play to halt and reverse that decline and allow London's children to enjoy all the benefits that playing offers them and their communities. It is an expression of London Play's core objective to enhance children's ability to participate in society and *"develop to their fullest as nature intended"*, according to Paul Hocker, development director for the initiative. However the issues that have caused this decline are significant and have a momentum that threaten to further diminish outdoor play. According to London Play:

> *Space for play is threatened by encroaching development and the dominance of traffic. Freedom to play is stifled by distorted perceptions of risk, and fear. Time for play is eroded by the competing demands of homework, scheduled activities and digital entertainment. Budgets for play workers and play spaces are shrinking.*
>
> (London Play website, undated)

The 2013 annual playday poll of 3,000 children, parents and adults capturing attitudes to play in the UK revealed that 53 per cent of adults thought traffic was a barrier to children playing out where they lived and 40 per cent cited *'stranger danger'* as a concern. Also of note was the anti-play culture this survey revealed. More than a quarter (28 per cent) of the parents questioned feared being judged by neighbours if they let their children play unsupervised outdoors and 32 per cent stated that they believed allowing their children to play ball games or make noise outdoors would cause problems with other residents (Play Day 2013).

To use the language of Chapter 3, these deterrents span the hardware of the city and the software of the community that occupies it. They work together to tip the 'balance of influences' on people's lives away from play, as the things discouraging street play are given greater weight than those things that are encouraging it. Thus they are creating a social and physical environment that is biased against playing on streets. This is a major issue given that streets are, almost by definition, on people's doorstep and comprise 80 per cent of the shared space in London (Transport for London 2013, reported in London Play 2014).

This has significant impacts that have the effect of isolating children in their houses and diminishing daily activity. Paul Hocker notes that although society has changed in a way that deters play, children haven't:

Their innate desire to play and make friends through play remains the same as it was 50 years ago. But the reality is that on an average day, most children play outside for less than 30 minutes—and one in five children does not play outside at all.

(pers. corr. 2017)

London Play describe themselves as promoters, defenders and deliverers of outdoor play opportunities for London's kids. They see their mission as providing a voice that can address these threats to play and allow London's children to have the best free play opportunities, near to where they live. They do this by supporting play providers in the voluntary, community, statutory and private sectors and directly providing play opportunities. They have a strong emphasis on engaging and facilitating communities and in particular children to create and enhance play opportunities. In order to address the institutional and cultural or orgware barriers that push play off the agenda, they are also tireless advocates for play, seeking *"to raise the profile of play with politicians, decision makers, parents, schools and other bodies who work with or influence children and young people—through the media, our publications and by contributing to policy-making structures"* (London Play website, undated).

Project Description

Play quarters are an evolution of the successful roll-out of play streets in London, or 'Play Streets Version 2.0', according to London Play. Play streets are normal, everyday residential streets that are closed to traffic for a few hours periodically to give children the chance to play freely and safely on their doorstep (Figure 6.1). The only essential physical props of play streets are street closed signs, supplied by the relevant Council. Play streets aren't top-down, imposed initiatives but are bottom up and happen if and when the people who share the street agree it is something they want to do. Sessions usually last for between two and five hours and can be held weekly, fortnightly or monthly; on week days after school; or during weekends, depending on whatever the residents decide (London Play 2014).

London Play provides advice and ongoing support to people hoping to set up a play street to see them through the bureaucratic hurdles, help them avoid pitfalls and address their concerns. They help co-ordinate with the local Council and provide training if required (for example in first aid or road safety). Under certain circumstances, they can fund play areas directly or otherwise they can help people to access the small pots of money available for community events from Councils and local businesses. They advise to typically start with a trial session to test the waters and then, if the trial is enjoyed and finds support more broadly within the community, extending it to a regular event.

At the time of writing there were play streets across 26 of the 33 London boroughs. Play quarters recognize that the diversity of play and social activity that contributes to community life can best be provided over multiple play streets across a neighbourhood.

They build on the existing network of play streets to strengthen their links with one another and with the surrounding community. The aim is to return to children some

Figure 6.1 Play Street

Source: photograph by Phil Rogers, courtesy of London Play

of the independence that has been lost in recent years—making walking with friends to school, the park, the shops or a neighbouring play street a normal, everyday occurrence.
(London Play 2014)

Paul told me that play quarters are a natural evolution of play streets and have happened as communities have become used to—and supportive of—multiple play streets in their neighbourhood.

London Play actively collect the experiences of play street organisers and participants and encourage them to inspire and recruit others to launch play streets in neighbouring areas. Paul felt this may have contributed to the clustering of play streets and points to the effectiveness of seeing them in action as an inspiration for their adoption by others.

Play quarters seek to further cultivate this 'organic' attitudinal change in an area so that its inhabitants see their shared surroundings as inviting children to participate in their neighbourhood. Play quarters do this through a range of co-ordinated measures that 'join up' clusters of existing play streets. These measures include:

- Doorstep play sessions are scheduled so children know where to go to play with their friends and neighbours can get to know each other (including intergenerational skill swaps, helping older people bond with the children in the area);
- Walk Groups are established so that children can get to the park safely at the weekend;
- Schools are encouraged to introduce play street sessions at the start and end of the school day and reduce school run traffic;
- Smartphone apps that map out local play streets, safe walking routes and supportive retailers;
- Working with play quarter partners—local retailers and food outlets—to create a discount scheme for healthy eating options; and
- Establishing 'safe points' in the quarter so children know where to find a trustworthy adult if they encounter a problem whilst playing out.

Paul stressed to me the importance of encouraging the active involvement of all in the community. This included the obvious—the police, retailers and local residents—and the not so obvious, such as street cleaners (*"they know everything that's going on"*) in order to build community support and approval for play streets and ensure their delivery can happen as smoothly as possible.

At time of writing, the first play quarter was being developed in Palmers Green in North London in the London Borough of Enfield (Figures 6.2–6.4). Although the concept is still evolving into its final form, the experience of taking it this far and of delivering play streets allow some observations to be made about some of difficulties that have been encountered and the benefits that play quarters will bring.

The Challenges to Play Streets and Quarters

The main source of resistance initially was from Councils and in particular from highway engineers, typically *"middle aged white guys called Paul"* according to Paul Hocker. For these people, the idea of closing streets is an anathema and the idea of encouraging play on the street seems reckless at best. However this resistance typically diminishes as staff at

Figure 6.2 Devonshire Road Play Street in the Palmers Green Play Quarter
Source: photograph by Phil Rogers, courtesy of London Play

Figure 6.3 Devonshire Road Play Street in the Palmers Green Play Quarter
Source: photograph by Phil Rogers, courtesy of London Play

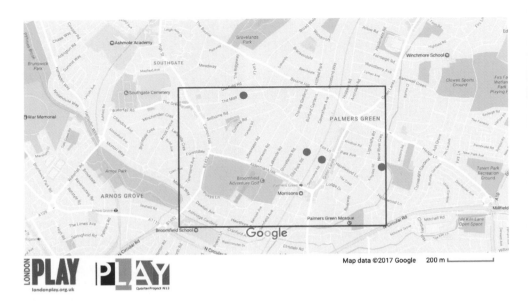

Figure 6.4 Map of the Palmers Green Quarter
Source: courtesy of London Play

London Play asked the highway engineers to recall their own childhood and their recollections of street play. In more recent times the growing track record of successful play streets provides compelling evidence that they work and are popular.

Another source of resistance has come from social media trolls looking to express discontentment and choosing to express it at play streets and quarters. Paul Hocker told me that although this form of attack has come from one person, it is particularly disappointing and has proved hurtful to the staff and volunteers who have committed so much emotional capital in making play streets and quarters happen.

Another (though small) focus of resistance to play quarters has come from some of the parents of children who are concerned that joining up play streets and advertising sessions will invite children and adults into the area who they don't know. Some parents fear this could potentially expose their community to bad behaviour from the visiting children and the risk of attack from these unknown adults.

Paul also added that parents who support the play quarter have their enthusiasm tinged by their own fears for their children's safety. He had heard *"that it is hard to let your child play freely when the media continuously pedals fear and terror"*.

Outcomes

Play London (2014) summarized their assessment that the benefits of play streets were:

> Active, happy children with friends next door;
> Friendlier, safer communities (where people know their neighbours); and
> Regular opportunities for everyone to have fun.

They also observed a sense of increased safety on play streets, as the social interactions they foster mean that people know more of their neighbours and therefore make it easier to spot outsiders.

In my conversation with Paul Hocker, he elaborated on these benefits. His extensive experience of play streets and the evident emotional capital he has invested in his work reveal themselves through his passionate and insightful observations. He stressed to me that play streets and quarters benefit and change all sections of the community, not just children. This change to the software and orgware of the community came about through the act of playing, in opportunities to participate in organizing the play streets, the incidental interactions that arise amongst adults watching the play, keeping an eye out for the children of the community and finding delight in their enjoyment.

He noted that these benefits leave a legacy on the neighbourhoods they are located within. They "*change the atmosphere*" and normally reserved English folk find it easier to talk to their neighbours in chance interactions. He also observed that play helps community cohesion, bringing together diverse elements of a community. Paul attributes this to the intoxicating effect of play, suggesting a play mate is a play mate before he or she is a member of a race or a believer in a religion, particularly for younger children. As such play doesn't 'buy in' to social prejudices that may otherwise blight community life and children playing together allows parents to focus on what they have in common and look beyond their differences.

He also stressed the importance of involving and empowering children and young people by allowing them to take responsibility and facilitate play sessions. He pointed to his observations that by respecting children and young people in this way, they have more reason to develop a sense of belonging to their community and are less likely to be involved in antisocial behaviour, which is an observation backed up by research such as Morris (2003).

Although the concept is still in an early stage of evolution, the initiative is gaining traction and support. It has won the support of Sadiq Khan, the mayor of London who saw it as an important contribution to "*reasserting the priority of people, rather than private vehicles, on the local streets where people spent much of their time*" (quoted in Palmers Green Community 2016).

Lessons Learnt

When I asked Paul what were the main factors that have contributed to the project's success, he told me that experiencing a play street is a delight and inspires others to take the idea back to their streets or council officers and councillors to adopt them: it is "*a nice contagion*", as he eloquently sums it up.

He noted the diverse opportunities that exist to make a play street happen are open to anyone and offer people the satisfaction of contributing to their community, echoing the sentiment in Chapter 1 that people feel good by doing good.

A related element that seems to have played a major part in the initiative's success is the emotional capital invested in it. The staff and volunteers really care about it and are motivated to apply all their evidently considerable resourcefulness to overcome almost any hurdle to see it happen. When Paul was telling me about the barriers put up by others, he said, "*but do you know what, we will win*" and his words weren't expressed with a tone of bloody mindedness but instead reflected a firm commitment that this was the right thing to do and could make the difference he felt was important and was in his power to make.

Paul recognized that this push to win streets back from cars, a critical part of enabling play on them, wasn't happening in a vacuum and there were other factors that opened people's minds to reducing car travel. He noted in particular a growing awareness that poor air quality is a major health issue. He noted there were the equivalent of around 9,400 deaths per year in London attributed to air quality-related illnesses, according to Transport for London (2016).

He stated that play quarters require the right circumstances to be successful. They have to have a degree of safety for play to even be considered, reflecting Bhalla et al.'s findings (2014) relating to walking and the primacy of safety reflected in the needs framework outlined in Chapter 2. They need to be of the 'Goldilocks size', neither too small nor too large. They need to be small enough to maintain a sense of neighbourhood but large enough to encourage children to extend their sense of what constitutes their home neighbourhood.

To return to the language of Chapter 3, play quarters might be seen as a way of cultivating emotional capital (the care that people have for their community) and turning some of it into social capital (strengthened bonds between people) and some of it into human capital (the skills and experiences developed through participating in play streets).

At its heart play quarters seek to achieve a fundamental reassessment of what streets are for and what community can mean to the people who share these streets.

> *It will, for some, take a leap of faith, perhaps a reflection upon the freedoms of their own childhood, to support the changes we all need to make to give children back some much needed independence in their childhoods. One of the big changes is to move from the idea that other people's children have little to do with us, to an understanding that they have everything to do with us. An investment in them is an investment in London's future, as they will inherit this city and become our future nurses, entrepreneurs, fire fighters, neighbours and teachers.*
>
> (London Play, reported on Palmers Green Community website)

References

Bhalla, K, Shotten, M, Cohen, A, Brauer, M, Shahraz, S, Burnett, R, Leach-Kemon, K, Freedman, G, and Murray, C (2014) *Transport for Health: The Global Burden of Disease From Motorized Road Transport*. Washington, DC: World Bank Group. Accessed June 2016, http://documents.worldbank.org/curated/en/984261468327002120/Transport-for-health-the-global-burden-of-disease-from-motorized-road-transport

Hocker, P (2017) *Personal Correspondence*.

London Play (undated) Accessed December 2016, www.londonplay.org.uk/

London Play (2014) *A Guide to Play Streets*. Accessed December 2016, www.londonplay.org.uk/resources/0000/1705/Play_Street_Guide_web.pdf

Morris, L (2003) *Sport, Physical Activity and Anti-Social Behaviour in Youth*. Australian Institute of Criminology Research and Public Policy Series No. 49. Accessed March 2016, www.aic.gov.au/media_library/publications/rpp/49/rpp49.pdf

Palmers Green Community (2016) *Play Quarters Palmers Green Leads the Way*. Accessed December 2016, www.palmersgreencommunity.org.uk/pgc/forums/forums-index/environmental-issues/575-play-quarters-palmers-green-leads-the-way

Play Day (2013) *Opinion Poll*. Play Day. Accessed January 2017, http://playday.gn.apc.org/2013-opinion-poll/

Transport for London (July 2013) *Roads Task Force Report*. Accessed December 2016, http://content.tfl.gov.uk/rtf-report-executive-summary.pdf

Transport for London (2016) *Mayor's Clean Air Action Plan*. Accessed December 2016, https://tfl.gov.uk/corporate/about-tfl/improving-air-quality?cid=transport-emissions#on-this-page-0

7 Benches Collective, Various Locations in The Netherlands and Overseas

Cultivating street life

The Netherlands are a small and densely populated country. One third of the country is below sea level and is only kept dry with significant communal sacrifice and the application of cutting-edge engineering techniques from the 1500s onwards. Given the preciousness of such land, Dutch cities have traditionally been compact and dense and houses small, with much life taking place outside on the stoep or street.

However the pressures and aspirations of modern life have eroded this tradition of sharing space. The appeal and imperative to spend time indoors or go elsewhere has grown and the relative appeal of spending time outdoors has diminished as safety concerns grow and time available has been squeezed by work, school and other commitments. With this trend away from sharing the street, the connections between neighbours and by extension the connection between people and place have diminished.

Benches Collective is an initiative that started in The Netherlands to reverse this decline and cultivate social connections. From the Benches Collective website:

> *The gap between rich and poor, immigrants and long-time locals and between low-skilled and highly educated people is growing every year. It is becoming increasingly more difficult to meet people who have a different background. The recent terror attacks worldwide and the tensed talks about refugees are making it one of the most urgent challenges of our time to combat structural inequality and promote mutual understanding. Diversity in ethnicity, culture, religion and sexual orientation is part of every neighborhood, in every dynamic city and even in many villages worldwide. But that doesn't always mean there's a natural sense connection and solidarity. It is no longer self-evident that you know your neighbours. Because honestly . . . Do you know all your neighbours?*

This was a matter of deep concern to Cathelijn de Reede, who works with *Springtime Studios* (a marketing studio with a social responsibility focus) and Jesse Jorg founder of *We the City* (an organization that seeks to change the way people view and use public space to increase social benefit). They both felt that without these connections an important avenue for self-expression, contribution and participation in one's community was denied. Consequently they sought to use their skills to bring back this sense that the sidewalk is a shared living room where people would choose to be.

Project Description

This imperative inspired them to launch the Benches Collective or Bankjes Collectief in 2013. The core of the idea was simple: to facilitate and inspire people to share the space in front of their house in a typically Dutch style. On 'Open-air café' days (initially every first Sunday of the month in summer), people would be invited to put out seats, benches, tables and the peripheral props outside their houses that passers-by would associate with cafés. Alternatively they would be invited or adopt a public bench for this purpose. The intention was that by making these ephemeral little interventions, almost anyone could help provide a warm and welcoming place for people to share the neighbourhood and enter into conversations that might not otherwise occur (Figures 7.1–7.3). In this way they provide settings to develop the bonds of friendship and community. From the Benches Collective website: *"Open air café days elevate the importance of streets and benches from pure utility to places of experimentation, community engagement, and placemaking."*

Benches Collective facilitate those who are inspired to take up this idea to advertise their chosen opening hours and an idea of the menu and activities they plan and, by doing so, extend an invitation to anyone to come and join them. Although food and drink and even 'smokable' items are available (with the price being agreed mutually between the host and the guest), the emphasis of these places isn't so much on their refreshment value as on their social value. In inviting people to linger amongst others who are sharing that experience, they allow those people to build up the number and the depth of interactions. The fond memories of such experiences leave a legacy in that place of positive associations that support the conclusion that it is part of a nurturing and friendly community. Opening hours are advertised on the website in order that people might combine hosting a bench with visiting other benches. In this way they could join their guests before or afterwards on a tour of other benches.

Figure 7.1 Open Bench 1

Source: photograph by Coco Plooijer, courtesy of Benches Collective

Figure 7.2 Open Bench 2
Source: photograph by Lilian Sijbesma, courtesy of Benches Collective

Figure 7.3 Open Bench 3
Source: photograph by Marika Kawaguchi, courtesy of Benches Collective

In keeping with the founders' creative backgrounds and in order to enhance the special-ness and memorability of a bench visit, the Collective has also sought to nurture compli-mentary private initiatives. An expression of this commitment is the encouragement they have given to innovative 'street services'. These include a person who travels to different benches to offer cocktails made with local flowers and weeds such as dandelion. Other street services include outdoor cinema, petanque courts, salsa classes, hairstyling, guaca-mole making, knitting courses and storytelling sessions for children.

In the first three years of the Collective, the benches days were on the same pre-determined days. This created a critical mass of active benches that mean that someone passing through a neighbourhood might come across several on one trip, helping to embed the idea of actively shared space more firmly in her or his mind. It also facilitates people to bench-hop and go between different benches, getting a better feel not just of their imme-diate neighbourhood but also of the wider community. However, in 2016, benches days were encouraged on whatever days the host(s) wanted between the opening of the season on Sunday, 5 June and closing on Sunday, 18 September.

Project Challenges

Cathelijn and Jesse informed me that the bureaucratic challenges presented some difficul-ties; whilst authorities were not averse to the idea, their initiative did not fit in well with the organizational structures or priorities of government. However their backgrounds in government and community development and the 'know-how' they have developed in these fields have allowed them to effectively convince the key stakeholders in Amsterdam to support the project, and in doing so created a conducive environment for the initiative to prosper.

Outcomes

If the uptake is a measure of their success, they have proved very successful, inspiring many people in The Netherlands and increasingly in other countries to host their own bench days. In the first year of the Collective, there were 163 benches over the benches season. In the following year, the number of benches doubled according to Caroline de Francqueville Hansen (2016), and since 2014 over 1,000 benches have opened in 17 coun-tries (Benches Collective, undated), giving weight to the Benches Collective's claim to be "*the world's largest open air cafe*".

The benches have provided entry-level experience of participating in and contributing to one's community which has had a lasting legacy. Research commissioned by Jesse Jorg found that almost 80 per cent of participants thought his/her bench was a success and 64 per cent of the people who meet each other during these events will keep seeing one another (Bankjes Collectief website undated). Other findings on the website suggests that in 57 per cent of cases, hosting a bench will motivate people to organize further activi-ties such as neighbourhood barbecues, starting a groepsapp (social media neighbourhood group) or starting a neighbourhood clean-up (ibid).

The analysis concluded, "*Benches Collective managed to comply with their three main goals; contributing to the inviting character of the street, strengthening the social structure of the neighbourhood and increasing feelings of safety, place attachment and apprecia-tion*" (ibid). The contribution that the enhanced community connections make to safety has attracted the attention of a number of insurance companies who are investigating sponsoring the Collective (Jesse Jorge May 2016, pers. corr.), motivated by a growing awareness that increased social capital is an effective preventative measure against crime (Weel and Akçomak (2008).

In talking to Cathelijn and Jesse in Amsterdam it was clear to me that perhaps the most significant contributor to the success of the program comes from their personal commitment and investment of emotional capital in the project. Their quite inspirational sense of the belief in the importance of person-to-person connections in determining happiness is evidently a powerful motivator. When coupled with their experience in community development and government, this has allowed them to design the initiative carefully and convince the governmental gatekeepers who need to be convinced to make the project happen.

Another contributor to the success of the initiative was that, for the reasons outlined in this chapter, Amsterdam has a tradition of sharing public space and conducting a significant amount of life in public; as such the concept was not entirely alien to Dutch people.

Lessons Learnt

Benches Collective provides an inspiring example of how public space can improve the human condition—not by government, housing corporations or project developers, but by the inhabitants themselves with minimal physical intervention. The inclusive and supportive nature of the Collective and the relatively easy and 'low-risk' interventions, grounded in a familiar although threatened aspect of Amsterdam life, has encouraged significant take up of the idea. It provides entry-level community activism that has helped facilitate other types of community engagement. The philosophical commitment to cultivating freedom of expression and the support offered for experimentation with themes has allowed many different types of benches to emerge. This has offered a wide variety of experiences to share and created the common ground for social capital to flourish.

References

Bankjes Collectief (undated) *Over Bankjes Collectief*. Accessed May 2016, www.bankjescollectief. nl/nl/about/

Benches Collective (undated) *About Benches Collective*. Accessed May 2016, www.bankjescollectief. nl/en/about/

Benches Collective (undated) *Benches Collective*. Accessed May 2016, www.bankjescollectief.nl/en/

de Francqueville Hansen, C (January 2016) *A Story of Benches*. Accessed May 2016, www.linkedin. com/pulse/story-benches-caroline-de-francqueville-hansen

Jorge, J (2016) *Personal Correspondence*.

Weel, B, and Akçomak, S (2008) *The Impact of Social Capital on Crime: Evidence From the Netherlands*. Institute for the Study of Labor. Accessed September 2016, http://ftp.iza.org/dp3603.pdf

8 Tower Hamlets Cemetery Park, London

Protecting and enhancing accessible wilderness

Tower Hamlets Cemetery Park (Figure 8.1) occupies 10.93 hectares of the otherwise intensely built-up London Borough of Tower Hamlets (Tower Hamlets undated), the local authority on the eastern edge of the City of London. The park had been one of London's 'Magnificent Seven' cemeteries between 1841 and 1966 when it was closed and gazetted as a park. By this time a history of neglect and war damage (Commonwealth War Graves Commission, undated) had given nature a chance to re-establish itself, as significant trees grew up amongst the graves. Initial plans envisaged redesigning the cemetery as a generic park, with its chapels demolished, its headstones cleared and many of its trees removed in favour of extensive areas of lawn. The attempted implementation of this plan by the Greater London Council (the upper tier of local government in London at the time) triggered determined community protests that resulted in the plans being abandoned.

In 1986 the responsibility for the park was transferred to Tower Hamlets. According to Ken Greenway, the very helpful park manager, ongoing concern about the management led to the founding of a Friends of Tower Hamlets Cemetery Park (FoTHCP, 'the Friends')

Figure 8.1 The Park and Its Setting
Source: adapted from Google maps

Figure 8.2 The Park's Natural Character Provides Relief to Its Intensely Urbanized Surroundings

who came together informally in 1986 and formally in May 1990. They saw their role as to protect and enhance the heritage and 'wild' natural woodland values of the park and share them with the people of the east end. Their vision saw the park as a piece of woodland in the city where people could escape the intensity of urban life, "*swap tower blocks for trees*" and recharge their emotional batteries (Figure 8.2). In May 2001 it was formally recognized as a Local Nature Reserve and in 2004 the Friends group took over the management of the park on behalf of the Council. The park has been added to twice in the 1990s, including a parcel known as 'Scrapyard Meadow' (Tower Hamlets website, undated).

Project Description

In stark contrast to its highly built-up surroundings, the park is an oasis of green, for the most part comprising dense woodland and clearings of meadow grasses. Despite its proximity to busy roads, railway lines and the intensity that comes from so many people nearby, the sense of seclusion and peace is striking. Once inside the tall perimeter walls of the cemetery era, the visitor would find their visual catchment dominated by trees that obscure the external world from most places in the park. On my visits to the park I recall a place where sunlight filtered through the canopy to dapple scattered monuments and wildflowers, illuminating some areas and casting others into deep shade (Figure 8.3). After a short time I found myself 'retuning' my eyes and ears to focus on the breeze in the trees and the fascinating industry of bees, butterflies, dragonflies and birds. To my mind this resonated with Berman et al.'s (2008) suggestion outlined in Chapter 2 that nature 'modestly' attracts people's attention and offers relief from more urban stimuli that 'dramatically' demand our attention.

Figure 8.3 Typical Scene

Ken Greenway described the Cemetery Park to me as "*a mosaic of habitats*" (pers. corr. 2015) that, according to the FTHCP website, have been managed to greatly diversify the woodland

> *with the gradual reduction of sycamore, new tree planting, and the development of a rich groundcover of grasses, bulbs and wildflowers. There are five wildlife ponds. About a third of the Local Nature Reserve is grassland, much of it flower rich meadow. Meadows are mostly cut annually in autumn. Each year some areas are cut twice, others not at all (to help overwintering insects). The areas change year by year.*

(undated)

At the northwest corner of the park is a collection of buildings which includes the offices and stores for the Friends and the Soanes Centre where Setpoint London East (a science and engineering charity) run science workshops. According to the Tower Hamlets website (undated), these are attended by over 8,000 school children every academic year. Most of these are based on the natural environment and study the ponds and the flower-rich woodlands and meadows in the park. All classes link to the National Curriculum and are offered for a small charge to schools in Tower Hamlets (ibid). The centre also provides a centre for a number of natural science- and history-based clubs and groups (Figure 8.4).

These contribute to the 170-plus events the Friends run each year to reveal its many different layers of meaning and maximize their contribution to the well-being of visitors. Others include guided walks, family-friendly events, history events, forest school and training courses (FTHCP website, undated). The park also hosts a range of festivals and fairs, which

Figure 8.4 Outdoor Classroom
Source: photograph courtesy of The Friends of Tower Hamlets Cemetery Park

helps provide funding and increases the appeal of the park, drawing more people in and exposing them to its exceptional character. One of the festivals is Shuffle Festival, an annual community event that involves film, natural science education, storytelling, performance art, architectural installations, walks, food, comedy and music. Part of the purpose of the festival is to experiment with spaces of the East End to find new uses and activities that respect and enhance the sites' values whilst meeting community needs. For the 2015 Shuffle Festival, sister organization Shuffle Regeneration commissioned and built four temporary pavilions in the park for use by local people and groups. These sought to inspire and show what was possible with a sensitive response to the setting by designing to celebrate the park rather than imposing upon it; 'privileging' the park as Ken eloquently put it. The pavilions were: *Symbiosis* (a treehouse restaurant) (Figure 8.5); a music pavilion; a 'homestead' pavilion; and the 'grounded den' (which celebrated rural crafts and country living).

Indicative of the festival's innovative and thought-provoking approach to celebrating the 'genus animi' (the soul of the place) was the choice of menu in the *Symbiosis* treehouse restaurant. Reflecting the science and local emphasis of the park and the festival, the menu showcased many unusual foods. These included locally sourced mealworms, foraged flowers from THCP and tree sap (Figure 8.6), successfully inviting experimentation by visitors and raising awareness of the park and its environmental values (Buck et al. 2015).

In operational terms the park is managed by the Friends via a Service Level Agreement (a contract) with Tower Hamlets Parks. The park is open from dawn till dusk and it is free to visit. The Friends have three full-time staff, and are supported by over 3,000 volunteers who take part in conservation work throughout the year (FTHCP website, undated b). The volunteers come from all sectors of society and include local residents, 'corporate

Figure 8.5 Symbiosis Pavilion

responsibility volunteers' from the nearby City of London, as well as addicts, the homeless and children. The Friends group also works closely with partner organizations such as Shuffle Regeneration and the Shuffle Festival.

Project Challenges

Ken told me that the park only exists as long as it enjoys the protection and support of key people at Tower Hamlets and other key stakeholders, and as long as it is liked by the community. An important component of maintaining this support is to have a strongly people-focussed perspective. This is a philosophy I saw manifested in the approachable nature of Ken and the others at the park and the informative and friendly tone of the signs around the park.

As a public space, the park has to deal with *"all the concerns/issues/problems that folk bring to the table from rough sleeping, to fires, and burnt-out bins, motorbikes, antisocial behaviour, and alfresco loving, to name but a few"* (pers. corr. 2015). Ken told me the

the symbiosis restaurant

3 COURSE MENU
£15
MUTUALISM
Maple Sour Brioche, Blue Cheese and Bitter Leaves (Yeast, bacteria and Tree Sap)

COMMENSALISM
Foraged Flowers, Pickles, Nori, Rice and Tofu Salad

MUTUALISM
Squid with wild Rocket, Chilli and Squid Ink Mayonnaise, (Aliivibrio Fischeri Bioluminescence providing light)

AMENALISM
Mealworm Dumplings, Fermented Chinese Vinegar, Nate De Coco and Kimchi

COMMENSALISM
Orzotto, Fungi, Algae, Squash and Parmesan

PARASITISM
Corn Smut Chicken Tacos, Corn and Refried Beans

MUTUALISM
Lemon and Gooseberry Posset with Violet and Crumb
--

MUTUALISM
Food waste composted by Black soldier flies

Figure 8.6 Symbiosis Menu
Source: The Friends of Tower Hamlets Cemetery Park

preferred way to deal with these issues was by negotiation and persuasion, which he felt has reduced the incidence of inappropriate behaviour and helped bolster local support.

Creating and maintaining this asset has not been easy. Although the park appears at first glance to be managed with only a light touch, Ken told me its wild character requires heavy intervention and a great deal of hard work to maintain the delicate balance that allows native flora and fauna to flourish. On top of this there is all the administration that comes with being a manager of land, a funding recipient and supplier of services to the Council.

The park has always faced difficulties finding funding to continue its operations. This gap has been met by cobbling together funding from a wide range of sources (including using the very atmospheric park as a setting for filming) and the investment of time, effort and emotional capital by volunteers and staff. Ken told me this has only been possible because it is *"more than a job"*. He added that the three staff and 3,000 volunteers were motivated by the *"chance to earn some satisfaction and do something that has a tangible and positive impact on the local community and wildlife"* (pers. corr. 2016).

Another challenge stems from the continued presence of the bodies buried in the park and the heightened emotional significance this generates for the friends, family members and the descendants of those interred. The assessment of the 2015 Shuffle Festival found that its former use as a cemetery discouraged some locals from visiting the park (Buck et al. 2015) and a commitment to respectful sensitivity limits what can happen there. In response to this the Friends developed and implemented management practices (Friends of Tower Hamlets Cemetery Park, undated-a) for themselves and partner organizations that have emphasized the respectful treatment of the graves and have contributed to documenting them (they have over 100 grave enquiries annually). This is reflected in their artistic policy which seeks to work with *"artists who unlock the joys of nature for urban people, and celebrate the diversity, lives and stories of the people interred here"* (ibid).

Outcomes

The park is a truly beautiful space that offers a wide range of opportunities for people to connect with one another and enjoy the benefits of a deeper engagement with nature. It allows a quality and depth of experience that seem likely to contribute to the values and priorities of the next generation, an aspiration of the Friends group. Its achievement has been recognized with multiple awards including the Observer Ethical Awards in the Ethical Wildlife category in 2015, which *"celebrate the people, organisations and campaigners who are leading the way to ensure we have an ethical future"* (*The Guardian* 3 July 2015). More recently they were the recipient of the Britain in Bloom Award for Wildlife and Conservation.

Achieving these outcomes was possible because:

The Friends' philosophy was one of *"privileging the site"*—letting its natural values inform the design agenda. It is also run to reflect the *"live and let live"* ethos of London's East End, according to Ken Greenway, placing great emphasis on respecting their neighbours and seeking to resolve conflicts through discussion rather than by imposition wherever possible.

This philosophy has helped inspire the exceptional commitment of staff and volunteers noted in the previous section and provides the park with considerable human and emotional capital that have helped fill in some of the gaps left by a paucity of financial capital. In particular the presence of the City of London nearby means that the park enjoys an ample supply of volunteers from corporate citizen programs and the support of some of their employers. Ken noted that the park probably couldn't function without the investment of these programs. He also noted the other key factors that supported the success of the park was the importance of the *"good guys"* at Council who created a supportive environment within which the park could operate.

In our conversations he further pointed to the importance of documenting and assessing things as they went along and sharing insights and responsibilities. This helps build up a body of knowledge and experience to ensure the park's continued success wasn't threatened if he or any other of the key people had to leave.

Lessons Learnt

To return to the language of Chapter 3, the park contributes greatly to the experience menu of the people of the East End. It offers them a range of 'nature' and 'people' experiences and opportunities that would otherwise be effectively unavailable.

The project tells us that its success owes as much to cultivating relationships between people as it does to cultivating the flora. The park's exceptional qualities and the welcoming nature of the Friends organization make it more likely that these opportunities transfer from people's experience menu to their experience diet. The park cultivates emotional capital amongst visitors, volunteers and workers by offering them a chance to enjoy, contribute and belong to something exceptional. As well as the intrinsic benefits of experiencing nature, its appeal to volunteers derives from a strong and consistently applied set of ethical values that are applied with great sensitivity and creativity. This support and the care taken to work with Council and other stakeholders has helped it to become embedded in the software and orgware of the community.

Many of the features of the park are quite unique and probably not replicable; for example few other places are of a scale or distinctiveness to be such good film sets, nor will many other sites be accessible to an almost inexhaustible pool of voluntary labour and professional skills. However the park's underlying strengths would seem to have more general relevance: 'privileging' the site and its natural values; the inspiration of leadership with an inclusive, strong and appealing vision that resonates with people; and offering a wide range of opportunities to engage and participate that suit different needs and capacities.

References

Berman, M, Jonides, J, and Kaplan, S (2008) The cognitive benefits of interacting with nature. *Psychological Science* 19(12): 1207–12. Accessed August 2016, http://journals.sagepub.com/doi/abs/10.1111/j.1467-9280.2008.02225.x

Buck, S, McKenzie, B, and Holtaway, J (2015) *Evaluation Report 2015 Shuffle Festival*. Flow 2015. Accessed November 2016, www.shufflefestival.com/2015-evaluation-report.

The Commonwealth War Graves Commission (undated) *City of London and Tower Hamlets Cemetery*. Accessed August 2016, www.cwgc.org/find-a-cemetery/cemetery/41902/city%20of%20london%20and%20tower%20hamlets%20cemetery

Friends of Tower Hamlets Cemetery Park (undated-a) *Artistic Policy*. Accessed August 2016, www.fothcp.org/Friends%20of%20Tower%20Hamlets%20Cemetery%20Park%20Artistic%20Policy.pdf

Friends of Tower Hamlets Cemetery Park (undated-b) *Volunteer*. Accessed December 2016, www.fothcp.org/volunteer

Greenway, K (2015) *Personal Correspondence*.

Greenway, K (2016) *Personal Correspondence*.

Tower Hamlets (undated) *Tower Hamlets Cemetery Park & Ackroyd Drive Green, Link Nature Reserve*. Accessed November 2016, www.towerhamlets.gov.uk/lgnl/leisure_and_culture/parks_and_open_spaces/cemetery_park.asp

9   De Ceuvel, Amsterdam

Inspiring waterside rehabilitation

Amsterdam has had a long and significant association with shipping. It is the largest city in The Netherlands and a major port in an export-oriented economy. Canals and harbours cover a quarter of the city's surface area (Amsterdam.info, undated). However, like all economies, the city has experienced change which has required its inhabitants to meet new challenges with old infrastructure.

One of the expressions of this change—and an inspiring response to the challenge—can be found at the former De Ceuvel shipyards, located on the van Hasselt Kanaal off the river IJ in Amsterdam's industrial north. The 5,000-square-metre site was a working yard from 1920 until 2000 when industry changes and plans to build a bridge downstream led to its closure. This left the waterfront site vacant but highly polluted, a legacy of its shipyard days and its previous use as a dump for Amsterdam's canal sludge (Schuetze 2014).

The potential of the site captured the imagination of architects Space&Matter and Marjolein Smeele, who share a commitment to social and ecological responsibility. When the city issued a tender for proposals to reuse of the site for a 10-year period, the architects brought together a multi-disciplinary group that developed the winning concept. The team included DELVA landscape architects (in conjunction with the University of Ghent) and Metabolic (a sustainable development agency who prepared the sustainability plan and feasibility study for the site). Innovation Network provided financial support and Bureau Broedplaatsen provided overall financing (De Ceuvel website, undated).

Description

The temporary nature of their tenure on the site and a low budget required the team to focus "*on developing an innovative concept where mobility and reuse were key*" (Space and Matter website, undated). Their idea was to use the site to create a dry harbour for 16 converted houseboats sitting above and protected from the contaminated soil that covered most of the site. This soil is remediated through phytoremediation (the use of soil-cleaning plants) that also provide an attractive landscape setting for the boats. Each of these have been converted into an atelier or studio for social enterprises or community organizations, drawn to the development by its designed qualities, inspirational setting and the interactions between the creative people who share it. The houseboats are connected by an elevated boardwalk that meanders through the emerging landscape and the trees that were part of the original boatyard (Figures 9.1 and 9.2). The path widens out at places where the site's setting can be best appreciated, such as its western aspect from where stunning views of the sun setting over the water can be enjoyed. The development also included a

Figure 9.1 Aerial Perspective
Source: adapted from Google maps

Figure 9.2 Typical Scene

waterside public space, a café and a boat landing, cultivating a sense that it is welcoming and orientated towards visitation.

Writing in the *New York Times* in 2014, Christopher Schuetze quoted project proponent and chief architect Sascha Glasl as saying houseboats were always the soul of the project. They reflected the site's former use and could be located without foundation on land best left untouched. They could *"be converted into innovative spaces before being towed up harbour and placed on the site by crane. This allowed the designers leeway, since city housing permits are not required to bring houseboats on land."*

The whole place was designed to embody a 'closed loop' philosophy and showcase regenerative urban development. Christopher Schuetz (2014) quotes Pieter Theuws, the lead landscape architect on the project, as saying: "*Our challenge is to connect streams of waste and energy and people into a circular city model.*" To this end the project is largely self-sufficient with bio water filters, a thermophilic compost and solar panels limiting further impact whilst the phytoremediation improves the site's ecological health. The café grows some of its menu on the roof and on floating rafts and most of the furniture is recycled. The human benefit comes from the inspiration of sharing ideas and spaces with like-minded people and is made possible by the contribution of "*lots of physical labour, a willingness to fight administrative bureaucracy and a desire to share the place with the public*" (ibid).

The innovative approach to the project extended to the selection of tenants who were

> *found through an advertisement on Marktplaats, a Dutch ad site, which asked potential tenants to choose one of the houseboats on sale that week, pretend that they could buy it for one euro and explain what they would do with it.*
>
> (ibid)

The development has an unambiguously experimental nature and places itself at the edge of what is possible, seeking to inspire and increase awareness. Sascha Glas describing it as a "*playground for us to experiment in city development*" (De Ceuvel website, undated). To this end, sustainability features are explained and results are reported through a series of informative signs, imparting the visitor with a clear message about the mechanisms by which sustainability might be achieved (Figure 9.3).

Figure 9.3 Interpretive Signage

Challenges

Such an innovative project did not fit easily into any particular administrative box and challenged many rules. Christopher Schuetz notes that *"although the project has been both financially and politically supported by the municipality . . . many of the team's ideas have run afoul of city bylaws"* (2014). He quotes American ecologist Eva Gladek, who stated, *"The site has no gas and no sewage connection; that itself is illegal."* She recounts how the intention to capture rainwater for drinking water had to be shelved because that would trigger a requirement

> *to licence the community as a drinking water provider—which was too complex and costly. In the end the community opted to bring in city water, although the ateliers are not connected to the sewer system. Commercial spaces and the cafe are connected.*
>
> (ibid)

Overcoming these challenges owed a great deal to the creativity of the project team and their ability to think their way around problems.

Outcomes

De Ceuvel is a beautiful and fascinating place that works on many levels that justify its claim to *"make sustainability tangible, understandable and fun"* (De Ceuvel website, undated). Its innovation has been recognized in a number of awards, including the 2014 Frame Public Dutch Design award. *"The annual prize, ultimately decided by a voting public (both online and at the Dutch Design week) is given to innovative designers. 'De Ceuvel gives the impression of a utopia that has actually been accomplished', wrote the prize selection committee"* (ibid).

The development has proved very popular with tenants and visitors but that popularity has brought its own challenges. Hans Karssenberg, founding partner of Stipo, a local urban strategy and development practice, told me that in the initial stage, the management of De Ceuvel was somewhat overwhelmed with the unexpected success of the development, which has become one of Amsterdam's tourist hotspots. This was great for De Ceuvel's name, but created access and parking problems for other local businesses. Fortunately these have now been resolved (pers. corr. 2015), partly by actively encouraging visitors to cycle there.

Contributory factors that influenced these outcomes were:

The site enjoys an accessible and valuable location, only 5-minutes' cycle from the ferry across the Ij and Amsterdam Central station.

Most of the houseboats could be acquired for a nominal sum of one Euro. Hans Karssenberg told me that Amsterdam's high environmental standards and rigorous local laws mean that the city's houseboats have a relatively short life and need recycling frequently (pers. corr. 2015). Furthermore, *"as Amsterdam's canals gentrify, and moorings are being leased by wealthier and more demanding residents, old boats are being scrapped to make way for new"* (Schuetze 2014). This meant that the project team's offer to take the boats for a Euro proved so popular that the team had to choose amongst offers (ibid).

The project had access to a deep pool of talent. Amsterdam has a rich culture of innovative design and an extensive network of creative professionals who are committed to social and ecological responsibility. The passion they brought to the project, with many unpaid hours of intellectual and physical labour, played a big part in making the project viable and getting it completed.

By establishing itself as a place to experiment, it has given itself licence to occupy the edges of what is possible and tolerate a few failures as opportunities to learn. For example, Hans Karssenberg told me that the phytoremediation was happening slower than expected but was providing a valuable case study into the practical use of plants to remediate contaminated soil (pers. Corr. 2015).

Lessons Learnt

To use the language of the first part of the book, De Ceuvel creates a positive relationship between people and place. It harnesses emotional capital (a passionate commitment to sustainability), human capital (skills, experience in many disciplines) and a little bit of financial capital. It cultivates these and turns them into a place that fosters social capital (strengthened bonds between people) and more human capital (through the work of its tenants and the conclusions drawn from its inherent experimental nature).

The development's setting, character, tenants and organization create an inspiring place for socially and ecologically responsible people and organizations to work. Furthermore its welcoming character, distinctiveness and commitment to showcasing the possibilities of ecological and social responsibility expose visitors to a wide range of ideas and insights. When the lease expires, the boats will be able to leave the site without any trace, leaving a legacy of land more valuable and biodiverse and a seed of inspiration planted in the hearts and minds of many who were drawn to visit the site.

References

Amsterdam.info (undated) *Canals*. Accessed December 2016, www.amsterdam.info/canals/

De Ceuvel (undated) *What Is De Ceuvel*. Accessed December 2016, http://deceuvel.nl/en/about/general-information/

Karssenberg, H (2015) *Personal Correspondence*.

Schuetze, CF (2014) Building a community on polluted land. *New York Times*, 19 November, 2014. Accessed December 2016, www.nytimes.com/2014/11/20/business/energy-environment/ex-shipyard-in-amsterdam-houses-shops-and-offices.html

Space and Matter (undated) *De Ceuvel*. Accessed December 2016, www.spaceandmatter.nl/de-ceuvel/

10 Woonerven, The Netherlands and Overseas

Hardwiring streets to be shared

Many countries have long struggled to reconcile cities that predate automobiles with their citizen's aspirations to own and use them. Until the 1970s, The Netherlands were making strenuous efforts to accommodate this aspiration by implementing a vigorous road-building program (Van der Zee 2015). However, as recounted in Chapter 4, a tragic and high-profile traffic accident triggered a campaign that caught people's attention and brought the Dutch government to reassess its approach to balancing cars and people. Part of this reassessment led to the creation of a new type of street, a 'woonerf' (plural 'woonerven'), literally 'living streets', first conceptualized by Dutch planner Niek De Boer (Van Gameren and Mooij undated). Woonerven sought to reduce the impact of vehicles on streets to ensure they didn't sterilize the streets they passed through and in doing so allow life to escape from within the adjoining dwellings. The first legally designated woonerf was built in Delft in 1976 and since then they have been adopted extensively elsewhere in The Netherlands and throughout Europe.

Description

Woonerven are distinctive street treatments (Figure 10.1) that break down rigid barriers between uses and dedicate little or no space solely to moving cars. Their central message is that cars are guests in that space, tolerated and accommodated to various degrees but not allowed to dominate or diminish the street's social potential (Figure 10.2). Recognizing the root of the problem lies as much with the legal framework within which streets were used, as with their design the early advocates drafted laws to enshrine the equal access of pedestrians and cyclists to streets designated as woonerven in order to *"extend citizens' rights over their home territorial space"* (Susskind and Elliot 1983).

There are six components found in most woonerven (Figure 10.3) (adapted from Hand 2010):

The first is to create distinct thresholds that tell the visitor that they are entering a woonerf. Typically these are compositions of signs that announce its legal status and other measures that frame and enhance the space as well as require traffic to slow down.

The second is variations and discontinuities in the travel lane to de-emphasize it, reducing its 'kinetic unity' (Cullen 1961).

The third is to design features that serve a dual purpose of slowing traffic to walking pace whilst also enhancing the quality of the pedestrian experience. Examples of such features would be benches, bollards, play equipment and vegetation.

The fourth is the elimination of continuous kerbs that creates a sense that the pedestrian domain has no edges and extends across the width of the street. *"This creates a situation*

Figure 10.1 Typical Woonerf

Figure 10.2 Balance of Priorities in a Woonerf

Elimination of kerbs to allow the pedestrian realm to extend into the street

Parking accommodated but not allowed to dominate

Streetscape features used to slow traffic and increase social value of space

Distinctive threshold and signage

Variations in travel lane

Figure 10.3 Key Elements of a Woonerf

where drivers and pedestrians are placed on the same level, and drivers are directed by bollards, street furniture, trees, and varied pavement treatment" (Hand 2010).

The fifth component is to accommodate parking but with intermittent spacing so that the street does not begin to feel like a parking lot.

The sixth relates to process: many woonerven were designed with a significant degree of community involvement and were implemented with the intention that the spaces 'won' from vehicles might be colonized by community uses.

More recent innovations have seen the woonerf concept evolve to encompass 'naked streets' based on the pioneering work of Hans Monderman (1945–2008). These are streets that are devoid of signage or edges that would otherwise dedicate space to a particular user, with no separate road, bike path, zebra crossings or footpath. In moving through such streets, an element of risk is deliberately introduced and eye contact between driver and pedestrians becomes the principal way of determining who has priority on each interaction. As Hans Monderman said, *"essentially, what it means is a transfer of power and responsibility from the state to the individual and the community"* (quoted in Project for Public Spaces 2009). His ideas have found application in many places in The Netherlands and beyond (Figure 10.4).

Challenges

Woonerven and similar streetscapes are estimated to cost 150 per cent more than conventional streets (Carr et al. 1992) and they raise more complex design and management issues. They require many people to think differently about streets and challenge them to reconsider their priorities. As Mike Biddulph found in relation to home zones (the UK equivalent of woonerven), they require *"a steep learning curve for engineers, partly because the concept itself challenges many values and approaches engineers hold dear"* (2003).

Furthermore, experience suggests that, for many people, diminishing parking or impeding traffic is too high a price to pay for most interventions, almost irrespective of their benefits. A study of home zones also identified concerns that they may adversely affect emergency services response times (Department for Transport 2005).

Figure 10.4 Exhibition Street Shared Space in Kensington, London
Source: Shutterstock 428535820

Outcomes

Research gathered by Mike Biddulph (2001) reveals that:

Woonerven and their counterparts are effective at reducing vehicular speed; the average speed of vehicles in woonerven in The Netherlands was between 13 and 25kph (8 to 16mph), with the closeness of the streetscape features having a significant impact on speed. This can improve safety; in concluding, Biddulph found that there is evidence to suggest that any initiative which dramatically calms traffic *"will have an impact on both the number and the severity of accidents"*. He adds:

> *Research from Germany and Denmark indicates that, over 10 years following the introduction of calming techniques, general fatalities in Germany reduced from 6.2 per 100,000 to 2.3 per 100,000, and that, in Denmark, a review of 600 schemes found the number of casualties had reduced by 43%.*

(ibid)

He also notes accidents between vehicles are no worse than on a conventional street (ibid).

He suggests that home zones can draw out life onto the street, noting that the pattern of activity seen in a home zone is more varied than that found in traditional neighbourhoods, with children playing out more and residents of all ages choosing to stay outside for longer periods and socializing more.

He also noted they may also contribute to improving the quality of the urban environment and help to increase the attractiveness of urban living, observing that "*80% of residents living in home zones in the UK find their living environment to be attractive or highly attractive*" (ibid).

Natalia Collarte further notes that "*while residents appreciate low traffic volumes and the absence of cut-through traffic, they considered the provision of larger play areas for children as well as the improvements to the street environment to be the most important benefits*" (2012).

Although woonerven and their equivalents offer significant benefits, they have proved controversial and are not without their drawbacks. In addition to their greater expense noted in the previous section, the additional landscaping and street furniture adds to maintenance responsibilities (Steinberg 2015).

> *Moreover, some critics have indicated that that service vehicles and drivers who are not familiar with the street have difficulties [to park and find] their way around. In addition, since some traffic is moved to adjusted streets, the implementation of a woonerf might have negative effect on its surrounding.*

> (ibid)

Susskind and Elliot (1983) also pointed out that their initial popularity meant that in some places they became generic and administrative convenience denied the community the potential to contribute to their design. Anecdotally the removal of kerbs and other physical characteristics of streets can compromise accessibility for the vision impaired who might use these features to navigate.

Thus, although woonerven have inspired similar interventions around the world they have gone out of favour in recent years as conventionally traffic-calmed roads have been found to be almost as good as reducing road traffic fatalities at much lower cost (Institute Of Highway Incorporated Engineers 2002).

In relation to Hans Monderman's shared spaces, the counterintuitive removal of safety measures such as signs, edges and designated crossings to improve safety has proved controversial. Research suggest they may yield some safety benefits (Edquist and Corben 2012) as well as create significant potential to improve amenity. However journalist Viveka van de Vliet noted that, whilst "*objectively, statistics show that Shared Space design increases traffic safety. Subjectively, residents of Shared Space areas report feeling less safe*" (2013). They also create concerns in local authorities about liability (ibid).

Some of the key factors that contribute to these outcomes are:

Woonerven are a product of their European and specifically Dutch context. The Netherlands has a long tradition of ambitious intervention in the built environment and a culture of sharing space. The characteristically fine-grained street network with narrow streets also supported the application of the concept, distributing traffic and ensuring that there were very many candidate streets that were appropriately short and lightly trafficked.

Changing the road surface is less difficult in The Netherlands than it would be in other countries; a third of the country is built on reclaimed land, including much of the cities. This causes irregular settlement, which means that brick paving set in sand has to be changed regularly anyway (Susskind and Elliot 1983).

According to Biddulph (2001), a woonerf or home zone works better in areas where there is resident support, existing street activity such as children playing on the streets, concern about traffic and little or no open spaces available close by. They also still need to be able to accommodate the traffic generated on that street without displacing it to other streets. He suggests this means they need to be used by fewer than 100 vehicles per hour at peak times, and notes existing practice that continuous treatments should be less than 600 metres in length (400 metres for a cul-de-sac).

He stresses, "*there appears to be no clear empirical basis for determining these limits, although Dutch experience suggests that the main justification for this is driver frustration at having to drive slowly through larger areas*" (ibid).

Lessons Learnt

Woonerven provide an inspiring example of 'and' thinking rather than 'or' thinking. They simultaneously calm traffic *and* improve the appeal of the streetscape for active occupation and enjoyment. In appropriate circumstances and embedded into a broader suite of streetscape measures, woonerven and home zones, etc. can communicate messages to the users that create a pro-pedestrian, pro-bicycle and pro-street life bias. However their costs can be prohibitive and will require judicious use to ensure their benefits are maximized.

References

Biddulph, M (2001) *Home Zones*. Bristol, UK: Policy Press.

Biddulph, M (October 2003) Towards successful home zones in the UK. *Journal of Urban Design* 8(3): 217–41.

Carr S, (1992) *Public Space*. Cambridge, UK: Cambridge University Press.

Collarte, N (2012) *The Woonerf Concept Rethinking a Residential Street in Somerville*. Tufts University. Accessed July 2016, http://nacto.org/docs/usdg/woonerf_concept_collarte.pdf

Cullen, G (1961) *Townscape*. London: Architectural Press.

Department for Transport (UK) (2005) *Homezones*, Department for Transport.

Edquist, J, and Corben, B (2012) *Potential Application of Shared Space Principles in Urban Road Design: Effects on Safety and Amenity*. Report to the NRMA-ACT Road Safety Trust Monash University Accident Research Centre. Accessed July 2016, www.roadsafetytrust.org.au/c/rtt?a=se ndfile&ft=p&fid=1339632202&sid

Hand, C (2010) *Woonerf: A Dutch Residential Streetscape*. University of Massachusetts. Accessed July 2016, http://people.umass.edu/latour/Netherlands/hand/

Project for Public Spaces (2009) *Hans Monderman*. www.pps.org/reference/hans-monderman/ Accessed June 2016.

Steinberg Lior (2015) *Woonerf: Inclusive and Livable Dutch Street*. Accessed November 2016, www.lvblcity.com/blog/2015/12/woonerf-inclusive-and-livable-dutch-street

Susskind, L, and Elliot, M (1983) *Paternalism, Conflict and Co-production*. Springer.

Van der Zee, R (2015) How Amsterdam became the bicycle capital of the world. *The Guardian*, May 2015. Accessed November 2016, www.theguardian.com/cities/2015/mayustraliardam-bicycle-capital-world-transport-cycling-kindermoord

van de Vliet, V (2013) *Space for People, Not for Cars*. Accessed November 2016, https://worksthatwork.com/1/shared-space

Van Gameren, D, and Mooij, H (undated) *The Heritage of the Woonerf*. DASH #03. Accessed November 2016, http://dash-journal.com/the-heritage-of-the-woonerf/

11 Christie Walk, Adelaide

Designing to inspire, community-led urban infill residential development

Until recently Australia's suburbia was overwhelmingly dominated by single-storey detached housing (.idcommunity 2012). This provided little choice in the housing market and consigned many people to unsustainable and unhealthy lifestyles, according to Paul Downton, architect of Christie Walk, a community-led urban infill residential development in Adelaide in South Australia. Christie Walk sought to challenge this problem and demonstrate how high(er) density urban living might simultaneously improve people's quality of life and diminish their ecological footprint. Christie Walk is the brainchild of Urban Ecology Australia (UEA), a not-for-profit organization founded in 1991 of which Paul was a co-founder. The goal of UEA was (and is) to draw attention to the inherently unsustainable and un-nurturing nature of Australian cities. It seeks to challenge the culture of the development industry and the planning system and in doing so inspire the transformation of conventional cities into ecological cities. UEA describes these as "*vibrant, equitable, socially supportive, ecologically sustaining and economically viable communities*" (UEA website, undated). Seeking to prove that this change was possible and offer an inspiring exemplar of what life would be like in such a place, UEA took the brave steps of becoming developers themselves and creating their own eco-development. After exploring several sites, the idea finally found a home at a former bottle recycling depot in the City of Adelaide. The site was developed between 1999 and 2006 and was named after Scott Christie, a local environmental and social activist.

Project Description

The irregular-shaped site is surrounded by a mix of different types of dwellings and businesses inside the Adelaide City 'square mile'. It is a predominantly residential development comprising 27 units, an office for UEA and 11 on-site car park spaces (considerably fewer than the city's planning provisions normally required at the time—which would have been at least one space per dwelling). The UEA website states that it is home for 40 people from the very young to those in their 80s (UEA, undated). The buildings are threaded together along a slightly meandering and well-landscaped, car-free path that connects with the surrounding street network at all three ends in a deliberate measure to stitch the development into the wider city and facilitate people to take short cuts through the area (Figure 11.1).

The buildings are between two and five storeys in height. Paul Downton told me they are constructed of straw bales or aerated concrete blockwork with extensive use of recycled and sustainably sourced timber. The five-storey apartment building also uses steel frames and pre-cast concrete. The colour scheme, variations in detail, frequent curves, relative absence of right angles or straight lines, and the emphasis placed on landscape gives the

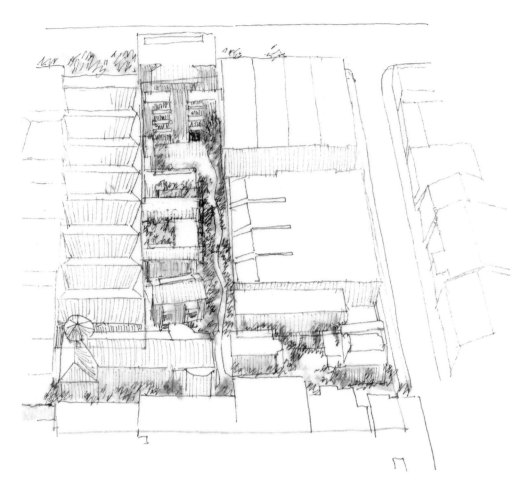

Figure 11.1 Aerial Perspective
Source: adapted from Google maps

whole development an earthy, organic feel whilst still being unambiguously urban (Figure 11.2). Internally the dwellings are relatively small and are designed to provide much of their amenity from the adjacent shared space. However privacy and security were also important design considerations. Windows overlooked by the walkway are buffered by semi-shared landscaped spaces visible from the public parts of Christie Walk but dedicated to the adjoining residence, minimizing views in but allowing views out.

A high standard of landscape design was seen as an important factor in maximizing the utility of the development and the amenity enjoyed by residents and visitors. It comprises a mix of native, indigenous, exotic and edible plants. The path bisects or is edged by a variety of convivial greened spaces that invite occupation of most of the nooks between the buildings. Coupled with the roof garden, the site offers a rich variety of shared places that support a range of individual or social activities. Some of these areas are destination spaces such as the roof garden, whilst others are both places to pass through or pause in,

Figure 11.2 Path Within Christie Walk

such as a variety of sized nooks along the access way (Figure 11.3). The productive community garden includes a small orchard.

The design seeks to make the most of the site and everything is designed to meet multiple needs. For example the roof garden was designed to be a proper, productive garden with deep soil (350mm) to not only enhance its productive value but also help insulate the

Figure 11.3 Multi-use 'Nook' Along Shared Path

apartments below from the baking Adelaide sun. The incidental nooks between buildings are maintained by the residents of the surrounding properties but can usually be used by all, enhancing choice, providing a variety of experiences and allowing residents to express themselves and gain satisfaction from the results of their work. This also reduces costs by diminishing the need for external contractors.

The development includes several collectively used assets. The community laundry helps with water and energy efficiency and there is a shared kitchen, library, meeting room, garden shed and bike shed for the use of all residents.

The philosophy espoused by Paul and UEA is one of cultivating ownership in an emotional sense as much as a legal sense. To do this the development seeks to give people a mix of pleasant and rewarding experiences and opportunities, facilitating them to work collaboratively (but not requiring them to do so) in order to enhance their chances of achieving eudemonic satisfaction as outlined in Chapter 1.

Challenges

In my discussions with Paul Downton between July and September 2015, he told me that finding funding or a builder willing to take on this brave vision proved difficult. In order to implement their vision in a way faithful to their principles and to minimize costs, UEA and the future residents formed two legal entities: Wirranendi, a private not-for-profit housing co-operative, to develop the site; and Ecocity Developments Pty Ltd, a non-profit company to build it. They set themselves challenging objectives relating to energy, water, land use, ecological and human health impacts, and pollution both during construction and in operation, as outlined in the UEA website (undated). Paul told me staying true to these standards added to the level of difficulty but also contributed to the level of inspiration and emotional capital they created in the stakeholders, who were involved in the planning, design and construction of the development. The CFMEU (a construction union) provided special memberships for the volunteers undertaking training on the site.

The extent to which the UEA vision departed from conventional planning and building practices also required them to challenge the rules and assumptions of many of the 'gatekeepers of development', such as Council's planners and engineers. For example the much lower rate of provision of car parking spaces than would normally be required in such a development. This required Council officers to make a leap of faith that was only possible because the philosophy of the scheme resonated with them, was well articulated by its proponents who had extensive skills and experience in this area.

Committing to bringing such a diverse group of stakeholders along on the design journey required going through the process in an incremental and transparent fashion, ensuring each step was signed off and broadly agreed to before moving to the next. This helped to ensure that the foundations of each design discussion were understood and shared, and that they allowed people to focus on the questions in hand.

Even so, the vast amounts of care and passion invested into the development meant that sometimes disagreements happened. Not surprisingly, much time and some frustration came with moving things forward with so many committed people, all with well-informed, passionately held but sometimes diverging views. For example the group differed about which paints they should use, some wanting mass-produced, more affordable paints whilst others favoured locally produced, more expensive eco-friendly paints. Paul noted these arguments only happened "*because people cared*" and were a good problem to have, mirroring the positive attitude that is reflected in UEA members and enshrined in their philosophy.

Outcomes

Although it was a challenging and sometimes frustrating design process (Australian Institute of Landscape Architects 2007), suffering all the disadvantages that come from being experimental, Christie Walk has succeeded and proves popular. In their assessment of the project, Sustainability Victoria (a government agency from a neighbouring state) noted that "*resale values have been strong, which, combined with anecdotal evidence, suggests a market demand for both the sustainability and community aspects of the development*" (undated). From Paul's perspective the development "*works better than dared hoped for*", with the residents coalescing into a community that has become well established and settled. In our discussions in September 2015, Sue Gilbey, then convener of the board of Urban Ecology Australia, told me of the close bonds of community that exist at Christie Walk. She told me that on more than one occasion, she came out from meetings there to find that someone had left bags of garden-grown produce for her on the seat of her stroller (walking aid). She doesn't know who does this but she considers it emblematic of the extent to which people look out for one another. She also told me of the informal babysitting that goes on in the development, where parents feel comfortable that their children are overseen by the community as much as any one individual. In talking to some of the residents, a theme I heard many times was that they were proud to live somewhere they considered beautiful with such a strong sense of community and such clear and inspiring principles.

The success of the scheme would seem to owe a great deal to the following factors:

The faithfulness to the ideals of the stakeholders. The clarity and uncompromising nature of the project philosophy, the commitment to community and the care taken in designing the development meant that every aspect reflected a consistent and inspiring set of principles. The commitment to an inclusive design process and involvement of co-op members in the building process has further strengthened the bonds between the residents and cultivated an increasing sense of shared ownership over the scheme as it emerged. This level of investment of emotional capital and shared belief that housing could be better meant that the emerging community had higher risk tolerance and willingness, even enthusiasm, to experiment at the edges of what was possible. This has allowed them to absorb the impacts of mistakes and create something more sustainable than would be possible by a conventional development (Sustainability Victoria, undated).

In his discussions with me, Paul also expressed the importance of not being bound by architectural convention or particular styles or fashion, thus creating something that was unique and timeless, informed both by traditional responses to climate and contemporary possibilities. He also stressed that although the design carries his name as the architect, it was created with input from many others, in particular his partner and co-initiator of the project, Chérie Hoyle.

Lessons Learnt

Such a development would not suit everyone, nor could it be done by everyone. However, for those who have the diverse skills and with whom these ideas resonate, it provides an inspiring example of what is possible. It required a significant degree of courage by the proponents to carry on after several setbacks and take the risks that arise from such an experimental project. However, the boldness of their ambition appears to have paid off and the development continues to attract incomers, drawn by its social and ecological values.

To use the language of Chapter 3, it required the investment of a great deal of emotional capital but this has yielded a return of greater emotional, social and financial capital. Sustainability Victoria concluded that this development has

> *demonstrated the possibilities for community-driven sustainable precinct development, both in design as well as business model and governance innovation. The lessons of Christie Walk present opportunities for other projects to recreate this approach with greater efficiency and subsequently greater potential value for participants.*
>
> (undated)

References

Australian Institute of Landscape Architects (2007) *Case Study #9 Eco-Village Christie Walk, 105 Sturt St, Adelaide.* Accessed January 2017, http://sustainablecanberra.aila.org.au/009-christie/default.htm

.idcommunity (2012) *Housing Types.* Accessed November 2016, http://profile.id.comustraliaalia/dwellings

Sustainability Victoria (undated) *Christie Walk, Adelaide Cooperative Approach Delivers Community-focused Eco-village.* Accessed January 2017, www.sustainability.vic.gov.au/-/ . . . /archive-building-the-business-case-adelaide.pdf?

Urban Ecology Australia (undated) *Inspiring Better Cities.* Accessed November 2016, www.urbanecology.org.au/

12 The Secular Pilgrimage and South Melbourne Commons, Melbourne

Recognizing and respecting the many layers of an inner-urban, gentrifying community

Despite its relatively short existence, South Melbourne has had a rich social history. Although long occupied by aboriginal people, its European history dates only from the 1840s when it became one of Melbourne's first suburbs. Located across the Yarra River from the city, the area was initially known as Emerald Hill, taking its name from the gentle rise that distinguished the area from the sand dunes and swamps elsewhere on the southern banks of the river. The emerging community soon established a patchwork character of small working-class cottages and larger middle-class houses amongst clusters of workshops and factories, attracted by the close proximity to the city, the river and the nearby Port of Melbourne. In common with many inner-urban communities, the area has experienced the ebb and flow of economic fortune and changes in industry which have triggered several cycles of growth and decline. In the post-war era, the decline was hastened as the recently developed, more spacious outer suburban communities found favour with the middle class and industry relocated to find more modern, less-constrained sites. The broader City of Port Phillip area (the local authority covering South Melbourne) became increasingly run down and soon associated with "*sly grog trading, cocaine smuggling, prostitution and organised crime*" (City of Port Phillip 2013).

The vacated residential properties were at first filled by immigrants, usually Greek or Italian, but by the 1970s these properties began to attract a returning middle class (Palen and London 1984). The area's characteristic mosaic of land uses and small lots occupied by old buildings—many of which are pretty Victorian houses on leafy streets with established urban villages, edged by beaches and parks, all adjacent to the CBD—has accelerated its de-industrialization and gentrification. The area has gone from being part of

> *a low-density working-class municipality dominated by families to a highly affluent, high density suburb populated by city professionals who predominately live alone. Port Phillip is now the fifth most advantaged Council in Victoria, populated by high income individuals and young renters.*
>
> (City of Port Phillip 2013)

The resulting rising prices, a parallel process of slum clearance and concentration of the disadvantaged in the community into large, multi-storey housing commission (public housing) flats, and a loss of jobs has eroded the older community and has brought about many social difficulties associated with gentrification. As the City of Port Phillip noted about this issue: "*Older long-term residents can be forced out, driven as much by the disappearance of familiar landmarks and memories as by rising rents, living costs and diminishing services. This can result in family or generational separation*" (City of Port

Phillip, undated). They note that for those who remain, there are reduced opportunities for community participation *"and there are well-documented links between social isolation and ill health, irrespective of income levels"* (ibid).

In their Municipal Public Health and Wellbeing Plan, the city noted that, despite the affluence of the incoming residents, *"marginalised communities, a high number of rooming houses, pockets of disadvantage and street sex work remain, evidence of the City's history as a cultural and societal melting pot"* (City of Port Phillip 2013).

The two projects covered in this chapter have sought to address aspects of this social divide. The Secular Pilgrimage sought to reveal, dignify and celebrate the hidden layers of meaning that these places had and share them with the wider world. The South Melbourne Commons created a community hub and shared space that could be enjoyed by all the community within a repurposed school.

The two projects were instigated by Father Bob Maguire, the retired parish priest for South Melbourne. His extensive (30-plus-year) experience of pastoral care as parish priest and subsequent founder and chair of the Father Bob Maguire Foundation (a not-for-profit charity whose by-line is 'who cares wins') gave him an insight into lives of the affluent incomers and the less well off, 'traditional' communities. These insights allowed him to see the human cost of living in a socially divided community. In his conversations with me (pers. corr. 2015, 2016) he spoke to me of the social disruption, drug-related violence and gang-related violence that he saw springing up amongst those who had little to hope for. He also noted that social exclusion wasn't just a problem for the poorer in the community. Wealthier incomers were often also affected, isolated in their flats in the new residential enclaves of Docklands and Southbank that have yet to develop social networks. In several of our conversations, he expressed his profound sadness at the impact of lives diminished by these largely invisible barriers between and amongst the haves and the have-nots. However he also noted the resilience of human kindness and commented on the many inspiring acts of courage, great humanity and compassion he has witnessed as people reached out to help one another.

The Secular Pilgrimage

Apart from some gang violence and organized thuggery, the history of the area has rarely warranted headlines. The layers of the past are instead made mostly from the delicate accretion of many fine layers of little history, the stories of personal human achievements, tragedies and the connections made or lost. Most of these stories have left little obvious trace. Sometimes they have been obscured by the comprehensive nature of subsequent development or because most people who live here now haven't tuned their eyes to see them, as is the case with the area's natural habitat values or the history of the indigenous inhabitants. Much of these stories are unavailable to us because the people who witnessed them are dead or have moved on. The built expression of these connections to place—the factories, orphanages, schools, churches, temporary dwellings, etc.—have been demolished or the houses gentrified and the factories, workshops and warehouses converted into apartments. However, despite this, many echoes and traces are still there. Much of this history has been documented and the relatively short and fast evolution of the area means that some of the people who witnessed these changes are still alive.

This Secular Pilgrimage seeks to provide a means by which the area's moving and fascinating social landscape might be revealed to all. The idea is grounded in a recognition of the power of a pilgrimage, a concept common to many faiths and increasingly finding

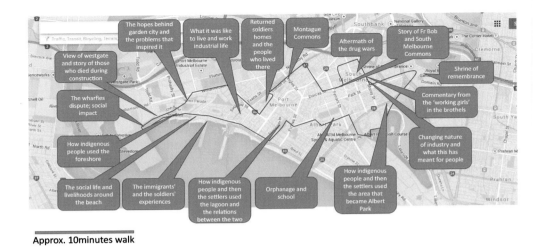

Approx. 10minutes walk

Figure 12.1 Secular Pilgrimage Route and the Stories It Reveals

application in the secular world. Pilgrimages might be seen as a sacrifice of time and effort dedicated to something of spiritual or otherwise profound importance. Unlike most other pilgrimages, this one is non-religious; the sacrifice of time and effort it represents is instead dedicated to a better and more respectful celebration of humanity.

The idea was developed by the author from the original idea of Father Bob Maguire in mid-2015. The proposed Secular Pilgrimage is a circuit walk of approximately 12km through South Melbourne and surrounding suburbs of Albert Park and Port Melbourne. The route takes people to and between 'story points'—places that are the focus of recollections of particular events. In this way it sought to reveal to pilgrims the little stories of humanity where they happened. It is hoped that it would allow the people who now live in the area or visit it to see their surroundings in a new light, as a setting for suffering, love, compassion and resilience, of differing but equally heartfelt meaning. It seeks to provide a symbol of reconciliation and recognition of those hurt by the hand of history that swept through the area and selectively pushed many aside. An indicative course for the pilgrimage is shown on Figure 12.1.

Our initial investigations revealed that, in addition to the stories indicated on this plan, there were other stories on or near the route that had left traces and told something important of the human condition. Some of these other stories include aboriginal sacred sites along the river, the sites of vanished factories, public houses and workmen's cottages, the sites of settler's churches and orphanages.

Pilgrims are directed around the route of the walk guided primarily by GPS-enabled smartphones (Figure 12.2). When pilgrims reach a 'story point', they can choose a number of ways to experience a story (written word on their smartphone screen, photographs of what was there before and in some cases the spoken word of those who experienced the events). In recognizing that there are usually many equally valid ways of seeing any subject and each adds light to the overall picture, the app was intended to give a choice of perspectives. It was envisaged that these perspective would include those of the traditional owners of the land, the Yalukut Willam Clan of the Boon Wurrungor (Eidelson 2014); the people

Route marker from the Camino, a pilgrimage in Spain. It is not essential to have some easily identifiable marker on the pilgrimage but it may help.

Next story 200m
Almost there!

Beaconsfield Parade

Kerferd Road

Turn left in 50m

Figure 12.2 Smartphone Navigation

who worked in, visited or were moved by a significant place; as well as the responses of other pilgrims (Figure 12.3).

The concept envisaged that the infrastructure for this pilgrimage is mainly web based but would be complemented by a few physical interventions. These would be mainly to mark the location of sites where stories are set and pique the interest of non-pilgrims (Figure 12.4). Recognizing that smartphones, though very common—in 2015 it was estimated that 79 per cent of Australians owned a smartphone (Deloittes 2015)—are not ubiquitous, the concept also envisaged producing these stories in a booklet.

Challenges

The project as I designed it and presented it to potential funders and implementers effectively focussed on the output and outcome, in the hope of capturing the imagination of those who had the resources to implement it. The concept described the pilgrimage, provided some direction about its components and shed some light on the tasks, such as the need to gather all the recollections and photographs of the area, process them and develop an app. It soon became clear that although it found support in principle and a great deal of enthusiasm was offered, the technical skills and time necessary to make it happen couldn't be found. Council feedback for the idea was that the project would have had

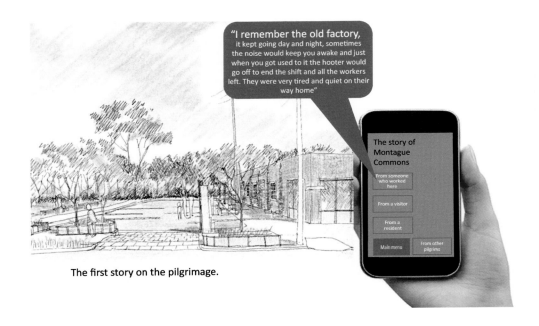

The first story on the pilgrimage.

Telling the stories

As well as the social history the app might also reveal the drier facts and figures history so people might be able to find out more about the place and put it into a historic context

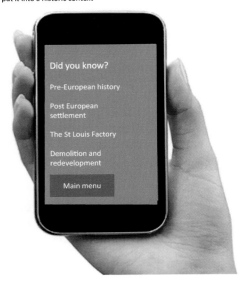

Figure 12.3 Each Story Point Can Be Experienced in Multiple Ways From Multiple Perspectives

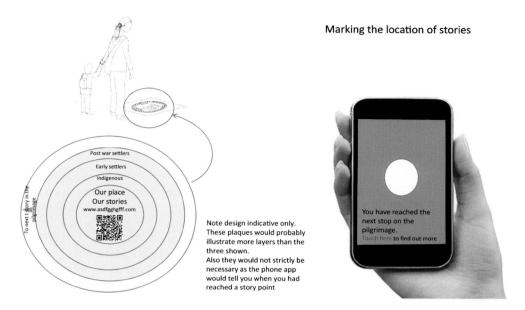

Figure 12.4 Marking the Locations of Stories

been eligible for local grants if we had the capacity to be the agents of implementation. As it was explained to me, the Council delivers a number of cultural heritage programs but also encourages the community to create activities, events and projects through support of historical societies, providing heritage resources and also a range of grant programs. Council recognizes the benefits of facilitating and supporting people to do things for themselves because of its multiple legacy benefits. These include the experience gained by community members, support of the local creative industries and increased responsiveness to the community.

The project also existed in an environment with several other projects that also sought to tell the stories of the local community in different formats; for example an exhibition of local photographs was being organized at the same time that this was drafted. This meant that those organizations that may have adopted the project and had expressed their support were already fully committed.

Outcomes

Despite the broad support in principle noted above, these challenges have so far proved insurmountable and the Secular Pilgrimage hasn't happened. Although recognized as a means to a desirable outcome, it lacked implementability. The 'what' and the 'why' of the project were adequate but the 'how' of the project just wasn't compelling. Having presented this idea and asked organizations to invest time and consideration into assessing the concept, there is a risk that future projects from myself or the foundation might be seen as being mere dreams, albeit pleasant ones, that are not resolved enough to be a good investment for funding agencies.

Lessons Learnt

The idea of experiencing a place from multiple perspectives and stringing these perspectives together to create a journey that was as much about moving the heart as the body was one that resonates with many people. The experience confirmed that ample care and commitment weren't enough to fill in the gaps left by an absence of other types of capital such as the intellectual capital of the app designers, historians, project managers, etc. Without the credibility that comes from the technical and administrative skills to make it happen or the time and resources to gather the stories, it couldn't be realized.

South Melbourne Commons

South Melbourne Commons (the Commons) sought to create a shared place that met multiple needs and did so in a way that facilitated people to connect across social fault lines. This project was a partnership of Father Bob Maguire, the South Melbourne Parish, the Friends of the Earth (FoE) and South Port Community Housing Group. It was a 'third way', social-enterprise development involving both public and private sectors but not led by either and was intended to deliver social benefits whilst covering its own costs economically. It could best be described as a 'community hub'. These are "*complex system of physical facilities, programs, and social networks that aim to improve people's quality of life. These services, networks and physical assets work together to form the foundation of a strong neighbourhood*" (Skraba 2010).

The Commons occupied the site of a former Catholic school that had been consolidated and relocated to more modern and appropriate premises nearby. The site is bounded by a church, roads and existing residential properties. It is within a block of two tram routes, near shops and healthcare facilities. Its walkable catchment (the area within 10 minutes' walk that did not require crossing a barrier to walking) extends through most of South Melbourne and significant parts of neighbouring suburbs. The site consisted of some beautiful old school buildings, some more recent buildings of little merit, and play and service areas.

The site has been developed in two parts: an area occupied by the former playgrounds and 1960s-era school buildings was cleared and redeveloped as 40 social housing units. These have been developed by the South Port Community Housing Group (SPCHG) for "*people on low incomes . . . who have faced homelessness, dislocation and social exclusion*" and aim to help "*the people housed to feel part of a community*" (SPCHG undated).

The balance of the site, comprising the original Victorian-era school buildings and surrounding spaces, were adapted by Friends of the Earth (Australia) for reuse as an 'eco-market' (a retail outlet for sustainably sourced food selling 70 per cent of the food-line items found in a supermarket), a café, hall, offices, several community spaces, play space and community gardens. These are all grouped around the landmark of a heritage-listed church and its established landscape (Figure 12.5). The net effect created was of an inspiring place that fits snugly into its physical and social context and was rich in opportunities.

The Features of the Commons

From the perspective that this book was written, one of the key characteristics of the Commons was the care taken to welcome visitors and offer them a wide range of experiences,

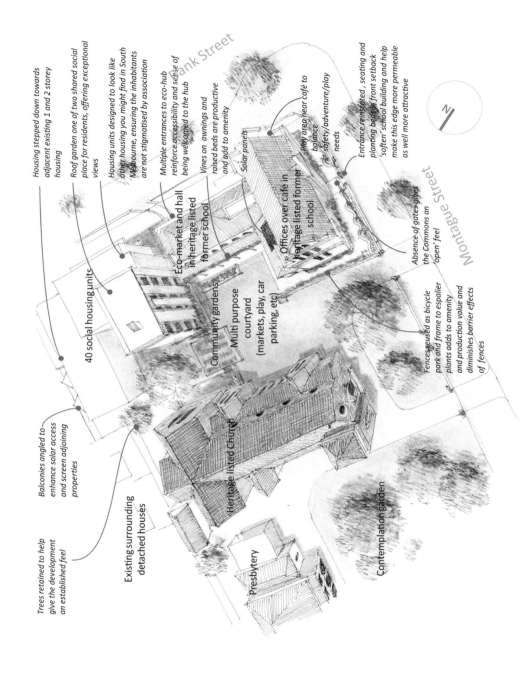

Trees retained to help give the development an established feel

Balconies angled to enhance solar access and screen adjoining properties

Existing surrounding detached houses

Housing stepped down towards adjacent existing 1 and 2 storey housing

Roof garden one of two shared social place for residents, offering exceptional views

Housing units designed to look like other housing you might find in South Melbourne, ensuring the inhabitants are not stigmatised by association

40 social housing units

Multiple entrances to eco-hub reinforce accessibility and sense of being welcomed to the hub

Eco-market and hall in heritage listed former school

Vines on awnings and raised beds are productive and add to amenity

Solar panels

Community gardens

Multi purpose courtyard (markets, play, car parking, etc)

Offices over café in heritage listed former school

Play area near café to balance safety/adventure/play needs

Entrance reinstated, seating and planting begin front setback 'soften' school building and help make this edge more permeable as well more attractive

Absence of gates gives the Commons an 'open' feel

Fences used as bicycle park and frame to espalier plants adds to amenity and production value and diminishes barrier effects of fences

Heritage listed Church

Presbytery

Contemplation garden

Bank Street

Montague Street

N

Figure 12.5 The Components of the Commons

Source: originally published in PIA Planning News Article by author (2013)

insights and inspiration that could be enjoyed almost as an incidental bonus to whatever might be the primary reason for visiting the Commons. A visitor might come to buy food but incidentally take away insights and ideas about how they can live sustainably, for example.

This required that the project paid careful attention to both 'big' and 'little' design decisions. Big design decisions are those by the architects (initially Nonda Katsalidis of Fender Katsalidis and then Ian Khoo of DesignInc) and the client that 'hard wired' the place physically, framing what can go on within it. Such 'big design decisions' include the distribution of the activities and the decision to design the social housing to have external standards that made them indistinguishable from nearby private apartments. The 'little design decisions' are those management and operational decisions in the hands of the people who use and operate the place rather than those who consciously designed it. Some of these 'little design decisions' that reinforced its ability to contribute to the quality of life of visitors and residents were:

Educational panels which were scattered throughout the site, explaining not just what people are looking at but why it is socially and ecologically beneficial.

The schedule of events, classes, markets, festivals, etc., most of which are free, drew people into the Commons and exposed them to a variety of ideas and opportunities. The eco-market provided free deliveries to ensure that not having a car is not a deterrent to accessing the food sold there. A library of sustainable living books was also to be found at the café.

The no longer required old school gates were removed and opportunities to get people involved sought so the Commons had an open and shared feel that would develop a sense of widespread ownership within the community (Figure 12.6).

These gave the place much of its welcoming feel. It seemed that for many people their experience of the Commons was influenced and enhanced by the way it was 'adorned' by the people in the café, the play area and by those tending the community gardens.

Together these 'big and little design' choices create a wide range of synergies that made the place what it is and facilitated a range of interactions (Figure 12.7).

Challenges

However, achieving this raised significant management and design challenges. Cam Walker (FoE) and Janet Goodwin (South Port Community Housing) mentioned to me that in management terms the sharing of spaces and the need to work across different agencies, each with different goals, had proved difficult, even given the co-operative approach of all parties. In design terms, providing buildings and spaces that can meet multiple objectives as well as responding to changing needs on a very tight budget also presented obvious challenges.

The surrounding community are very articulate and understandably protective of the areas high standard of liveability. Protecting this amenity in this heavily built-up area was a key challenge, not only because the City Council required it but because of the clients' and designers' ethical values.

The project was the first of its type and required the respective parties to go way outside their comfort zones. In particular Friends of the Earth had to venture into retail management and the Parish Council ventured bravely into major development projects, a world they had little experience in.

The project was also heavily focussed around the vision and driving force of Father Bob. Priests are given a high degree of autonomy in the Catholic Archdiocese of Melbourne and

Figure 12.6 The Reinstatement of an Entry to Montague Street, Installation of Planting Beds, a Play
Area and Café Seats Have Made the Formerly Grand But Rather Severe School Building More Open, Welcoming and Accessible

Source: by author, originally published in PIA Planning News Article (2013)

as long as he remained priest he could contribute greatly to creating a supportive environment for the project. However, when he retired, he no longer could provide this support.

Outcomes

For a while the inspiring ambition of the concept seemed to pay off. The social housing
units were built and continue to house people who would have otherwise lost their connection to the area or suffer intolerable housing stress. The café flourished, the hall was
often booked and the eco-store sold a wide variety of high-quality, sustainably sourced

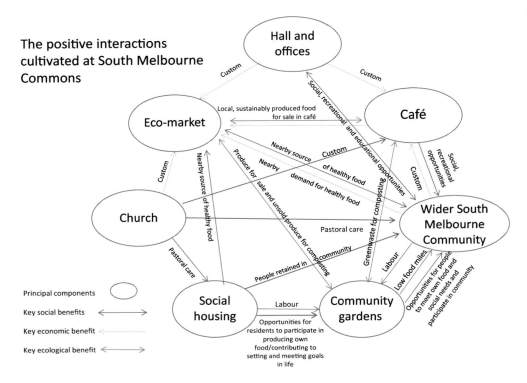

Figure 12.7 A Hypothetical Model of the Interactions Facilitated by South Melbourne Commons
Source: by author, originally published in PIA Planning News Article (2013)

food. The attention to programmatic and built measures ensured people could benefit from and contribute to the activities, opportunities and experiences the place had to offer.

Unfortunately most aspects of the Commons haven't withstood the test of time. By late 2012, when the Friends of the Earth did not have their lease renewed, the project had already suffered a series of reversals. With the retirement of Father Bob in 2012, the project lost its co-ordinating force. The new parish priest held a different vision for the site and the various elements of the project fell by the wayside, one by one. The shop failed, its initial location was felt to be too isolated at the rear of the site. It moved to a smaller site on the street front but was too constrained there to offer a variety of goods to compete with more conventional stores. The café has succeeded under different ownership and continues to draw customers—no mean feat in the competitive world of Melbourne cafés. Although it provides an attractive setting and offers great coffee, it is no more or less a social hub than any of the other cafés that can be found throughout the area. The positive interactions it was intended to facilitate between diverse activities largely don't take place. The gardens thrive but with a more ornamental than productive character, now tended carefully by three diligent volunteers as a quid pro quo for using the hall for weekly exercise classes.

A second attempt was made to create a 'Commons' when a lease was secured on another property, this time on the industrial/residential interface elsewhere in South

Melbourne. Unfortunately again the concept fell afoul of external forces when a change in the planning provisions saw the land suddenly jump in value, triggering a wave of redevelopment that resulted in this site, known as Montague Commons, also failing to get its lease renewed.

Lessons Learnt

The Commons offer several lessons for those considering collaborative, cross-sector projects to create bricks-and-mortar changes in their community. It demonstrates what a committed group of people can do when they break free of the constraints of public/private/community sectors to create assets relevant to the local community in a way that the market arguably cannot. Janet Goodwin, Cam Walker and David Cox (of architects DesignInc) identified the following factors as essential in getting the scheme realized and at least for a while achieving a good outcome:

- **Emotional capital.** The care of the people and organizations involved, the willingness to go the extra mile and desire to achieve a good outcome (where the definition of good extends to the social outcome) was critical to achieving and sustaining the project. It also helped fill in the gaps that would normally be filled by more conventional sources of capital.
- **The site.** The location of the site meant it was in an area of overlap for the diverse communities it was intended to serve. Its size and shape and a co-operative land owner made it ideal for this type of co-ordinated development.
- **Vision.** The project wouldn't have been possible without the energy, drive and commitment of the scheme's stakeholders, in particular Father Bob Maguire, Cam Walker, the Commons staff, the community reference group and volunteers at Friends of the Earth (Australia), and Janet Goodwin of the South Port Community Housing.
- **Active co-operation.** Such a complex and multi-agency project requires the active support and collaboration of all critical stakeholders: the Council (Port Phillip), Catholic Church and architects Nonda Katsalidis of Fender Katsalidis and later David Cox and Ian Khoo of DesignInc, who saw the social housing project through until completion.
- **Co-ordination.** Careful co-ordination was needed to organize and coalesce the diverse people, agencies and businesses needed to get the project built.
- **High sustainability standards.** These inspired people and helped gather support as well as improve its resilience.
- **Responding to the area's heritage and landscape values.** Retaining the existing mature landscape and heritage wall, referring to the colours of the wall in the new buildings and providing adequate setbacks to adjoining dwellings and screening were critical components in getting the project approved.
- **Respectful engagement with the local community.** The project was initially controversial and met with some resistance from neighbours; however, the community concerns were addressed by one-on-one meetings with surrounding residents and a series of 'community open days' that explained the design and demonstrated a willingness to adapt emerging designs.
- **Fostering a sense of community.** The design of the social housing units incorporated shared social spaces for the residents on the roof and at the entrance and great

care was taken in selecting people for the units to ensure a sense of community amongst the residents can grow. This helped to increase the stability, sense of settledness and engagement amongst the residents as well as fostering a greater sense of stewardship over the development and the wider area.

(adapted from an earlier article by the author
published in *Planning News* March 2013)

However, the project also shows the vulnerability of such interventions to outside forces and the potential weaknesses of a community-led approach. Investing emotional capital in a big, inspiring idea can achieve a great deal, but it can't achieve everything.

The importance of embedding a project in a legal and administrative structure that gives a project secure tenure and allows it to continue when key personnel leave are obvious lessons to take away (though very difficult to respond to).

Cam Walker suggested a key lesson was the need for community groups to do a careful 'audit' of the necessary financial, governance, professional and logistics skills in their group and seek to fill any gaps rather than 'battling on' with what they have. Architects, planners and other allied professionals can help provide these insights and ensure that the final outcome does not just meet the intended primary objective but can also meet a suite of other objectives that might help the community.

References

City of Port Phillip (undated) *Understanding Gentrification.* Accessed July 2014, www.portphillip. vic.gov.au/print_understanding_gentrification.htm

City of Port Phillip (2013) *Municipal Public Health and Wellbeing Plan.* Accessed July 2014, www. portphillip.vic.gov.au/COPP_Health_and_Wellbeing_Plan.pdf

Deloittes (2015) *Mobile Consumer Survey 2015—The Australian Cut.* Accessed July 2014, http:// landing.deloitte.com.au/rs/761-IBL-328/images/deloitte-au-tmt-mobile-consumer-survey-2015-291015.pdf

Eidelson, M (2014) *Yalukit Willam: The River People of of Port Phillip.* City of Port Phillip.

Maguire, Bob (2015) *Personal Correspondence.*

Maguire, Bob (2016) *Personal Correspondence.*

Palen, J, and London, B (Eds.) (1984) *Gentrification, Displacement and Neighborhood Revitalization.* Albany, NY: State University of New York Press.

Skraba, A (2010) *Thinking Economics When Planning for Community Hubs.* Accessed July 2014, www.planning.org.au/documents/item/2049

South Port Community Housing Group (SPCHG) (undated) *Who We Are.* Accessed July 2014, www.spchg.org.au/

13 Stewartstown Road Centre, Belfast

Softening the barriers between communities

Suffolk and Lenadoon are two adjacent communities in Belfast's outer west that have suffered greatly on either side of Northern Ireland's sectarian divide. To generalize, on one side of this divide are those who aspire to a united and independent Ireland (Nationalists), many of whom see their rights and identity undermined by Northern Ireland's inclusion in the UK. On the other side are those who see this connection as integral to their collective identity (Unionists). Conflict between the two communities has varied greatly in intensity over the centuries but flared up significantly in the period known as the 'the troubles' from the late 1960s. This brought with it outbreaks of violence with atrocities committed by extremists on both sides and led to significant displacement of people who sought refuge amongst those who shared their cultural identity (Hall 2008). This reinforced the polarization of the two communities, increasingly separating Northern Ireland (NI) into a patchwork of Nationalist and Unionist areas. Unionist Suffolk and Nationalist Lenadoon face one another on either side of the Stewartstown Road, which has been one of many flashpoints of conflict during the troubles, "*characterised by high levels of inter-community violence, fear, mistrust and division, which included shootings, bombings and large-scale rioting*" (ibid).

In an attempt to separate the two communities, a variety of barriers were built that have grown progressively more extensive, higher and more permanent in nature (Northern Ireland Foundation, undated) (Figures 13.1, 13.2). Although 'the troubles' are generally agreed to have ended in the late 1990s after a series of ceasefires and the signing of the Good Friday agreement in 1998, a study in 2011 revealed the construction of these barriers continued apace and at the time numbered 99 (Belfast Interface Project 2013). However whilst they have reassured those who feel protected by them (Northern Ireland Foundation, undated), they have blighted land (ibid) and created hard edges that divide people into 'us' and 'them'. They demarcate land, not just as places where Nationalists or Unionists live, but as Nationalist or Unionist places. This creates frontlines where the enemy is anyone on the other side and allies are everyone on this side. "*By creating clear physical indicators where one community 'begins' and another community 'ends', barriers have sometimes served as magnets for exploiting or expressing community tensions for political ends*" (CRC 2008, quoted in Bell et al. 2010, p. 13) (Figure 13.3). They have become the settings for 'recreational rioting' amongst disaffected youth on the interface with the traditional enemy as a way of alleviating boredom; "*the buzz they get from being on those interfaces, you could bottle that*" (Interface worker, quoted in Pierson 2011, p. 25). The *Belfast Telegraph* reported in 2014 that 200 officers were required

Figure 13.1 Examples of Peace Walls and Barriers
Source: Shutterstock 586265999

Figure 13.2 Examples of Peace Walls and Barriers
Source: Shutterstock 586265999

Figure 13.3 Barriers to Protect Against Recreational Rioting
Source: Shutterstock 586265999

nightly during the summer months when tensions peak to keep the peace at these interfaces (McAleese 2014).

The Northern Ireland Foundation (NIF) found that, as well as the walls, there are

> *other ways and means by which segregating boundaries are marked out. This includes the numerous low-level yellow barriers used to enclose roads and entries; redevelopment which separates residential areas by the construction of industrial and commercial zones; new road lay-out or developments; and even the numerous examples of grills and bars used to protect domestic properties.*
>
> (NIF undated)

It is testament to the resilience and humanity of the people throughout Northern Ireland that despite this conflict and the mistrust it has generated, courageous individuals and groups on both sides have reached out across the sectarian divide, stood firm despite accusations of disloyalty to their own community (Belfast Telegraph 2015) and have sought to find ways of working together. The Suffolk Lenadoon Interface Group (SLIG), a community development and peacebuilding organization, is one such group. SLIG and its colleague organization, Stewartstown Road Regeneration Project (SRRP), are owned by the two main community organizations in the area: the Suffolk Community Forum and the Lenadoon Community Forum (SRRP website undated). Jean Brown (co-founder of SLIG), John Hoey (manager of the Stewartstown Road Regeneration Project) and Suzanne Lavery (peace walls project worker) were all kind enough to share their time and insights with me about the work of the group.

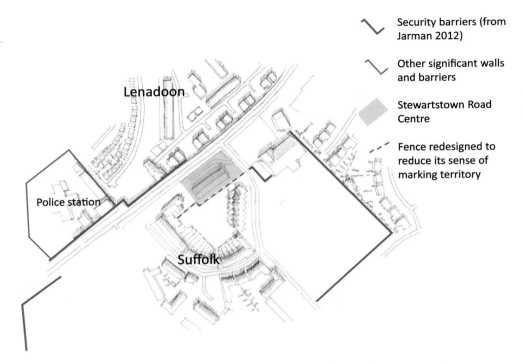

Figure 13.4 The Stewartstown Road Regeneration Project and Immediate Surroundings

Through an impressive combination of faith, trust and co-operation, with help from the NI government, European Social Fund and Atlantic Philanthropies, SLIG and SRRP have created many functioning and mutually beneficial links that span the divide. Principal amongst these is the creation of a shared community centre with shops, offices, community facilities and a childcare centre on the Stewartstown Road Interface. This approach reflects the philosophy of Oxford professor of psychology and Young Foundation fellow Miles Hewstone, who has explored inter-community relations in conflict areas. He *"suggests that so long as there is contact (which isn't always the case) diverse populations can develop understanding and less discomfort between different groups"* (Young Foundation 2010). He notes that *"this challenges the more popularly accepted (within the UK) 'threat' theory which proposes that more diversity leads to more misunderstanding and competition, and increased prejudice"* (ibid). Since the development of the centre, the interface has gone from being a blighted and contested no man's land to being a shared and valued place where the two communities can overlap (Donovan 2013). However its geography still requires the Unionist community to pass through a peace barrier that had 'defended' the Suffolk community from this interface but now separates it from the Stewartstown Road centre (Figure 13.4).

Description

In 2014 the SRRP rebuilt this wall and replaced it with a wall of somewhat more domestic, less militaristic character in conjunction with improvements to landscaping and lighting (Figures 13.5, 13.6). In doing so they sought to diminish the barriers' impact as a divider

Figure 13.5 Rear Fence and Landscaping, Before and After (Stewartstown Road Regeneration Project)

Figure 13.6 Rear Fence and Landscaping, Before and After (Stewartstown Road Regeneration Project)

and reminder of conflict whilst recognizing that removing the walls completely would not be acceptable to a community that still valued the protection and reassurance it offered. John Hoey, SRRP manager, told me that the initial designs prepared by the architects had emphasized *"park benches and picnic tables"* (pers. corr. 2015). However he noted the community felt this missed the mark and reflected the designer's priorities rather than the community's, who just wanted footpaths, lighting, improved all-abilities access and a sense that the area was being looked after. The eventual, simpler design was adopted after extensive discussions with local community members.

Subsequently, in 2013, the Northern Ireland government announced their intent to remove all barriers by 2023 (Northern Ireland Executive 2013) in an effort to facilitate greater integration and trust.

Outcomes

Suzanne Lavery told me that initial responses to the new permeable fences, lighting and improved landscaping has been positive and John Hoey spoke of the reduction in anti-social behaviour in this area since the new fence was installed. At the time of writing, only one other example of 'barrier softening' (International Fund for Ireland 2016) has been successfully implemented. Despite a broad recognition that these barriers had negative effects and should go eventually (Geoghegan 2015), other initiatives have faced reluctance in the community as many fear that if the barriers were removed they would lose the reassurance the barriers offer them (ibid) and for some because of their incidental effects, such as removing traffic.

The Suffolk/Lenadoon experience brought Suzanne Lavery to conclude that although peace walls *"are critical to the viability of Suffolk"* (pers. corr. 2016)—a small community hemmed in by demographics and geography—with time it might be possible to change the barrier's character to be less exclusionary. She speculated that where these boundaries are aligned along natural features, they may contribute to the amenity of both communities. She also pointed to the examples of where they are aligned through shared facilities, in particular local allotments (community gardens), where anecdotal evidence suggested they might provide a positive setting for interaction between the two communities.

Contributory Factors

The NIF have found that *"barriers can provide psychological security and help to create a stronger feeling of communal identity and solidarity"* (undated). This is a view backed up by Suzanne Lavery, who told me the barriers are just the physical expression of deeper psychological distinctions. For many the blight and inconvenience they impose are a small price to pay for the reassurance they bring (pers. corr. 2016). The fact that progress of a sort has been possible at the Suffolk Lenadoon Interface is because SLIG has created a strong network and links across boundaries which have given people experience of co-operating and building up trust.

Suzanne Lavery also told me that the upkeep of the environment around the walls is important, and the lighting and landscaping associated with rebuilding the wall has helped diminish the sense that the land is blighted but instead feels cared for.

Lessons Learnt

Change will be slow and will require a great deal of emotional capital. A sensitive but rigid social landscape and a history of conflict make the walls very resilient, both as physical structures and as symbols, their justification firm in many people's minds. When change does occur, if it is to be a positive, nurturing change, it will be because it has been well thought through, respectfully discussed and is actively supported by both communities as part of a larger program of reconciliation. As noted by Allen McAdam, board member of the International Fund for Ireland, *"the removal of a wall is not a starting point nor an end point, but a significant milestone on the journey towards a positive future"* (International Fund for Ireland website 2016). For this to happen, good design will be important, but what represents good design is unlikely to be the innovative design that might excite designers. It is more likely to be the reassuring, familiar characteristics that define normality for those who live there and create tangible evidence that they have been listened to.

References

Belfast Interface Project (2013) *Interfaces Map and Database—Overview.* Accessed October 2015, www.belfastinterfaceproject.org/interfaces-map-and-database-overview

Belfast Telegraph (2015) *In an Inspirational Story of Friendship Across the Divide, How Jean and Renee Worked Tirelessly to Unite Their Two Communities* 09/07/2015. Accessed October 2015, www.belfasttelegraph.co.uk/life/features/in-an-inspirational-story-of-friendship-across-the-divide-how-jean-and-renee-worked-tirelessly-to-unite-their-two-communities-31362725.html #comments

Bell, J, Jarman, N, and Harvey, B (2010) *Beyond Belfast.* Community Relations Council and Rural Community Network. Accessed December 2011, www.conflictresearch.org.uk/Resources/Documents/CRC%20Beyond%20Belfast%20(Web).pdf

Community Relations Council (2008) *Towards Sustainable Security: Interface Barriers and the Legacy of Segregation in Belfast.* Belfast: CRC.

Donovan, J (2013) *Designing to Heal.* Clayton, Australia: CSIRO Publishing.

Geoghegan, P (2015) *Will Belfast ever have a Berlin Wall moment and tear down its 'peace walls'?* Accessed March 2016 https://www.theguardian.com/cities/2015/sep/29/belfast-berlin-wall-moment-permanent-peace-walls

Hall, M (2008) *Self-help at the Grassroots, How Communities Responded to the Northern Ireland, Troubles.* Island Pamphlets no. 90, Island Publications, Newtownabbey, Northern Ireland.

Hoey, J (2015) *Personal Correspondence.*

International Fund for Ireland (2016) *Community Celebrates Peace Wall Removal.* Accessed August 11th, 2016, www.internationalfundforireland.com/media-centre/124-press-releases-2016/720-community-celebrates-peace-wall-removal

Lavery, S (2015) *Personal Correspondence.*

McAleese, D (2014) Interfaces bleed PSNI resources: 200 officers required nightly to keep the peace at Belfast flashpoint areas. *Belfast Telegraph*, November 28th. Accessed August 2016, www.belfasttelegraph.co.uk/news/northern-ireland/interfaces-bleed-psni-resources-200-officers-required-nightly-to-keep-the-peace-at-belfast-flashpoint-areas-30780142.html

Northern Ireland Executive (2013) *Together: Building a United Community Strategy.* Accessed August 2016, www.executiveoffice-ni.gov.uk/sites/default/files/publications/ofmdfm_dev/together-building-a-united-community-strategy.pdf

Northern Ireland Foundation (undated) *Peace Walls.* Accessed August 2016, https://northernireland.foundation/sharedfuture/research/peace-walls/

Pierson, C (2011) *The CitySide Initiative—Community Based Peacebuilding in North Belfast.* Belfast: The Institute of Conflict Research.

Stewartstown Road Regeneration Project (undated) *A local inter-community business stimulating and promoting economic and social regeneration.* Accessed May 2015. http://www.srrp.net/introduction.htm

The Young Foundation (August 2010) *The World in Our Neighbourhood.* Accessed June 2015. https://youngfoundation.org/publications/the-world-in-our-neighbourhood/

14 UN Habitat Placemaking Projects in West Bank Villages, Palestine

Self-determination 101

The West Bank has been *"under temporary belligerent occupation"* by Israel since 1967 according to Israeli planning rights organization Bimkom (2008) and now is home to two very distinct communities, the indigenous Palestinians who inhabit the established towns and villages, and the more recent Israeli settlers, who inhabit 135 new settlements and outposts (at time of writing) scattered throughout the austere but beautiful landscape.

As in Northern Ireland, both communities have a strong sense of territoriality, every scrap of land is claimed and tinted with political allegiance, either Palestinian or Israeli. Places where Israeli people live become Israeli places and places where Palestinians live remain Palestinian places. In such an environment both sides see active occupation of the land as important, simultaneously claiming it for their own community and denying it to the other.

However this competition to assert a right to land is strongly skewed by the asymmetric balance of power between the two peoples. An International Advisory Board established to assess this issue from a planning perspective (UN-Habitat 2015) found that the planning system and its assertive enforcement by the Israeli Civil Administration (ICA) has been used to deny Palestinians the ability to plan or develop whilst facilitating Israeli development for settlements and military purposes. This influences both the extent of the land occupied by both communities and the quality of life that occupation affords.

This planning practice is particularly evident in those parts designated 'Area C' in the Oslo accords (signed in 1993 and 1995) within which the settlements are generally located and the Israeli government retains security control (Figure 14.1). Bimkom found that most Palestinian residents of Area C

> *have no regular access to water, electricity, sewage and roads, and there is a distinct lack of public services such as schools, health clinics or employment zones. Even the construction of agricultural infrastructure is prohibited in most cases by the Israeli Civil Administration.*
>
> (2008)

As of 2014 only 20 (of 180) Palestinian villages in Area C have approved local outline plans (Karni-Kohn 2014) which offer any degree of protection or ability to plan for the future. Hence most Palestinians find their surroundings qualitatively and quantitatively inadequate, offering few opportunities and experiences to meet needs or express their identity (Figure 14.2).

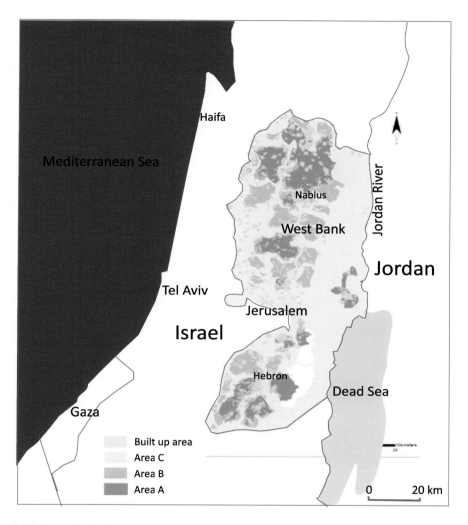

Figure 14.1 Areas A, B, C
Source: adapted from UN Habitat

Description

UN Resolution 23/2 (April 2011) called upon UN Habitat to begin "*improving the housing and human settlement conditions of Palestinians, addressing the urbanization challenges, supporting the building of a Palestinian State, humanitarian action and peace-building, in the areas where there are acute humanitarian and development needs*" (unpublished project Terms of Reference, 2014). One strand of this support was to undertake exemplar placemaking projects with the community to offer them a means of asserting their identity and reclaiming underused spaces and turning them into meaningful places (Figure 14.3). This was to be achieved through taking these communities through a process of 'learning

Figure 14.2 A Typical Village Space, Offering Little to the Quality of Life of the People Who Live
       Nearby

Source: adapted from Marsh et al. (2018)

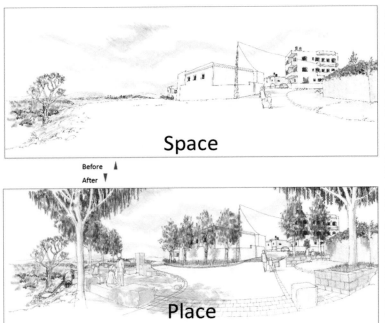

A small public space in Um Lahem, near Bethlehem. The community expressed an aspiration (amongst other things) to have a place for people to gather, a place for children to play and to create a legacy that they could be proud of that reflected the esteem with which they held their village. They wanted shade and valued the contribution that trees made to the landscape. The community also expressed their concern about traffic accidents. This concept seeks to create a place where people will want to gather, that deters dangerous driving, 'wins' previously rarely used land for community life and will enable local people to see their surroundings in a new light.

Figure 14.3 Turning Spaces Into Places

Source: adapted from image prepared by the author for UN Habitat

by doing' with a team of local and international UN staff and an overseas advisor. I was fortunate enough to be appointed to this role in 2014. My 'mission' with UN Habitat (to use UN terminology) was to collaboratively develop implementable plans for 14 villages and in doing so enhance their liveability, create a sense of empowerment and create positive momentum (adapted from unpublished Project Terms of Reference, UN 2014).

These plans were prepared using a process that had proven effective elsewhere (UN Habitat 2013), amended in consultation with local staff. This process sought to share responsibility between the community and the UN team (Palestinian and international) in a way that empowered the community whilst meeting high technical standards. We saw our role being to facilitate the emergence of ideas from the community and use our skills to create relevant and engaging built form and programmatic responses. This required the team to reconcile strategic objectives, determine the requirements of funding agencies, and facilitate the community to implement and maintain the interventions. To this end we sought to encourage 'communities of implementation' of local people and stakeholders who had made significant emotional investment in making it happen. This emphasis on emotional capital was intended to minimize dependence on limited financial capital and instead give greater weight to a local community's skills and materials to make positive progress.

Great care was taken to ensure the whole process and its component stages were made transparent and explained as best we could. Each step, from analysis and visioning to preparation of a strategy, was tested with the community who were invited to amend or veto the emerging projects as they saw fit. Responses were invited verbally, either individually or in the workshop sessions or through response forms, to create multiple avenues of engagement.

The plans we prepared recognized that many of the issues raised by the community fell outside the essentially small scale and scope of locally implementable placemaking proposals, instead requiring major or significant infrastructure/engineering works. Rather than ignore them, our reports were divided into two sections: the placemaking proposals and a summary of other issues; and their rationale and impacts that might help inform the agendas of donors and other funding agencies.

Challenges

The project was undertaken against a very complex and dynamic backdrop. Apart from the agenda of the Israeli authorities, there were many agencies, local and international, who were pursuing a variety of agendas in Area C. Reconciling our work with these agencies and the priorities of the local communities added another level of complexity that called on all my local colleagues' skill of diplomacy and persuasion.

As is common in Arab cultures, men and women would form into single sex groups in the workshops to discuss ideas that often stemmed from very different priorities. This required great care in these workshops to ensure that the perspectives of both genders could be given equal weight.

In several of the communities, 'consultation fatigue' and cynicism was evident; people had been consulted many times by a plethora of different agencies. They had often been asked apparently similar questions at each of these meetings but nothing (or very little) seemed to be achieved. Hopes were raised only to be dashed. We addressed this as best we could by being upfront about the limitations and scope of the project, seeking to make the process interactive, making extensive use of accessible maps and graphics and in particular through the use of before-and-after sketches to create a strong image of what we believed was possible. We also built in reporting mechanisms to demonstrate that people had been heard, explained the path to implementation clearly and openly recognized limitations.

The representativeness of the participants at the workshops may also have been an issue. We were aware that other perspectives existed to those that had been asserted but recognized that to seek them would risk causing offence. Hence we took the pragmatic view that any extension of self-determination through a community was better than no extension.

Outcomes

The plans and the methodology behind them were successful in winning funds for implementation from the EU for the first four communities. These have now been constructed. Initial feedback (Johannes, pers. corr. 2015; D'hondt, pers. corr. 2015) suggests:

These plans have indeed enabled some people to look upon their surroundings as catalysts for hope, better expressions of their own values and cultural identity and affirmation of their ongoing connection to the land.

They provided an accessible model for communities to 'cut their teeth' on making decisions and co-ordinating work.

The persuasive and clear articulation of the ideas, the values on which they were based and the process by which they were defined all raised interest with potential donors.

Although small in scale, they offer a 'first step' towards empowering people to stake their claim on their land and accrue the experience to make bigger interventions.

However:

Only the first four villages were funded and implemented. Although hopes were cultivated in several communities, the articulation of concepts before a budget is confirmed can lead to those hopes being dashed and make people wary that the process may not come to anything. For many, this may just reinforce a sense that consultation like this is meaningless.

There is little evidence that these initiatives have caught the imagination of the wider community.

The patchy resonance of the projects may be put down to a number of factors:

On reflection my role of demonstrating and facilitating a 'translation mechanism' from social issue to 'built form' response may have been overly tinted by my own aesthetic and social values. Although I committed myself to the task as best I could, at the end of the day I am still an outsider and may not have achieved the correct balance between designer and advisor. This leads me to conclude that in some communities the concepts rang true with community members only in as far as they were happy to approve the proposals but not enough to inspire them to go through all the challenges to actually get them built.

We also noted that in some communities placemaking failed to gain traction because of inaccurate assumptions about the scope of the project, with some questioning the value of placemaking, considering it only an aesthetic consideration or a collaborationist distraction (D'hondt, pers. corr. 2015). Conversely in other communities people were inclined to just say what they thought we wanted to hear—say yes or thank you to whatever they perceived we were offering and 'not rock the boat'.

Lessons Learnt

Using placemaking projects to provide 'entry-level' community development opportunities that fosters hope appears to have merit. However on reflection future projects may benefit from:

More obvious leadership by local placemakers. This was always the intention for future placemaking projects but perhaps this could have been made clearer.

Clarification of the role of placemaking in order to avoid the recurring suspicion that placemaking was being 'pushed' on them as a substitute for water, electricity, etc.

A colleague, Frank D'hondt, also suggested their impact on the momentum of the community might be enhanced if they were incorporated into 'placemaking activism'. These are short, intense periods of design and immediate implementation. These would incorporate on-site, inclusive planning processes with

> *a component to mobilize local forces to clean up the village, do some acupunctural interventions such as tree and flower planting, temporary bins, cultural placemaking events, youth/women mobilizing events, temporary street interventions to calm traffic or mark a future public space etc.*

(D'hondt, pers. corr. 2015)

References

Bimkom (2008) *The Prohibited Zone Israeli Planning Policy in the Palestinian Villages in Area C*. Jerusalem, Israel: Bimkom.

D'hondt, F (2015) *Personal Correspondence*.

Johannes, J (2015) *Personal Correspondence*.

Karni-Kohn (September 2014) *A Response to the State of Israel's Report to the United Nations Regarding the Implementation of the Covenant on Civil and Political Rights*. Bimkom—Planners for Planning Rights. Accessed October 2015, http://bimkom.org/eng/wp-content/uploads/shadow-report.pdf

Marsh, G Ahmed, I Mulligan, M, Donovan, J Barton, S 2018 *Community Engagement in Post-Disaster Recovery*. Abingdon, UK: Routledge.

UN General Assembly (2011) *Resolution 23/2: Human Settlements Development in the Occupied Palestinian Territory*. Accessed January 2017, https://unispal.un.org/DPA/DPR/unispal.nsf/0/22D B3FF1E77A0499852578E70051BEEE

UN-Habitat (2013) *Turning Spaces Into Places*. UN Habitat. Accessed March 2008, www. unhabi-tat-kosovo.org/repository/docs/UN-habitat_Turning_spac-es_into_places-c_478833.pdf

UN-Habitat (2015) *Spatial Planning in Area C of the Israeli Occupied West Bank of the Palestinian Territory: Report of an International Advisory Board*. Accessed December 2016, http://unhabitat. org/spatial-planning-in-area-c-of-the-israeli-occupied-west-bank-of-the-palestinian-territory/

15 The Obstacles and Pitfalls to Creating Places Where People Thrive

This final part of the book seeks to gather the lessons of the projects covered in these pages and puts forward some ideas about how we can use urban design to help cultivate a more nurturing relationship between 'people' and 'place'. Perhaps one of the most important observations that can be made is that despite the inspiring commitment of their proponents, they have met with varying degrees of resistance and success. This chapter seeks to outline some of these challenges and the lessons they offer.

Volatile Emotional Capital

Emotional capital, though significant, is a difficult force to control. It cannot be taken for granted that it will be directed at achieving shared strategic goals or indeed is directed in the same way by everyone in any given community. The Young Foundation (2010) found that when this motivating force coalesces in community organizations that are developed outside the conventional administrative framework, they can become *"thorns in the side of local institutions"*. They go on to conclude that care is needed to find a balance *"between the creation of social infrastructure that nurtures yet controls communities—setting limits on problematic behaviour for example—and the need to let natural dynamism flourish"*.

Almost inevitably there will be a diversity of perspectives about what the ideal design solution might be for any site, as a whole or in detail (Chapter 11). Designing interventions that everyone (or at least most people) will recognize as resonating with their views is challenging. It will require a process that is sensitive to the perspectives of those who will experience the development, seeks to understand and align their values, and cultivates visions within the community that are grounded in these aligned values. Done well, this allows the designer(s) to create a compelling link between the generally agreed issues and the outcome. It isn't always possible and what sections of the community may consider to be an improvement may be greeted with fear, disappointment or disapproval by others (Chapter 13).

Lack of Financial Resources

Perhaps the most obvious and often most significant obstacle is that it is difficult to find the money to make these projects happen. The benefits that arise from creating nurturing places accrue broadly to the community rather than specifically to capital interests. Hence they don't appeal to typical investors. This means not only are they challenging to build, they cannot compete for land against 'big capital'. For the most part, conventional commercially orientated developments would be able to outbid compassionate design projects, denying all but the least attractive sites to such projects. Furthermore, if such projects can find a home, they may find their tenure insecure, as landowners understandably will be swayed when a better offer comes along (Chapter 12).

There is also the challenge of finding the time resources needed to engage a community, prime them, and go through a process that leaves a legacy of greater understanding, empowerment and satisfaction. This challenge is often met by many in civic society and sympathetic professionals offering their time and insight voluntarily or at highly discounted rates. At other times businesses and professionals may choose to cross-subsidize such 'compassionate' projects with income from profitable ones (and/or their day jobs) or by offering their skills and the time of their employees (Chapter 8). However many professionals and businesses just cannot afford to forego the time required to develop the rapport and understanding with a community needed to take a compassionate project to completion. Without such insight, achieving compassionate design outcomes can be somewhat hit and miss, even with the best will in the world.

Lack of Experience and Know-How

In most cities almost all development is done by 'big capital' interests. Very little is what you might call community development. Consequently only a small minority of the experience of development and the attendant upskilling this brings will accrue to the community sector. Without the benefits of this experience the process of every project becomes more of an experiment than it would otherwise be, with a greater likelihood of mistakes and potentially setbacks.

When discussing their experience of cultivating community involvement and empowerment, Laura Hansen, managing director Neighborhood Plaza Partnerships in New York (pers. corr. 2015), and Graham Duxbury of Groundwork in the UK (pers. corr. 2015) pointed out that although there are numerous examples of local communities being given permission through legislation to utilize this emotional capital to get things done, not all were equally equipped to do so. Communities with more resources (better-off, more organized and more educated communities with greater insights into the planning and development systems) can make better use of the opportunities provided, but those in communities with less access to the system, that were less well organized or less well educated may find the challenges too daunting and the risks of making discouraging mistakes too great. Thus giving power to local people, without other empowering measures to address underlying injustices, may amplify those injustices and steepen the social gradient of invitation, to use the language of Chapter 4.

Furthermore, even in well-resourced communities, there are substantial risks that come from experimental/pathfinding projects that swim against the tide. When they don't work, hopes are dashed and the emotional capital invested in making them happen may find expression as frustration and anger and the experience may be seen as providing compelling if incorrect evidence that the whole approach doesn't work.

Disproportionate Emphasis on Risks

In keeping with Max Neef's observations about the primacy given to safety and security as a basic need as outlined in Chapter 2, we tend to attach greater weight to risks that challenge this need than we do to potential positive outcomes, as outlined in Chapter 3.

This often means we will put up with significant detrimental impacts to our quality of life if we think it keeps us safe. Thus the fear that an initiative will expose people to risk is a powerful motivator to reject it, even if it may bring significant potential benefits.

For many people this leads them to take positions, which whilst understandable, fail to support their welfare. These are things such as preferring to drive children to school or discouraging them from playing outside, as Chapter 6 noted. Parents that hold these views are unlikely to encourage their children to take up the opportunities to walk or cycle even if these opportunities are created. Parents that challenge these social positions by encouraging their older children to walk/cycle to school or play on the street face the disapproval of their neighbours (Chapter 6).

Losses in Translation

The inclusive nature of these projects, spanning sectors and industries, is likely to require input or approval from many different people. Each will have their own perspective. What is good design to one group may be far from good design for another. In passing ideas back and forward between different disciplines and community groups to add their contribution, there will always be a risk of misinterpretation or misalignment of values. This can create a tension between professional and resident expectations with a (usually unwarranted) perception that the professionals are only hearing what they want to hear. Unchecked, this may erode trust and confidence between the parties, as demonstrated in the Suffolk and Lenadoon interface project (Chapter 13).

Incompatible Administrative Systems

Council officers, insurance companies and other gatekeepers of the development process are likely to have a familiar, 'well-trodden path' for getting things done that is governed by an understood set of rules and budgets that they are likely to have grown familiar with over time. The radical nature of compassionate city interventions—spanning the physical environment, health promotion and social policy—will often mean that the city's administrators, its orgware, will not have a box to fit them in. This can create institutional resistance that can slow a process down or derail it. It is important to note that such challenges can happen even when the gatekeepers personally support a project but the system they work within has difficulty accommodating it, as the De Ceuvel (Chapter 9) and the Benches Collective (Chapter 7) pathfinder projects demonstrate.

Another administrative issue that can derail compassionate city projects is the accountancy practices of development funding bodies. Cultivating trust and creating a shared, implementable, beneficial plan with diverse stakeholders may take a lot of time, involving multiple points of contact between professionals and community members. When such projects are built, their emphasis on low-cost, locally produced interventions often means that the ratio of implementation costs to design costs will differ from conventional projects in that they cost relatively little to build but a significant amount to design. Unfortunately for many funding agencies, only the implementation costs are considered investments in the community; the design costs are considered administration costs. In accountancy terms, spending a lot on administration and relatively little on implementation does not look good, as noted in the Palestine pathfinder project (Chapter 14).

Piecing Together the Jigsaw of Diverse Resources

A characteristic of many of the pathfinder projects is that they often rely on cobbling together a variety of 'hard' resources such as donated and recovered materials and 'soft' resources of skills and enthusiasm. These often have to be tied together with a variety of funding sources (Chapter 8). Assessing and administering these diverse resources, managing a workforce that might include volunteers and utilizing them to achieve a particular goal will be a significant challenge in its own right.

Burn Out/Turnover of Key Individuals

All the pathfinder projects explored in this book owe a great deal to the attitude, commitment, extraordinarily hard work and often courage of their proponents. However the investment of emotional capital this demands can be exhausting and stressful. Furthermore these projects often demand a significant voluntary component which takes people away from earning a living to keep themselves and their families. For many this is not sustainable; the level of emotional investment may lead to significant distress and disillusionment when setbacks occur and can lead to burn out and a high turnover, which can diminish organizational effectiveness. Furthermore any project tied to a person becomes vulnerable when that person leaves. The South Melbourne Commons (Chapter 12) provides an example of what can happen with the retirement of an inspirational project leader and the consequent loss of the protective space he created for the whole project.

Unexpected and Inappropriate Behaviours

As noted in Chapter 2, everyone will interpret their surroundings differently. Interventions intended to invite a particular behaviour may in some people's minds invite other, perhaps incompatible behaviours. For example Mike Biddulph points out in *Home Zones* planning and design handbook (2001) that measures to slow down vehicles by narrowing or deflecting traffic lanes might be interpreted as creating a challenge that invites drivers (particularly young male drivers) to drive faster to test themselves.

References

Biddulph, M (2001) *Home Zones*. Bristol, UK: Policy Press.
Duxbury, G (2015) *Personal Correspondence*.
Hansen, L (2015) *Personal Correspondence*.

16 Designing the Compassionate City

This chapter suggests a set of principles and a process that may help designers make informed design decisions and avoid or overcome the obstacles noted in the previous chapter. The ideas here are not intended as the last word on how to design. Instead they are offered as a pair of spectacles by which design issues can be revealed and people's relationship with their surroundings given due consideration.

Design Principles

The values that designers bring to their work echoes in the outcome of that work. Embedding messages into the built environment that help people to meet their needs suggests a commitment to the following values:

Facilitate Choice

The compassionate city facilitates people to self-determine where and how they can best meet their needs. This has two dimensions:

The first requires that every person can get to places where they can access a wide variety of experiences and opportunities that allow them to meet whatever needs are most pressing at the time. The second requires that wherever possible each of the places can be used in more than one way without conflict. In turn this also means the people using these public places can feel confident that their rights will be respected and they are aware that they have a responsibility to share that space with others who might use it differently.

Privilege Needs-Fulfilling Behaviours

As noted throughout this book, people typically interpret their surroundings as inviting particular behaviours and discouraging others which happen under sufferance, if at all. The inhabitants of many towns and cities might be forgiven for feeling that the urban space they share reflects their government and the wider community's *preference* that they drive and play indoors. They may feel that walking, cycling or playing outside was frowned upon.

In the compassionate city, the messages broadcast by the built environment explicitly and implicitly prioritize needs-fulfilling behaviours (Figures 16.1, 16.2), either as the principal characteristic for an intervention (for example creating a playground) or an incidental characteristic (such as a street that can also be used for playing) (Figure 16.3).

Figure 16.1 Privileging Walking in Porto, Portugal

Figure 16.2 Privileging Walking in Amsterdam, The Netherlands

Get the Balance Right Between the Designer, Stakeholders and the Wider Community

The default position of the compassionate city is that decisions are made at the closest competent level to those impacted by actioning that decision, reflecting the principle of subsidiarity. Professional urban designers have design and organizational skills that can be harnessed to help people to move towards realizing a shared, exciting, implementable and enduring vision for their community. For this to happen these skills need to be applied in a respectful and sensitive manner and at the appropriate times in a process that also makes the best use of the skills and insights of the community. Achieving this raises many challenges.

The design process should promote the inclusion of all parties, particularly those who tend not to get involved and feel participation is not for them, without forcing it on

Figure 16.3 Privileging Play Over Vehicles, Northmoor, Manchester, UK

anyone. In different contexts, those excluded can be women, children and minorities of different types. The designer(s) will need to lead all the participants through a process of clarifying the issues and envisaging what positive and sustainable change means for them and then outline a pathway to realizing that change. From this perspective the urban designer's role is to be an accessible two-way conduit, sharing information, revealing the process so people can see how each step leads to the next and cultivating a shared vision that excites or reassures people about what will happen, as far as is possible. This will require the designer to understand and then align diverse agendas where possible, reassure those with diverging views and create a conducive environment for people to make their own contribution.

The process requires a careful balancing act. The designer(s) have to have intellectual humility, valuing the inputs of everyone. This requires that the designers invest emotional capital into ensuring people feel engaged and respected. There are many considerations to achieving this but experience suggests that the key elements are ensuring the process is explained and understood, everyone's roles and responsibilities are made clear, and their contributions are treated with respect. Designers will also need to demonstrate they are willing to adapt their views as new information comes to hand and take the time to explain changes and confirm their understanding with the participants.

However, as urban designers, we also need to back ourselves. We will (hopefully) have insights that lay people will not have. We serve no one by merely unquestioningly taking a shopping list of objectives if they are unrealistic, irreconcilable or incompatible with our strategic responsibilities and ethical values. Thus a key element of keeping the right balance between the designer and the wider community is to ensure that, as projects progress, the balance of inputs between professionals and community can change so that these professional insights can inform the process at the right stage and that the experience leaves a legacy of community empowerment (Figure 16.4).

Create a Low Threshold of Engagement

Unfortunately for many people living in many cities, management policies, cost, lack of confidence, poor awareness, inexperience, bureaucracy or professional opacity effectively concentrate the power to change things in a relatively small, often distant group of professionals and politicians. In such a place, the point at which it becomes possible to participate in and contribute to civic life—the 'threshold of engagement'—is high and can't be reached with the skills and resources of most people.

The compassionate city seeks to diminish these barriers and in doing so lower the threshold and enable more people to accrue experience of taking control and achieving satisfaction from contributing to their well-being and that of their families and communities.

This requires that projects have many figurative 'front doors', offering a variety of opportunities to contribute and share a project in its planning, implementation, use or management. The Tower Hamlets Cemetery Park is an excellent example of a project that has a low threshold of engagement. Its inclusive management philosophy and the variety of tasks needed to maintain it allows opportunities to engage at many different levels of skill and availability.

Recognize the Significance of the Social Landscape

As noted in Chapter 3, the physical and social landscape interact and influence one another. From a compassionate design perspective, both are equally important. Spaces acquire meaning and become places because of the uses they are put to and the hopes and fears they inspire. Good design is only possible when the designers seek to consider the impact of their work on the geography of the values, hopes and fears of the people affected by the realization of these designs. Whilst we should never presume to feel what someone else feels, by seeking to gain a respectful insight into the community's perspective or perspectives and confirming this understanding with them, we can then give it its due consideration.

Experience suggests this requires a willingness for the designer to immerse themselves in the local values, issues and aesthetics of the people they are designing for and communicate with them in terms they will understand. For this reason, good compassionate design may sometimes not look like 'good design' as it is envisaged in the landscape or architectural journals that are based on a different set of values.

Understanding the social landscape will reveal if there are any deep fault lines between communities or sections of communities. As Chapter 13 indicated, it is important to recognize this diversity of opinion to help ensure interventions can be sensitively designed to avoid exacerbating community conflicts, ossifying divisions or increasing a sense of injustice that can happen when people feel they haven't been listened to but others have.

The changing balance of inputs into the design process

Getting the right balance of professional and the community
Compassionate design requires harnessing the skills and experience of **designers and managers** to find solutions to a set of issues that were identified with **the community**. This requires a discussion between all parties to ensure emerging solutions are the best one for the problem, are achievable and make efficient use of scarce resources.
As a project moves towards completion the balance of inputs between professionals and community will change to ensure that decisions are made at the most appropriate level and that the community is **empowered.**

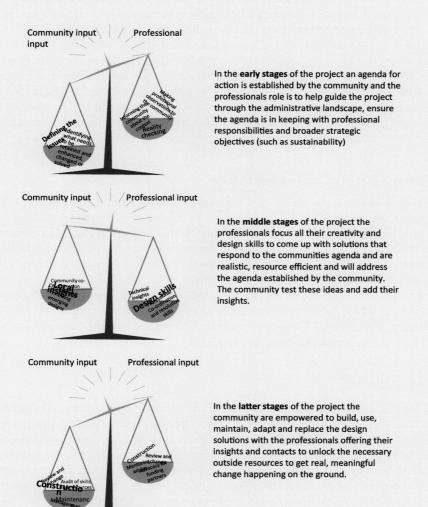

In the **early stages** of the project an agenda for action is established by the community and the professionals role is to help guide the project through the administrative landscape, ensure the agenda is in keeping with professional responsibilities and broader strategic objectives (such as sustainability)

In the **middle stages** of the project the professionals focus all their creativity and design skills to come up with solutions that respond to the communities agenda and are realistic, resource efficient and will address the agenda established by the community. The community test these ideas and add their insights.

In the **latter stages** of the project the community are empowered to build, use, maintain, adapt and replace the design solutions with the professionals offering their insights and contacts to unlock the necessary outside resources to get real, meaningful change happening on the ground.

Figure 16.4 The Evolving Balance of Community and Professional Input
Source: adapted from work by the author for UN Habitat (2014)

Emphasize and Cultivate Emotional Capital

Designers have the power to 'fire up' a community by creating and bringing into sharp focus a shared vision that can nurture hope and provoke a reciprocal sense of commitment from others who can help make a project happen. Experience suggests cultivating this emotional capital demands that the designer is respectful, invests significant attentional capacity in the project, speaks from the heart and takes the time to explain emerging designs in ways that demonstrate a link between proposal and the community's values and concerns. This can inspire offers of informal resources unavailable to conventional projects such as voluntary labour, skills, materials and the positive disposition of Council and government officials. Such inspiration can act 'like a nice contagion', to borrow a phrase from Paul Hocker (Chapter 6), and can help people make the leap of faith necessary to ensure effective and co-ordinated changes that otherwise wouldn't happen.

Cultivating the seed of care and concern that most people will have for their community can bear fruit in many, often unexpected ways. In my experience the inspiration that comes from involvement in a shared project can create fertile ground for people to come up with their own ideas and find their own ways around the challenges they face. Although emotional capital can be difficult to co-ordinate, unsuited to specialist or highly technical projects, it is a very real resource and harnessing it can make the difference between a project being viable or not viable.

Cultivate Bridging as Well as Bonding Capital

It is relatively easy to create places that facilitate bonding capital (that strengthen connections within a group). This can be achieved by almost any degree of making a place exclusive or separate. This will mark out its inhabitants as having that area in common, of it being *their* land. This need not be a problem in itself, but if it is achieved by isolating people completely, it can diminish bridging capital (the bonds between different groups). The compassionate city seeks to keep connections open across boundaries of abilities, race, religion, gender, sexuality, political allegiance or class. It does this by cultivating a sense that valued territory can and should be shared with people from other sections of the community. The Benches Collective project (Chapter 7) and the Stewartstown Road centre (Chapter 13) address this issue in particular.

Take Responsibility

The multi-faceted impacts of interventions can echo through generations and over a much wider area than their site. Designing the compassionate city requires that the designers, managers and users of buildings think about these impacts and consider the externalities of their actions. We have a responsibility to ensure our interventions contribute to the human experience of the public realm by sustainably adding life to it rather than just displacing it from somewhere else or robbing it from future generations. This means we have a responsibility to consider the needs and perspectives of more than just the immediate clients, those who attend meetings/respond to questionnaires, participate in making things happen or fund interventions. The unrepresented others might be living elsewhere, unaware of the changes that might be wrought on their lives; do not feel able to attend; or are too young, too old or not yet born. If they will be impacted, they should be considered too. This calls on the designer to be aware of the likely needs of those who are excluded from the design process,

Before   After

Figure 16.5 Before and After Visualizations
Source: adapted from unpublished work for UN Habitat

try and engage them where this is possible and speak up for them where it isn't, based on research and professional insight. It also means that wherever possible that interventions are designed to meet multiple needs, be adaptable and resonate with different perspectives.

We also need to be aware of the inherent dignity of these clients. When exercising this responsibility suggests that challenging a belief is needed (for example as often happens when a community initially suggest that increasing car parking should be the designers' priority), great care should be taken to explain the implications of what this means and efforts made to find other ways to address the underlying problem, seeking to convince rather than impose. Of course this isn't always possible, but that should not stop us trying. Visualizing what positive change can mean and explaining it in terms the community can understand can provide a useful means of cultivating a shared vision and aligning aspirations (Figure 16.5).

Little Design Rather Than Big Design, Where Possible

'Little design' interventions are those that can be made by those who occupy a place and look after it. Typically they are things such as tree planting, landscape works, footpath improvements, murals, signs, etc. made at least partly with local skills, using local materials and employing local people in design and management (Figure 16.6). 'Big design' is capital intensive, uses industrialized processes to generalized standards and is usually done by people outside the community. The compassionate city encourages little design where possible and allows it to escape its traditional niche of the front garden to contribute more broadly to the public realm.

Little design offers a 'low threshold of engagement' (as explored in the section of the same name previously in this chapter), privileges local inputs, creates metaphorical and sometimes literal pathways for communities to upskill themselves and leaves a legacy of empowerment. Little design can therefore provide a means of capturing economic benefits and experiences that can serve the community well in the future. Such interventions can often be achieved quickly and are cheaper than larger, engineering-based solutions that require significant capital and often incur long-term debt. Little design interventions can also usually be removed/changed more easily if they prove not to work. They offer the people who make them happen the satisfaction of having achieved something themselves (Thin 2012), quite apart from the benefits of enjoying the spaces that result from these interventions.

Figure 16.6 Example of Little Design Interventions in a London Mews

Think Legacy

Compassionate design is about looking beyond the output of urban design to consider the outcome on the lives of those who experience it. These impacts can happen at all steps in the process, not just when a space is in use. With appropriate professional support, nearly every step creates opportunities to positively change a community's hardware, software or orgware. To take the example of converting a standard street to a woonerf-type street:

The planning and design phases can cultivate the motivating power of hope, create a community of interest and reveal the processes and issues that need to be considered to make informed design choices. Gathering the permissions can give people a chance to develop advocacy skills and experience of finding the best way through the labyrinth of bureaucracy. Implementing the project can offer opportunities to gather building/project-management skills. The shared use of the places that result may facilitate many outcomes such as friendships made, a greater sense of pride in one's surroundings and a greater awareness of the importance and fun of sharing outdoor space. Facilitating outdoor play will help children realize their potential in many ways: physical and emotional health, cognitive development, safety skills, resilience, and social and moral development (Donovan 2016). Providing a safe and familiar place that reassures older people they can get out and stay active will help them stay healthy and engaged in their community longer. Offering people a positive experience of a place will make them more likely to want to go there again and thus it can become part of their actively shared environment (Chapter 3).

Managing and reviewing the design once it has been there a while creates opportunities and challenges to weigh up priorities and critically analyze the intervention. It also raises questions about what happens with the assets (paving, plants, signage, etc.) that are being changed/removed. Thinking about how these things may be reused provides another avenue for expression and upskilling. In giving people a shared focus and experience in overcoming problems, the community can learn how best to work together. This can optimize the web of nurturing relationships, reinforcing the bonds of community (Figure 16.7).

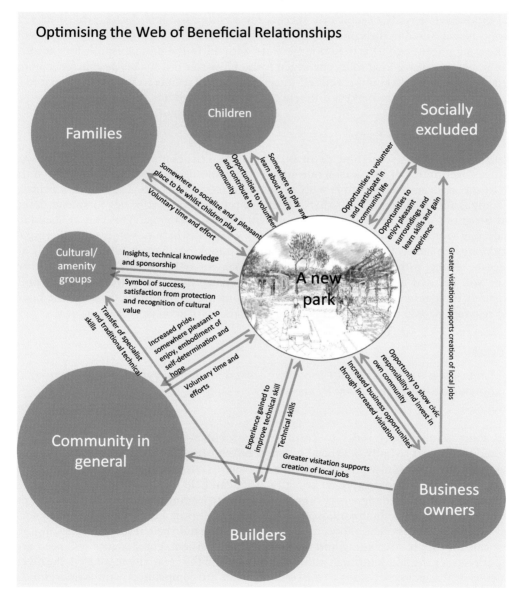

Figure 16.7 The Web of Nurturing Relationships
Source: adapted from UN Habitat (2014)

However it is always worth remembering that every project will almost inevitably bring with it disagreements, misunderstandings, frustration and setbacks which will take an emotional toll. However when these can be faced as opportunities to learn and not a sign of failure, merely a consequence of many different people all investing a great deal of passion into a shared task, then they can be put into perspective. This was illustrated in the inspiring philosophy employed in Christie Walk (Chapter 11).

Several of the projects covered in these pages reveal the power of inspiring and innovative design to cultivate a change in people's hearts and minds as much as on the ground. They can plant a seed in people's consciousness that can grow to bear fruit in many new and innovative ways. Consequently success for a compassionate design project may not always be measured in the same way as it would a conventional project. It probably won't make a significant profit, it may not resonate with all in the design establishment and it may not even survive long in its envisaged form. However if it makes people feel empowered, more secure, offers improved self-esteem or enables people to feel better prepared for the next time they try to make a difference, then arguably it has been a success.

Allow Interventions to Evolve

Every intervention is something of an experiment and the context within which we work changes over time. For this reason our interventions should be capable of alteration if they are to stay relevant to the people whose lives are affected by them. The final key principle of compassionate design then is that it does not preclude opportunities to amend designs and programs as the demands placed on them change over time. This can be facilitated by designing interventions so they can be easily adapted where possible, empowering the community to assess the project and contribute to making changes when needed. It also suggests testing with temporary interventions that not only provide evidence of how a place will be used but also allow people to see change happening from an early point. Experience suggests this can create a sense of momentum, of getting 'runs on the board' and reassure people that their contribution has (and will) achieve something real.

Process

> Cities have the capability of providing something for everybody, only because, and only when, they are created by everybody.
>
> —Jane Jacobs (1962)

The compassionate city seeks to ensure that its hardware, software and orgware are aligned to support socially beneficial outcomes. Achieving this requires that the designers and the wider community go down a path together to come up with a vision that they all share (or at least broadly support) and all parties can help realize.

To do this the urban designers or others charged with leading a project will need to be part advocate, mediator, facilitator, messenger, leader and follower. He or she will need to devise and explain a process that allows all parties to understand their responsibilities and how they can contribute to creating and realizing a shared vision. The designer will need great empathy to see the issues through many sets of eyes and the creativity to address the diverse issues as well as advocacy skills so the resulting ideas are compelling to authorities, funding agencies and (where possible) commercial interests. This will require integrity and sometimes courage to explain potential solutions to the stakeholders or explain why it might not be possible to pursue certain paths in terms the participants will understand. This section outlines some of the key characteristics of a design process that will facilitate this outcome.

Creating a Conducive Orgware and Software Environment

The projects included in this book reveal that compassionate city projects can flourish at almost any point on the spectrum of support from civic administrators—from discouragement, indifference through to enthusiastic backing—as long as other factors are conducive. However it is worth thinking about the optimum administrative climate for these projects to succeed. Groundwork in the UK asked a similar question in relation to creating the ideal conditions for green spaces to be recognized as a vital national asset and shared resource, worthy of protection with enduring rights of public enjoyment. To this end they commissioned the *Grey Places Need Green Spaces* report by Julian Dobson (2012) to examine this question and make recommendations. In his report he outlined the strong evidence for investing in the UK's natural assets and lays out 13 recommendations that seek to ensure governance decisions are made in line with the evidence rather than contrary to it.

Amongst his insightful recommendations, the report contained several ideas that may help create the compassionate city. These could help change a place's administrative framework and priorities (its orgware, using the language of Chapter 3) so greater awareness and emphasis is placed on creating more nurturing places. These ideas are (adapted from Dobson 2012):

The passing of an Enabling Act to establish the framework within which the diverse elements of creating a compassionate city can be co-ordinated. This should enshrine in law the responsibility of stewardship for all shared spaces currently open to the public, whether or not they are publicly owned. Such an act should facilitate government, businesses and local authorities to work together to incentivize and reward public involvement and embed a requirement that the commissioners of works to these spaces consider social value through procurement rather than simply opting for the lowest cost.

Such an act should also ensure that the social capital generated through green and shared spaces is adequately valued. This means that social capital is monitored, which will require that robust indicators of social value can be readily used by commissioners of services.

This act (or subsidiary legislation) may also be used to facilitate the establishment of a national level, independently run endowment fund, financed by business and philanthropic contributions, to match funding of community-led programmatic and physical initiatives that improve the relationship between people and place. This fund (and the agency that will administer it) can be used to showcase inspiring and innovative initiatives in conjunction with existing community environmental improvement organizations. This may provide a means to promote compassionate design interventions and 'prime' communities to be aware of the possibilities and responsibilities that come with this approach to urban design.

These legislative changes may create a conducive environment for the following to happen:

- Interventions to be considered from a placemaking or 'total place' perspective encompassing physical and programmatic interventions. This will make it more likely that all the messages received by the occupants of a place are aligned to invite them to make choices that enhance their quality of life and help them meet their needs.

- Changes in the insurance industry to enable the initiators of little design interventions to access affordable and relevant insurance. Supporting people to forge social bonds and get together to look after their surroundings can be in the insurance industry's best interest, as explored in the next chapter. Places that broadcast a sense that they are cared for and have greater social cohesion have lower rates of crime and anti-social behaviour (Weel and Akçomak 2008).
- Local authorities to pilot 'green improvement districts'. These can bring together local stakeholders and residents to take concerted action where green spaces are neglected or failing and community members report a high level of dissatisfaction with their shared surroundings. The plans for these districts should seek to link interventions directly with training and employment opportunities.
- The savings in future health costs that arise from creating more nurturing places may support local authorities and health services to create 'community well-being budgets' and fund interventions through social impact or social benefit bonds. These are financial instruments that pay a return based on achieving agreed beneficial social outcomes. They are based on private investors providing working capital to deliver an intervention. *"If the provider achieves an agreed social outcome, this can result in savings to the government in the form of future avoided costs"* (NSW Govt undated). These savings may then be used to repay the upfront investment plus an agreed financial return. Although focussed on social services rather than environmental improvements, initial trials of these bonds in Australia reveal they are viable, have earnt a competitive yield and have achieved positive outcomes (KPMG 2014). The same report noted that they created interest amongst 'impact investors' (investors interested in cultivating positive social and environmental change). As such, although in a relatively early stage of development and not without their problems (Dobson, pers. corr. 2017), such bonds *may* provide one way of investing funds held by Treasury, pension funds, insurers, housing providers, and local authorities and others interested in averting negative social impacts.
- Each process to be documented and the lessons learnt. The experimental nature of these projects and the inevitable turnover of their proponents will result in some spaces becoming abandoned or lead to other unexpected or even adverse outcomes. To this end, the endowment fund and its administrative agency (as outlined previously in this section) might gather further evidence of what makes a successful space and the optimal process for reviewing and responding to failed interventions. This will enable each project to then contribute to the body of evidence that suggests a more compassionate approach is both important and possible.

Resourcing the Process

As noted in Chapter 15, compassionate city projects may take longer to design than conventional processes and may need a wider range of inputs. Consequently the compassionate design process will need to factor in adequate time and skills in facilitating the engagement and upskilling of the community members, particularly those traditionally excluded and disadvantaged. This may well call on skills in facilitation and public health promotion to be added to those of designers, engineers and all the traditional built environment professionals.

Furthermore, compassionate city projects are unlikely to attract conventional market-orientated funding. Experience suggests that projects are much better equipped to compete for the funds that are available when they are presented well with meaningful graphics and the ideas are explicitly explained in relation to the funding agencies' priorities.

Key Features of a Model Process

Every project will be different, but experience and the lessons of the projects covered in this book suggest that, if a project is to be successful, the process by which it was developed should follow a process as illustrated in Figure 16.8 and embody the following key characteristics:

- The stakeholders are adequately primed, understand the process, understand their responsibilities and have realistic expectations. They need to be aware that broad community involvement is essential and that the project will have to fulfil strategic responsibilities (such as sustainability and implementing other planning objectives).
- The designers/facilitators will need to 'look people in the eye'. This requires making a commitment to the community at each stage of the process to cultivate a sense that a successful design will be a collaborative process and that the designer is going into bat for them.
- Pre-conceived design solutions are left at the door. When this is understood it creates a more conducive environment to identify and focus on the underlying issues and minimizes the chances of people investing pride and personal prestige in taking a position on potential interventions that may turn out to not be the best solutions.
- Contingency is made to ensure the project can progress at a pace that the community are happy with, providing a good chance for each step to be bedded down before progressing to the next.
- The community have multiple ways of contributing ideas and observations and giving feedback to ensure they are more likely to find a way that suits them. In particular it is important that there is a way in which people can provide feedback anonymously if necessary.
- The facilitator balances authority with approachability and sensitivity.
- Actions are based on an explicit 'design agenda' established collaboratively between the community and outside experts that lays out a metaphorical pathway to achieving a broadly shared and non-divisive vision.
- The community have the opportunity and responsibility to sign off each stage.
- Care is taken by the professional advisors to listen and carefully consider all the observations made by the community and respond to them, taking particular care to explain why ideas have not been adopted if that is the case.
- Drawings are used effectively to tell the story. A picture is worth a thousand words and if done well require no translation. Experience suggests that before-and-after perspective drawings are powerful tools in cultivating a shared vision and demonstrating the differences that can be achieved.
- Each proposal should include a what, who and why: what the intervention is (plans, visualizations, specifications); who is responsible for implementing different aspects of the proposal; and why it is being proposed, the issues it addresses.
- Ideas are tested in the real world where possible with mock ups and temporary interventions.

Compassionate Design

Getting the process right is very important to ensure the community and the professionals who help them can move together to arrive at relevant and broadly supported set of design proposals

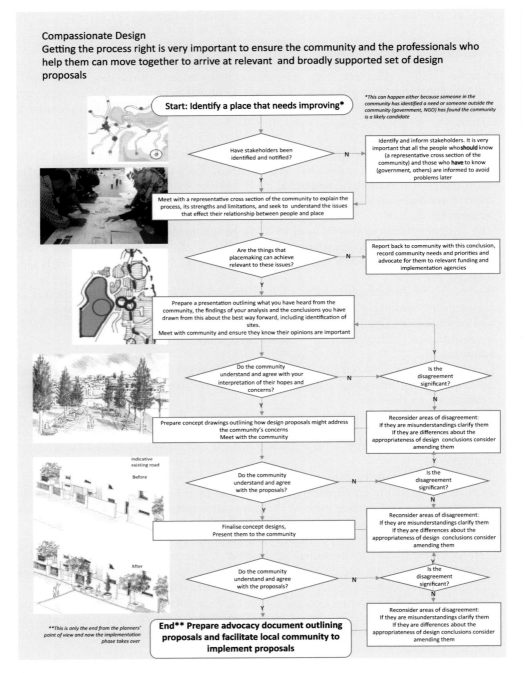

Figure 16.8 Compassionate Design Flowchart

Source: adapted from UN Habitat (2014)

- Implementing designs should utilize local skills and materials wherever possible to create a low threshold of engagement and maximize the amount of investment within the community.
- The completion of the design should be celebrated by the professional advisors and the community together to provide the process with a momentum and cultivate a sense that it mattered to all its participants; it is more than just another job.
- The implementation phase is assisted by ongoing advice from the team that helped generate the design to help engender a sense of consistency and ensure the project benefits from the team's experience.

References

Dobson, J (2012) *Grey Places Need Green Spaces* Groundwork. https://www.groundwork.org.uk/grey-places-need-green-spaces-uk Accessed June 2016.

Dobson, J (2017) *Personal Correspondence.*

Donovan, J (August 2016) *Enabling Play Friendly Places.* Australian Institute of Architects, EDG 87 JD.

Jacobs, J (1962) *The Death and Life of Great American Cities.* New York, NY: Random House.

KPMG (January 2014) *KPMG Evaluation of the Joint Development Phase of the NSW Social Benefit Bonds Trial.* Prepared by KPMG NSW Government Advisory Service.

New South Wales Government (undated) *Social Benefit Bonds.* www.osii.nsw.gov.au/initiatives/social-benefit-bonds/

Thin, N (2012) *Social Happiness: Research Into Policy and Practice.* Bristol: Policy Press.

Weel, B, and Akçomak, S (2008) *The Impact of Social Capital on Crime: Evidence From the Netherlands.* Institute for the Study of Labor. Accessed September 2016. http://ftp.iza.org/dp3603.pdf

17 The Characteristics of the Compassionate City

Designing the compassionate city is distinguished from conventional approaches to design by the things it emphasizes (Figure 17.1). These priorities seek to ensure that everyone has access to an extensive 'menu' of experiences and opportunities and the healthy, rewarding behaviours on that menu are more appealing than the unhealthy ones, most of the time. This chapter suggests some built form characteristics that may help achieve this outcome, both by virtue of their intrinsic qualities and the ephemeral/programmed activities they make possible. These characteristics are broken into two; the structural characteristics that provide the underlying foundations that make a city potentially compassionate and the detailed characteristics that realize this potential and facilitate people to interpret their surroundings as nurturing.

Structural Characteristics

Optimize Density of Experiences

A key influence on our experience menu is variety of experiences our surroundings offer us. The area we can cover by active transport is limited, even with good design, and so that area needs to cram in many opportunities and experiences if it is to help us meet our diverse needs. Higher population densities contribute to making local businesses and services viable and support a wide range of community activities within walking distance (Udell et al. 2014) (Figure 17.2). If a population is spread thinly, so too are the shared facilities, opportunities and experiences that facilitate community life. Consequently, designing the compassionate city places great weight on the efficient use of space and seeks to maximize the density of people and experiences where possible.

Strategic Active Transport Links

The bones of the compassionate city are made up of strategic links that tie its component parts together and provide conduits that make walking or cycling realistic options to get to places outside a person's immediate neighbourhood (Figure 17.3). These are important because distance is not the only factor in determining walking and cycling range. In their consideration of what is considered a reasonable walking distance, The Planning Institute of Australia found that far from the generally accepted view that a reasonable walking distance is around 400m (5-minute walk) *"recent studies have shown that people are willing to walk much greater distances if the walking environment is favourable (an average of 1.2 kilometres in good conditions)"* (2009).

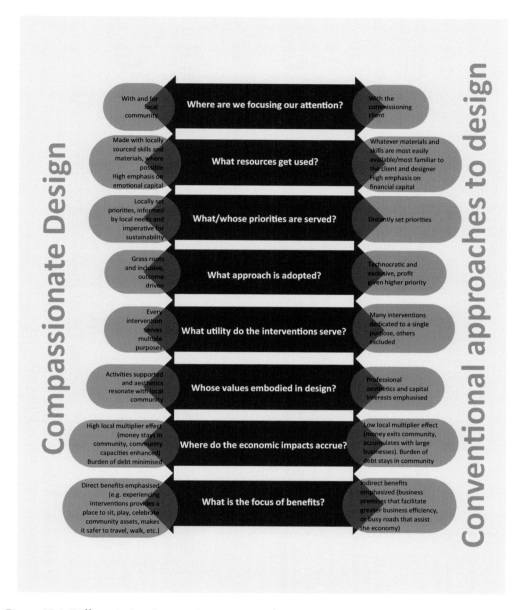

Figure 17.1 Differentiating Compassionate Design from Conventional Design
Source: adapted from Donovan (2015)

The distance at which a destination becomes 'too far' varies with the destination, design quality on the journey, sense of safety and the familiarity that people have with their surroundings, amongst other variables (Donovan 2014). Consequently concentrating efforts on creating safe, attractive, visually interesting green conduits that are aligned with key destinations may work in multiple ways to tip many people's balance of influences

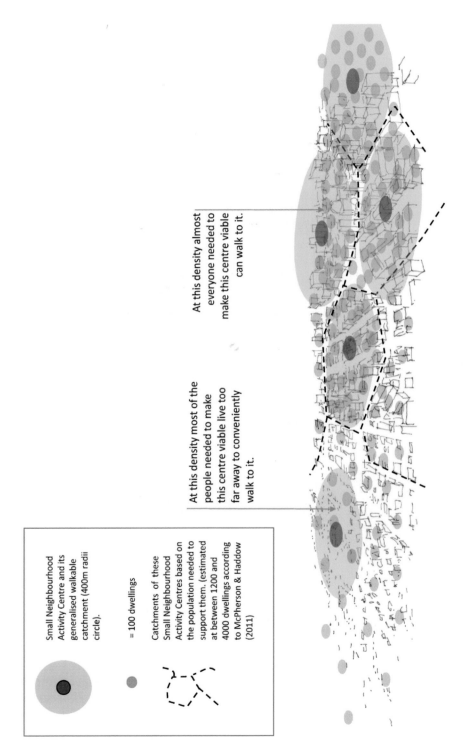

Small Neighbourhood
Activity Centre and its
generalised walkable
catchment (400m radii
circle).

= 100 dwellings

Catchments of these
Small Neighbourhood
Activity Centres based on
the population needed to
support them. (estimated
at between 1200 and
4000 dwellings according
to McPherson & Haddow
(2011)

At this density almost
everyone needed to
make this centre viable
can walk to it.

At this density most of the
people needed to make
this centre viable live too
far away to conveniently
walk to it.

Figure 17.2 Different Densities in a Hypothetical Town Illustrating the Ease of Walking to Their Nearest 'Small Neighbourhood Activity Centre' at Different Densities

Figure 17.3 Strategic Link Offering a Continuous Active Transport 'Hardware Bias' to Facilitate Longer Active Transport Journeys

(Chapter 3) so that walking and cycling become attractive options for more and longer journeys than would otherwise be the case.

Gridded and Integrated Network

Grid systems with good footpath connectivity have higher rates of walking than non-grid areas with poor footpath connectivity (Hoehner et al. 2005; Saelens et al. 2003). Grid systems allow choice so people may choose to take a route that best suits their needs at the time (Figure 17.4) or avoid a route they associate with an unpleasant experience. Gridded networks also allow the closure of a street for community events with minimal disruption to the wider network.

Co-ordinate Fronts and Backs

Some activities and some parts of buildings contribute to the public realm. These are things such as the windows of habitable rooms (with appropriate safeguards to maintain privacy), shop displays and principal pedestrian entrances to buildings of all sorts. However, some activities and parts of buildings do not contribute to the public realm even though they may be critical to its function. These are things such as utility cabinets, rubbish and storage areas, and parking areas. Other functions such as private spaces are often too sensitive to be placed adjacent to the public realm. To avoid tainting other

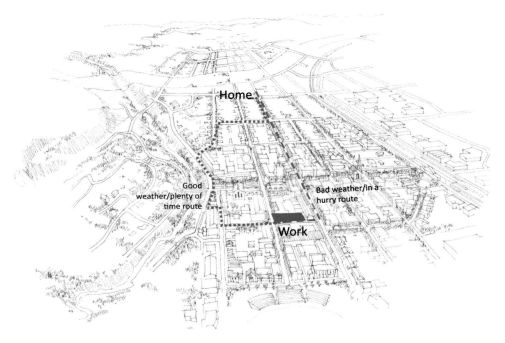

Figure 17.4 Gridded Network

people's experience of a space, amenity-prioritizing fronts should be grouped and utility-prioritizing rears should be grouped wherever possible, reflecting Bentley et al.'s concept of 'perimeter blocks' (1985). In practical terms, this may indicate the provision of rear lanes to provide the focus of these utility functions freeing the fronts of blocks from having to accommodate these uses and (in residential areas) provide further play opportunities within a relatively robust environment (Figure 17.5).

Incidentality

A needs-fulfilling behaviour is more likely to go from someone's experience menu into their experience diet when the time, effort and psychological degree of difficulty engaging in that behaviour—the opportunity cost—is minimized.

It follows that we can make it easier for people to meet needs that often go unmet (such as experiencing nature) by minimizing their opportunity cost. This suggests aligning experiences so that undertaking what Jan Gehl (1996) describes as necessary activities (such as walking to school, shops, work, etc.) exposes people to opportunities that meet other needs, such as experiencing nature, social interaction or opportunities for physical activity. Thus they incur no or little additional effort, at least to access them—in other words they are incidental (Figure 17.6).

Another example of this is provided by a plan prepared by David Lock Associates (Australia) for Bacchus Marsh, a town in Melbourne's peri-urban hinterland. The plan sought to privilege pedestrian movement to the station and favour needs fulfilment by creating a 'greenway' that offered a range of experiences to engage the passer-by along

Figure 17.5 Laneways Can Provide a Relatively Robust Environment for Play and Free Fronts From Being Dominated by Garages

Figure 17.6 Example of Incidentality: Offering People the Experience of Nature Without Going out of Their Way

Figure 17.7 Bacchus Marsh Greenway

a pedestrian-orientated, high-amenity route through the town's growth area between the station and the town centre, approximately a kilometre distant (Figure 17.7).

Detailed Characteristics

Places that embody the strategic characteristics described in the previous section are potentially compassionate. For this potential to be realized, they need to also embody a range of detailed characteristics that will influence people's lived experience of their surroundings. This section describes these characteristics, grouped together under the objectives they may help to meet.

A Welcoming Built Environment

A welcoming built environment is one that broadcasts messages to the people that experience it that their physical and psychological well-being has been considered in the design of that place. Inviting people into a space and then making them comfortable there increases the chances of them staying long enough to be there when other people pass through. Thus welcoming places invite chance and planned encounters in actively shared space, to use the terminology of Chapter 3.

Supporting physical well-being requires that people can interpret their surroundings as offering opportunities to meet basic physiological needs, such as comfortable places to rest

Figure 17.8 Access Marker Designed to Create a Welcoming Threshold Rather Than an Exclusionary Gateway

Source: adapted from work by the author for the City of Sydney walking and cycling strategy 2012

and gain respite from climactic extremes. Supporting psychological well-being requires the built environment to affirm their right to be there (assuming that right exists) and avoids broadcasting any messages that make an individual feel their presence there exposes them to a particular risk of accident, attack or confrontation. It also requires the promise of a positive experience in that place, something pleasant, inspiring and/or interesting.

One of the techniques for making a place more welcoming is by defining it by means that avoid cultivating a sense of 'us and them', which happens when a person is required to cross into what feels like the exclusive territory of the other. Experience suggests explicitly welcoming people to a place can create a sense of threshold rather than gateway, emphasizing a place is different but not exclusive (Figure 17.8). Other welcoming characteristics include helpful signage, a friendly tone taken to communicate rules and responsibilities (Chapter 8), and well-designed and maintained street furniture and landscape that facilitate a diversity of experiences in a place (Figure 17.9). Well-designed and ample landscape may also help ameliorate climactic extremes, expose people to nature and provide diverse opportunities for play and learning that contribute to the promise of occupying that place.

Provide Legibility

Helping people to get a sense of where they are and the options available to them can be very reassuring (see Chapter 4). It can safeguard against the fear that every step may be a step in the wrong direction and ensure choices can be made with greater confidence.

Figure 17.9 Inviting Streetscape That Communicates a Sense That the Visitor Is Welcome to Linger and Can Enjoy a Range of Engaging Experiences Without Conflict With Others

Providing legibility requires that places are rich with helpful messages that allow people to orientate themselves with little difficulty. Building lightly on the influential work of Bentley et al. (1985), places may be made intrinsically legible when they are embedded with a hierarchy of landmarks that enable people to place themselves in the right direction, neighbourhood or vicinity (Figure 17.10) and when buildings respect a convention that tells the observer what their function is. Experience suggests that locating minor landmarks—effectively any designed characteristic that distinguishes that point from the norm at particular decision points such as corners—will help people navigate around a place: *"turn left at the corner with the little pocket park"*.

Another means of enhancing legibility is by the use of signage and mapping that require little effort to relate to the reader's own mental map and allow people to make informed choices as to where they are going. An excellent example of this is the mapping system employed by the City of Bristol, UK as part of their *Bristol Legible City* initiative. The maps, which are themselves minor landmarks in public space, provide a 'heads-up' viewpoint of

Examples of a hierarchy of landmarks. Major landmarks allow us to confidently set off in the right direction (top), or tell us we are in the right vicinity (middle) and minor landmarks (bottom) can be very helpful in marking different stages in a journey. The minor landmarks here might provide useful points of orientation, "turn left where the street narrows" or "turn right at the school".

Figure 17.10 Landmark Hierarchy and Role

Figure 17.11 Bristol Map
Source: photograph by Aoife Doherty

pedestrian maps (rather than the traditional north at the top) and include graphic represen-
tations of three-dimensional landmarks. They offer a great depth of detail, but the detail is
presented in a consistent and intuitive hierarchy that means they can easily be read to the
level of detail needed without having to sift through extraneous information (Figure 17.11).

Provide Reassurance

Fear has a significant weight on the balance of influences on people's behaviour, deterring
people from engaging in many needs-fulfilling activities such as walking, cycling, playing

(Chapters 2, 3, 4 and 6). The compassionate city is designed to provide ample evidence that potentially threatening behaviours (accidental or deliberate) are curtailed and to support its inhabitants to put the residual risks into perspective. This is not to aim for perfect safety, as this is neither possible nor desirable. A single-minded pursuit of safety leads to design that precludes other objectives and isolates people (CABE 2008).

As noted in Chapter 2, different people have different sensitivities to risk. On the whole, older people feel more vulnerable than younger people; women feel more vulnerable than men. In keeping with the philosophy of this book, the compassionate city should seek to calibrate the reassurance it offers to those most vulnerable. The built environment can lift the burden of fear and reassure people when it incorporates 'passive surveillance'—the quality a place has that can deter attackers because of the likelihood an attack will be witnessed or people might intervene. Reassurance is cultivated when a place gives off messages that effectively say potentially dangerous or unpleasant appropriating uses are discouraged or otherwise limited (Figure 17.12). It is also facilitated through a strong sense of community cohesion that is an effective deterrent to anti-social behaviour (Sampson and Raudenbush 1999). The findings of Southworth and Ben-Joseph (2003) back up the evidence of experience which suggests that cultivating the sense that people care about what goes on in the world around them is also greatly reassuring: "*In particular, well-maintained properties and streets seem to reduce crime, particularly when combined with passive surveillance.*"

Reassurance is also provided by the lived experience of a place as reliably safe. It only needs one mishap for an older person to feel less confident in a place. To this end, ensuring busy streetscapes have a continuous and consistent zone that is wide enough to accommodate significant peaks in pedestrian movements and is reliably free of seats, displays, bicycles, mooring points for awnings, etc. will allow many to face the outside world with greater confidence. This is particularly so if street names, building entrances and pedestrian-orientated signage are clearly visible from this safe zone and it directly adjoins shaded seating areas.

Reflect Well on the Occupant

As noted in Chapter 1 and observed by Glen Gourlay (2007), "*The negative labelling and resulting stigmatisation of a neighbourhood exerts a powerful influence on the material and psychological wellbeing of residents, which contributes towards their experience of exclusion from important aspects of economic, social and cultural life.*" It seems part of this problem is a sense that communities get the design standards 'they deserve'. The compassionate city seeks to give people evidence that they are valued and reassure them and the wider world they are considered worthy of design effort, as in the South Melbourne Commons case study. Experience suggests achieving this is strongly associated with high standards of maintenance and care. Places that have more pride put into them inspire more pride in those who experience them.

Create Adornable Spaces

The compassionate city provides its inhabitants with many blank canvases that have intrinsic quality as they are but can be enhanced—'adorned'—by the people who share them, by the things they do in it or the interventions they put within them. These actions add something uniquely of that place, add interest, allow people to use 'little design' interventions (see Chapter 16) to express themselves, feel engaged in that space and contribute to the quality of experience for passers-by (Figures 17.13–17.15). Creating adornable space requires the urban designer, architect, etc. to build in a degree of flexibility and

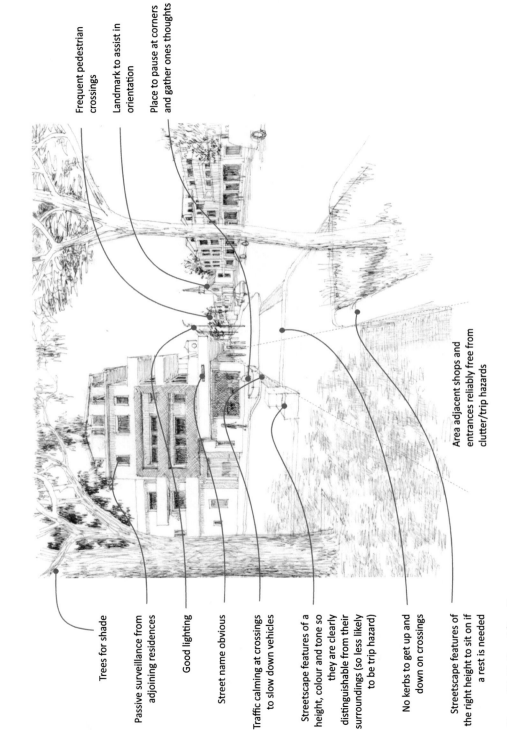

Frequent pedestrian crossings

Landmark to assist in orientation

Place to pause at corners and gather ones thoughts

Area adjacent shops and entrances reliably free from clutter/trip hazards

Trees for shade

Passive surveillance from adjoining residences

Good lighting

Street name obvious

Traffic calming at crossings to slow down vehicles

Streetscape features of a height, colour and tone so they are clearly distinguishable from their surroundings (so less likely to be trip hazard)

No kerbs to get up and down on crossings

Streetscape features of the right height to sit on if a rest is needed

Figure 17.12 Providing Reassurance

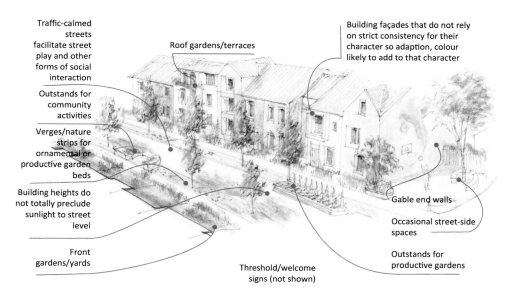

Traffic-calmed streets facilitate street play and other forms of social interaction

Outstands for community activities

Verges/nature strips for ornamental or productive garden beds

Building heights do not totally preclude sunlight to street level

Front gardens/yards

Roof gardens/terraces

Threshold/welcome signs (not shown)

Building façades that do not rely on strict consistency for their character so adaption, colour likely to add to that character

Gable end walls

Occasional street-side spaces

Outstands for productive gardens

Figure 17.13 Examples of Characteristics That Help Create Adornable Spaces

Figure 17.14 Reykjavik Wall Adorned by Adaption
Source: photograph Stephen Ingrouille

Figure 17.15 Melbourne Street Adorned by Usage

robustness in the public realm and ensure the public realm is not appropriated by another use (such as traffic) that would stifle social use. It also requires the community to be able to make informed choices as to where to locate interventions so they do nothing to diminish a space's function but add a great deal to its appeal. Of course the nature of that adornment might prove controversial, as it does with many forms of street art, and not all forms of expression are socially beneficial (such as tagging). However it is contended that facilitating people to make their mark, on balance and within norms established with the wider community, contributes more than it detracts.

Engage People, Gently

Meeting needs requires the Goldilocks level of stimulation: too little or too much can be stressful (Chapter 4). The compassionate city offers its occupants a wide range of interesting, thought-provoking stimuli that can provide a pleasant distraction as they move through shared spaces should they wish to engage with these qualities. This reflects what Jan Gehl (2006) has called the 5km/hour environment, a richness of experience and level of detail that is designed to be experienced at walking pace. This echoes the conclusions of psychologist William James over a century ago, who found, "*in general, a time filled with varied and interesting experiences seems short in passing, but long as we look back. On*

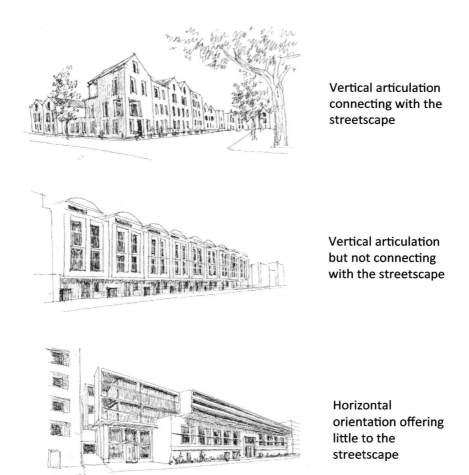

Vertical articulation connecting with the streetscape

Vertical articulation but not connecting with the streetscape

Horizontal orientation offering little to the streetscape

Figure 17.16 Horizontal Versus Vertical Articulation

the other hand a tract of time empty of experiences seems long in passing, but in retrospect short" (1892).

Creating environments that offer distinguishable patterns or regular variations and points of interest in the public realm can contribute to providing visual interest and offer subtle stimulation. Given the human experience is generally one of walking along the base of buildings rather than moving up them vertically, buildings that offer vertical articulation and allow the life within the buildings to find expression at street level will provide a richer experience than buildings that offer only horizontal articulation or blank façades at street level (Figure 17.16). (Thanks to Mark Sheppard for sharing this observation.)

Importantly engaging people will require more than just physical interventions. It is greatly assisted by the promotion of a wide range of opportunities for people to participate in programmed and non-programmed community activities, in this way allowing people to share, learn, be proud of, value or otherwise connect with their community.

Importantly, it is the responsibility of the compassionate city to inspire people to engage in its component places rather than force them to. Consequently the experiences embodied into the compassionate city should offer an invitation to engage, never demand a response. Creating space for landscaping to survive, mature and maximize its contribution to the public realm will provide a foil for the more assertive demands that the man-made environment makes on our attention. The Tower Hamlets Cemetery Park provides a good example of a place that engages people at many levels, offering a variety of opportunities to experience the place, be nurtured by the restorative effects of exposure to nature and participate in looking after it in ways that meet multiple needs.

Offer Resonance

As noted in Chapter 4, almost any intervention in any city happens in a place that people have grown familiar with and who will have their own established view of what represents good design. Even if change is objectively positive, if it challenges these familiar characteristics and patterns it can be disruptive, provoking a sense of loss for the people whose lives are most directly affected. In the compassionate city, this emotional impact is given weight and it is not enough to disregard this sense of loss because the community 'will get used to it', even if this may be true.

By designing new development mindful of community values, a sense of familiarity may be cultivated, so change may be seen as evolutionary rather than disruptive. This isn't to suggest that new places should be a slavish reproduction of what was there before, but they should be responsive to the area's identity and character where possible. How this resonance is expressed is a matter for the designer to establish with the community and other stakeholders. It may be a matter of its dedication to a person or group, its appearance, use, materials, relationship to its surroundings, its landscape character, the challenges it addresses, the skills it calls on, all of these things or none of them. If resonance can't be achieved (and there are many strategic reasons why new development will need to depart radically from what was there before), careful and sensitive explanation for this departure is needed and tokenistic references should be avoided.

Offer Delight and Playfulness

The promise of fun is a powerful motivator that offers by-products of physical activity, affection and mental stimulation, as noted in Chapters 2 and 4. Fun, delight and playfulness are doorways to deeper connections between people and between people and their surroundings. Such experiences lift life out of the mundane and utilitarian and affirm our humanity.

The compassionate city invites people to do things just for the fun of it. It offers many engaging and playful experiences throughout the public realm rather than just in dedicated places of fun and recreation (parks, play areas, social places, etc.). It enables people to have fun in many different ways, by passively enjoying a space and the theatre of the streets, by engaging only with their eyes (as in the Tirana repainting project in Chapter 4), their ears (Figure 17.4) or whole body (as the Gap Filler Dance-O-Mat in Chapter 4). Creating conducive circumstances for fun and playfulness requires that a place has the following qualities:

Play-stifling characteristics are diminished. Traffic, safety concerns and competition for space from other uses can stop fun colonizing the public realm. As explored in Chapter 10, reducing the area dedicated to mono-purpose vehicle space can help diminish traffic speed and hence its intrusion. It also wins space that can be used for play. Offering lived

Figure 17.17 Play-Friendly Melbourne Street Edge

evidence that play is valued and contributes to all in the community can help give play greater weight and emphasis when considered against competing uses.

Careful choice of materials, separation from avoidable sources of risk, good maintenance, adequate passive surveillance and protection from climatic extremes all contribute to reassuring people that the risks of spending time playing or supervising play are minimized. Providing wide footpaths and nature strips (verges) that can be occupied by children playing without conflict with other passers-by both adorns the streets and facilitates shared outdoor play (Figure 17.17).

Co-locating private open spaces can facilitate more substantial landscaping than would otherwise be possible in smaller, more 'broken up' spaces. Creating buffer spaces such as verandahs or stoops between private dwellings and associated open spaces can provide a place to keep muddy boots, footballs and other play equipment so they won't be a problem inside the house (Figure 17.18). Explicitly inviting fun and giving it a high profile (Figure 17.19) may offer an unwritten licence to join in and enjoy.

Given the impracticability of putting props dedicated solely for play everywhere, the compassionate city also seeks to ensure fun and delight are at least a secondary characteristic of many interventions. Elements such as signs, streets, paving materials and retaining walls, intended primarily to serve another purpose, can also complement the range of locally available play opportunities with appropriate design and placement (Figure 17.20).

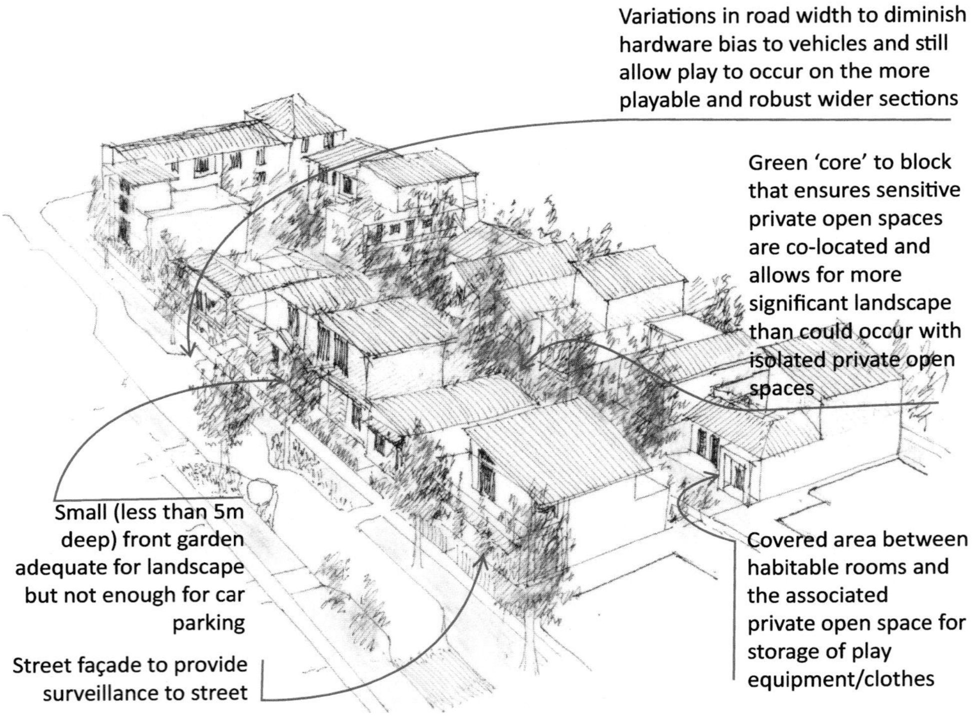

Variations in road width to diminish hardware bias to vehicles and still allow play to occur on the more playable and robust wider sections

Green 'core' to block that ensures sensitive private open spaces are co-located and allows for more significant landscape than could occur with isolated private open spaces

Small (less than 5m deep) front garden adequate for landscape but not enough for car parking

Street façade to provide surveillance to street

Covered area between habitable rooms and the associated private open space for storage of play equipment/clothes

Figure 17.18 Play-Friendly Blocks
Source: adapted from Donovan (2016)

Figure 17.19 'Play Me, I'm Yours'; Inviting Fun
Source: Shutterstock 302598683

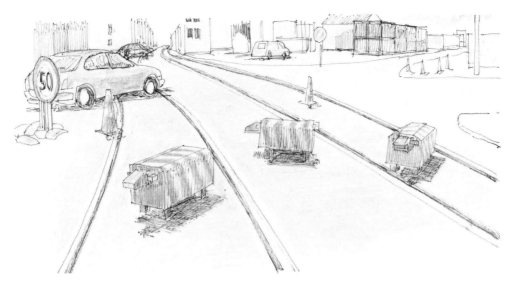

Figure 17.20 Playful Traffic Control, Seats in Christchurch, NZ

Another important characteristic of playability is to ensure parents, carers and other non-players are looked after too. Installing seats and seating opportunities overlooking playable features and play spaces in multiple shaded, high-amenity settings allows carers to see their children and sit and chat as well as allowing children to rest. This minimizes the potential for discomfort or tiredness to deter play or bring it to a premature conclusion.

The diverse range and intensity of play activities suggests that, where possible, loose-fit, robust, multi-purpose spaces are provided that can be colonized for a range of activities. Such places are defined by permeable, fuzzy edges such as planting, seats, landscape features and changes of level (Figure 17.21). Appropriately designed, such places provide a place to 'let the play out' for children and delight people of all ages by being adorned by children in use and by virtue of their intrinsic design values when they are not being actively used.

Furthermore the software and orgware of the compassionate city—its culture—needs to be permissive of play. This happens when the importance of fun and play is broadly understood and facilitated. This might arise from education, promotion, cultivating a 'game-friendly' environment, facilitating people to form teams or close streets or public spaces to allow games to take place.

Safeguard Against Blighting

On accident or on purpose, some uses, people or activities have the capacity to blight the space around them. The compassionate city seeks to safeguard against this, not necessarily by excluding these people and uses but preferably by managing their impact.

As noted in Chapter 4, two of the most significant causes of blight come from the impact that vehicles have on the space around them and our fear of what other people might do. Safeguarding against blighting by vehicles requires slowing speed, diminishing their presence in urban spaces and reducing the need for people to make so many car-borne trips.

Figure 17.21 Example of Loose-Fit Space, Birrarung Marr, Melbourne

Woonerven provide a great example of minimizing the intrusion of vehicles by changing the implied priorities of residential streets, privileging pedestrians and street life over cars. They do this by dedicating little or no space solely to moving vehicles and breaking up what Gordon Cullen (1961) described as the kinetic unity of the street (Figure 17.22). This allows the space within which play and community life can occur to spread onto the road.

Higher densities with mixed uses put more destinations in walking distance, giving people a degree of choice about how they make those journeys.

As noted in Chapter 4, a territorial claim made by a group over a space need not necessarily be a problem. However, when it leads to the exclusion of others and fragments society, it can become one. Safeguarding against this blighting by groups means ensuring places can be actively shared and the lived experience of that place refutes the conclusion that it belongs solely to a particular group. Holland et al. (2007), writing for the Joseph Rowntree Foundation, noted that spaces that continuously attracted people through offering interest, stimulation, comfort and amenity acquired positive experiences and resisted this sense of 'belonging' to just one group.

Another effective mechanism to safeguard against appropriation by a group or individuals is to ensure adequate passive surveillance of the public realm. For a person walking alone at night, the presence of one other person may trigger a fear that they may be an assailant. However, if there are several people nearby (as long as they are not perceived as part of the same group or gang), then the individual can draw reassurance from the knowledge someone may intervene or at least be a witness and so perhaps deter a potential assailant. These potential helpers could either be sharing the footpath or looking out from nearby buildings.

Figure 17.22 Street Designed to Minimize the Dominance of Vehicles

As noted in the section 'Provide Reassurance' previously in this chapter, strong community cohesion and a high standard of maintenance broadcasts messages that are interpreted as signs that other people care about what happens in that place. This can act as a deterrent to crime and anti-social behaviour (Southworth and Ben-Joseph 2003) that may otherwise blight a place.

Ensuring that houses are set back from the public realm less than 5m (on conventional streets) will provide adequate space for some quite significant landscaping but is small enough to facilitate good passive surveillance and deter the conversion of front gardens to parking spaces and the attendant domination of footpaths by crossovers.

Facilitate Connections With Nature

The compassionate city places a great emphasis on nature. It seeks to present people with ample opportunities to deepen their engagement with it and so enjoy the stress relief, visual interest, play, sustenance, socializing and educational opportunities that nature affords, as explored throughout this book. Sun and shade, wind and drainage are all carefully considered to keep people comfortable and their surroundings healthy.

The compassionate city seeks to give nature a high profile, emphasizing its contribution to the lived experience of the city and its capacity to gently distract the viewer. As noted in Chapter 3, our ability to hear sounds is very distance sensitive and visual acuity is not evenly distributed across our field of vision. Consequently we are more aware of things that are closer to us or near the centre of our field of vision. This and the evidence of experience suggests that we can accentuate landscape and nature by careful placement so it has a presence framing or at the centre of the viewer's vision, impacts on the skyline or casts an interesting shade-scape around us (Figure 17.23). It also suggests that the exposure of natural processes at street level with interventions such as swales, rain

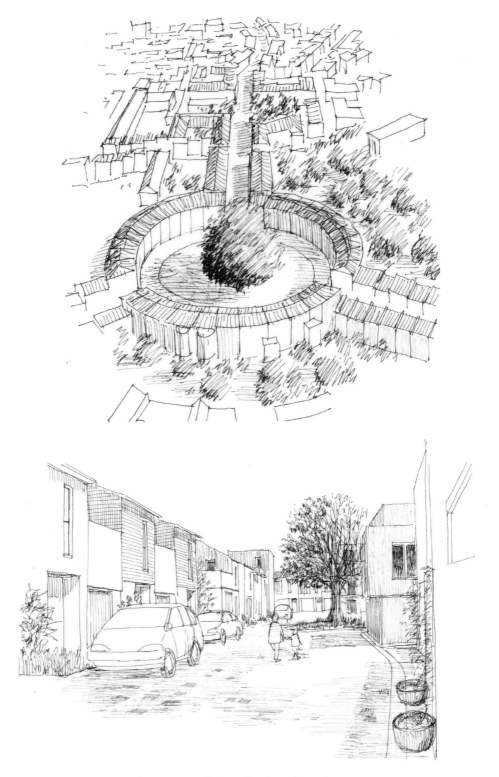

Figure 17.23 Maximizing the Impact and Contribution of Landscape

gardens and mini nature reserves can make experiencing nature incidental to meeting other needs.

The compassionate city seeks to ensure that rich and balanced ecosystems can develop and the investments we make in installing landscape assets survive long enough to maximize their contribution. This has important orgware implications. Continuous commitment is needed over many years to ensure trees can mature enough to have a presence on the skyline and offer micro-climactic mitigation to the surrounding streetscape. This means ensuring they aren't stressed or over pruned; their roots aren't likely to be cut when services are put in or taken out; and soil quality, depth and irrigation are considered. These are all obvious things, but nonetheless are so often overlooked when nature/landscape is pushed down the list of priorities.

Importantly, if these assets are to maximize their contribution, they need to reveal and celebrate their function and the natural processes they serve. This requires high-quality, informative interpretive signage (see the section 'Provide Opportunities to Learn') and careful consideration of how we might allow people to experience natural processes they wouldn't normally be able to (Figure 17.24).

Provide Opportunities to Learn

The built environment and the communities that occupy them are like books; with a little ability and effort they can be read and the ideas, values and stories they hold can be revealed. The compassionate city seeks to share these stories and facilitate people to connect with other people and the place they share. De Ceuvel (Chapter 9) and the Secular Pilgrimage (Chapter 12) provide examples of how these stories can be told and celebrated that facilitate a deeper connection with one's surroundings and enable people to see those surroundings in a new light.

In order to provide the foundations for this software layer, a city's orgware needs to commit adequate resources to gathering and valuing these stories of connection between people and place and the hardware to tell these stories.

Facilitate Co-operation

The compassionate city seeks to create opportunities for people to share in activities where the ends *and* the means contribute to their well-being and leave a legacy of empowerment and closer bonds with people who have shared that activity.

Experience suggests that witnessing shared activity is probably the most effective way of inspiring people to take it up themselves. To this end the compassionate city gives these things a high profile and celebrates them. Thus presenting people with evidence that participating in the production and shared use of the public realm is a common and (hopefully) rewarding experience.

An inspiring example of co-operation as a catalyst for improved well-being comes from 'garden colonies' (allotments/community gardens) in Germany. Journalist Christine Lepisto (2017) pointed out the growing incidence of refugees taking out leases on plots in these garden colonies has benefitted the native German gardeners as well as the incoming refugee gardeners. This has happened through *"the exchange of ideas between gardeners that serves as an important opportunity for integration and community building"*. She also noted that a shared interest in gardening has furthered *"the integration effort by giving people whose lives have been interrupted renewed purpose"* (2017). She observed that a common underlying theme in

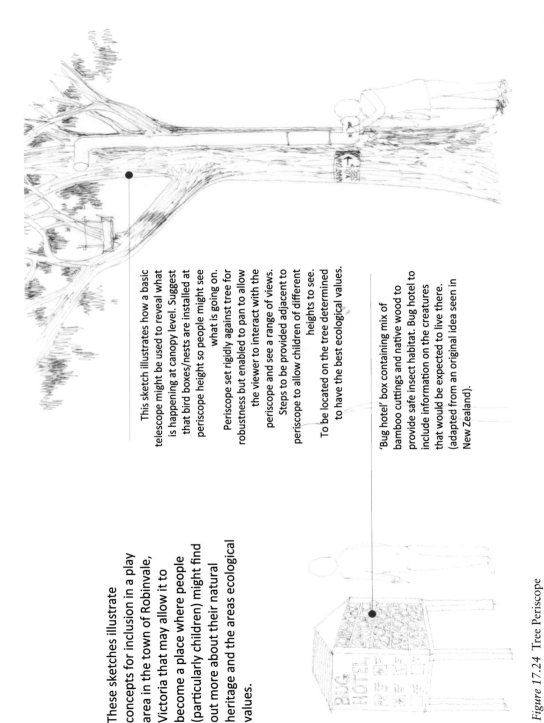

These sketches illustrate concepts for inclusion in a play area in the town of Robinvale, Victoria that may allow it to become a place where people (particularly children) might find out more about their natural heritage and the areas ecological values.

This sketch illustrates how a basic telescope might be used to reveal what is happening at canopy level. Suggest that bird boxes/nests are installed at periscope height so people might see what is going on.

Periscope set rigidly against tree for robustness but enabled to pan to allow the viewer to interact with the periscope and see a range of views.

Steps to be provided adjacent to periscope to allow children of different heights to see.

To be located on the tree determined to have the best ecological values.

'Bug hotel' box containing mix of bamboo cuttings and native wood to provide safe insect habitat. Bug hotel to include information on the creatures that would be expected to live there. (adapted from an original idea seen in New Zealand).

Figure 17.24 Tree Periscope

Source: adapted from a project by the author for the Swan Hill Rural City Council the gardens where this had been noted was that established inhabitants *"reach out proactively to make their community gardens an inviting space for the newcomers"* (ibid).

Polyvalence

As noted throughout this book, every public space in any city is likely to be occupied at any given time by people with diverse needs and priorities. Polyvalence is a term adopted and adapted from chemistry to mean the ability of something to have multiple values. In design terms, it is taken as meaning a quality that a place or intervention has that enables it to be interpreted in more than one way, where each intervention meets multiple needs (Figures 17.25, 17.26) and each need can be met by many features (Figure 17.27). Thus places with polyvalence increase the chances of an individual interpreting their surroundings as being relevant to their needs. In the examples illustrated, passers-by are invited to interpret the place as somewhere good to sit, play, walk past, chat or relax according to their needs at the time.

Figure 17.25 Seat or Window Display, Depending on the Priorities of the Viewer

Figure 17.26 Seat, Planting Bed or Minor Landmark, Depending on the Perception of the Viewer

Figure 17.27 Need Somewhere to Sit?

Note polyvalence is not ambiguity. Ambiguous places are unclear in their purpose and the passers-by might interpret them as not meeting any purpose very well. However a polyvalent place will be experienced by each person as inviting a particular use, and different people will see it as inviting different uses. Woonerven provide an example of this quality in that they invite a child to interpret them principally as places to play whereas an adult may see them as a focus of community life or a place to pass through depending on their priorities.

At a more detailed scale, Douglas Nutall offers the example of simple concrete boxes placed in front of each home in his deck-access housing:

> *They carried the number plate and located the entrance. They offered covered space in which to leave deliveries. They were just right for propping a bicycle against. There were the right sort of height for sitting on and chatting to your neighbours, and so on and so on.*
> (pers. corr. 2015)

Another expression of polyvalence might be the creation of streetscape spaces that make nature strip gardening possible and an orgware culture that is permissive of this happening. To passers-by, this offers visual interest, the experience of seasonal change and an insight into the people who live nearby. To those who tend these little gardens, they see them as a source of fresh food and satisfaction at having grown something themselves, a chance to show off their horticultural skills and perhaps express their aesthetic abilities.

Figure 17.28 Gardens at Alhambra

A memorable example of polyvalance is provided in the gardens of the palace at Alhambra (Figure 17.28) in what was the Moorish emirate of Al Andalus in Spain. These were designed to simultaneously express their owners' (Islamic Emirs and later Christian kings) refinement to visitors, provide a place for relaxation and reflection for those at court, offer comfort in the harsh climate and provide a ready supply of fresh food: figs, citrus and olives, as well as fish from the ponds.

Allow People to Set Themselves Achievable Challenges

People have diverse skill sets and aspirations. The compassionate city seeks to enable as many of its inhabitants as possible to look around their surroundings and feel invited to stretch themselves, express their identity, earn satisfaction from their labours, and make their contribution to their surroundings and their community. This requires offering a diversity of challenges and opportunities so people can find the size and type of challenge that best allows them to take the next step towards a sense of self-fulfilment.

This characteristic is expressed in environments that create choices and allow people to plan their progress along their self-determined path to fulfilling their potential. It might be achieved by landmarks that facilitate people to set their own fitness goals; *"today I will run to the nearest pond in the park and back, tomorrow I will run to the furthest"*. For children (or the young at heart), places can be embedded with challenges such as retaining walls terraced low enough to jump off and stepping stones placed far enough away to require effort and a degree of skill to jump between. In Figure 17.29, the challenge was producing a pleasant tune from the sonic play feature.

Figure 17.29 Sonic Play, Christchurch, NZ

For older people, tiredness may typically deter them from challenging themselves. The compassionate city would offer them the reassurance that if they decide to walk farther than usual, they will be able to find shaded seats at regular intervals where they can enjoy a well-earnt rest.

Importantly the compassionate city also cultivates confidence that people can participate not only in using the city around them but also in creating it. Of particular importance are the 'entry-level challenges' that allow people and communities to cut their teeth and build confidence in their abilities. For example nature strips (verges) that can be used as a productive or ornamental garden bed can enable people individually or collaboratively to set themselves challenges in relation to their contribution to the public realm. Projects such as the Tower Hamlets Cemetery Park (Chapter 8) provide an excellent example of how a project can be designed to co-ordinate many different challenges and equip many different people to address them. The Benches Collective (Chapter 7) provides another excellent example of this quality in that it sets a challenge—to open a bench—but it leaves it up to the people taking that challenge to decide how far they go with it.

Reward People for Doing the Right Thing

The compassionate city is rich in messages that invite people to make informed choices about how they can act compassionately and rewards them for doing so (Figure 17.30). Experience and anecdotal evidence suggest that inviting people to make behavioural choices to express their highest ideals is rewarding in itself, is a strong influence on

Figure 17.30 Fostering a Sense of Connection Between an Observer and Their Surroundings
Source: Shutterstock 563535922

behaviour and leaves a legacy that helps people connect more deeply within the place where those choices were made.

References

Bentley, I, Alcock, A, Murrain, P, McGlynn, S, and Smith, G (1985) *Responsive Environments*. Oxford: Architectural Press.

Commission for Architecture and the Built Environment (2008) *Inclusion By Design: Equality, Diversity and the Built Environment*. CABE. Accessed January 2015, www.designcouncil.org.uk/sites/default/files/asset/document/inclusion-by-design.pdf

Cullen, G (1961) *Townscape*. Oxford: Architectural Press.

Donovan, J (2014) *Overcoming the Tyranny of Distance*. MUEN-D-14-00014R1. www.icevirtual library.com/content/serial/muen/fasttrack

Donovan, J (2015) *Placemaking Projects Final Report*. Internal UN Report.

Donovan, J (August 2016) *Enabling Play Friendly Places*. Australian Institute of Architects, EDG 87 JD.

Gehl, J (1996) *Life Between Buildings*. Hørsholm: The Danish Architectural Press.

Gourlay, G (2007) *Approaching Stigma as a Distinct Focus of Neighbourhood Regeneration Initiatives*. Paper presented at the EURA Conference, 'The Vital City' 12–14 September 2007, Glasgow. Accessed January 2017, www.gla.ac.uk/media/media_47940_en.pdf

Hoehner, CM, Ramirez, LKB, Elliott, MB, Handy, SL, and Brownson, RC (2005) Perceived and objective environmental measures and physical activity among urban adults. *American Journal of Preventive Medicine* 28(2): 105–16. Accessed January 2017, www.ncbi.nlm.nih.gov/pubmed/15694518

Holland, C, Clark, A, Katz, J, and Peace, S (2007) *Social Interactions in Urban Public Places*. York, UK: Joseph Rowntree Foundation.

James, W (1892) *Psychology, Briefer Course*. Cambridge, MA: Harvard University Press.

Lepisto, C (2017) Gardens make 'bad hombres' into good neighbors. *Treehugger*, February 28th, 2017. Accessed March 2017, www.treehugger.com/lawn-garden/gardens-make-bad-hombres-good-neighbors.html

McPherson, S, and Haddow, A (2011) *Shall We Dense?* Policy Potentials, SJB Urban Australia and SJB Architects Australia.

Nuttall, D (2015) *Personal Correspondence*.

Planning Institute of Australia (2009) *Healthy Spaces and Places*. www.healthyplaces.org.au/userfiles/file/Connectivity%20June09.pdf

Saelens, BE, Sallis, JF, and Frank, LD (2003) Environmental correlates of walking and cycling: Findings from the transportation, urban design, and planning literatures. *Annals of Behavioral Medicine* 25: 80. doi:10.1207/S15324796ABM2502_03

Sampson, R, and Raudenbush, W (1999) Systematic social observation of public spaces: A new look at disorder in urban neighborhoods. *American Journal of Sociology* 105(3): 603–51. Accessed March 2017, https://dash.harvard.edu/bitstream/handle/1/3226951/Sampson_Systematic SocialObservation.pdf?sequence=2

Sheppard, M (2016) *Personal Correspondence*.

Southworth, M, and Ben-Joseph, E (2003) *Streets and the Shaping of Towns and Cities*. Island Press.

Udell, T, Daley, M, Johnson, B, and Tolley, R (2014) *Does Density Matter?* National Heart Foundation of Australia. Accessed November 2016, www.heartfoundation.org.au/images/uploads/publications/Heart_Foundation__Does_density_matter_FINAL2014.pdf

18 Applying Compassionate City Principles

In his inspirational and insightful book *Livable Streets* (1981), Donald Appleyard set a challenge: "*We should raise our sights for the moment. What could a residential street—a street on which our children are brought up, adults live, and old people spend their last days—what could such a street be like?*" This section speculates about what such streets would be like, and furthers the challenge to consider what the other parts of a town or city might be like if they were designed to reflect the ideas in this book and Donald Appleyard's aspiration to create places where life can flourish.

- Figure 18.1 illustrates the structural characteristics of the compassionate city: compact, gridded, offering a diversity of different spaces and qualities with many key uses aligned along a high-amenity, pedestrian- and cyclist-focussed greenway.
- Figure 18.2 illustrates a hypothetical street of less than 600m in length (Chapter 10). It seeks to provide an attractive setting for a range of social and recreational activities, as well as enhance ecological values whilst still accommodating necessary vehicle movements. (It is based on the assumption that car parking spaces will still be required adjacent to each dwelling.)
- Figure 18.3 illustrates the arterial links that play a role in tying together different parts of the compassionate city. It seeks to ensure the necessary vehicle movements don't blight their surroundings and also to provide for safe and pleasant pedestrian movement and public transport usage. It is based on the assumption that car parking is provided from rear lanes.
- Figure 18.4 illustrates how central city spaces can be read as welcoming, distinctive and vibrant spaces where the design of the buildings and spaces reflect and amplify the social significance of the city centre.
- Figure 18.5 illustrates the conduits for high-volume pedestrian and cyclist movement to a range of key destinations. These seek to make the journey safe and pleasant, and to allow people to incidentally meet a wide range of other needs when using them. It is based on the assumption that car parking is provided from rear lanes or from adjacent side streets.
- Figure 18.6 illustrates the destination for meeting many day-to-day needs. These would accommodate shop(s), community offices, shared workplaces, local education facilities such as computer labs or kitchens, cafés, meeting rooms, places of religious observance and housing, as appropriate. The adjoining space would widen the range of experiences on offer and reflect and amplify the social significance of the place through its design standards.
- Figure 18.7 illustrates a conceptual public transport stop that is designed to make the experience of using public transport more pleasant and less stigmatizing.

Indicative expressions of compassionate design

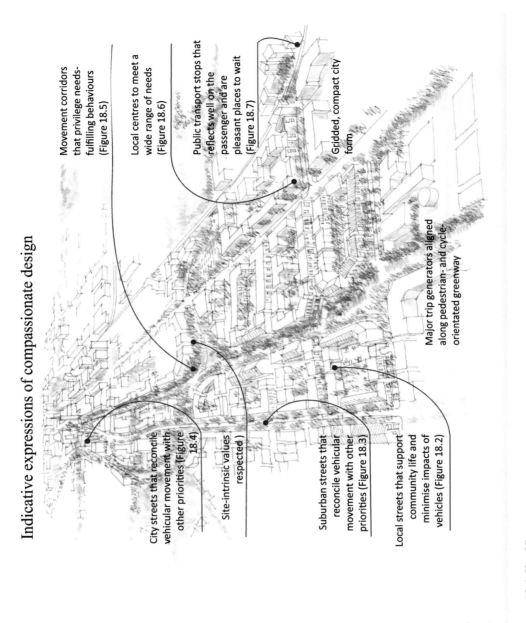

Movement corridors that privilege needs-fulfilling behaviours (Figure 18.5)

Local centres to meet a wide range of needs (Figure 18.6)

Public transport stops that reflects well on the passenger and are pleasant places to wait (Figure 18.7)

Gridded, compact city form

Major trip generators aligned along pedestrian- and cycle-orientated greenway

City streets that reconcile vehicular movement with other priorities (Figure 18.4)

Site-intrinsic values respected)

Suburban streets that reconcile vehicular movement with other priorities (Figure 18.3)

Local streets that support community life and minimise impacts of vehicles (Figure 18.2)

Figure 18.1 Key View

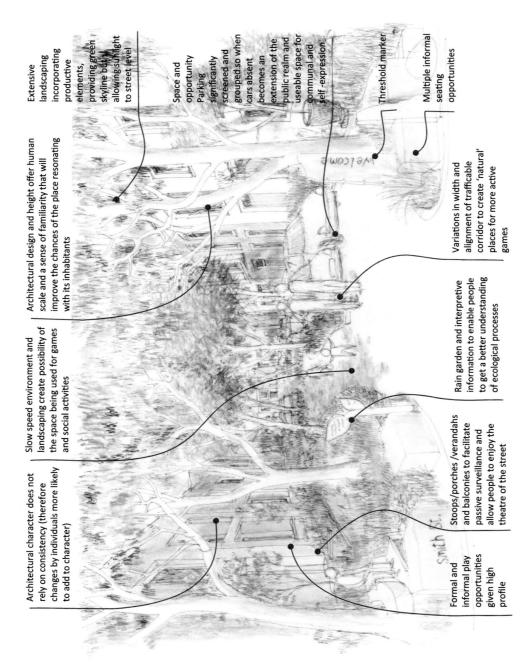

Extensive landscaping incorporating productive elements, providing green skyline but allowing sunlight to street level

Space and opportunity Parking significantly screened and grouped so when cars absent becomes an extension of the public realm and useable space for communal and self-expression

Threshold marker

Multiple informal seating opportunities

Architectural design and height offer human scale and a sense of familiarity that will improve the chances of the place resonating with its inhabitants

Slow speed environment and landscaping create possibility of the space being used for games and social activities

Architectural character does not rely on consistency (therefore changes by individuals more likely to add to character)

Variations in width and alignment of trafficable corridor to create 'natural' places for more active games

Rain garden and interpretive information to enable people to get a better understanding of ecological processes

Stoops/porches /verandahs and balconies to facilitate passive surveillance and allow people to enjoy the theatre of the street

Formal and informal play opportunities given high profile

Figure 18.2 Minor Residential Street

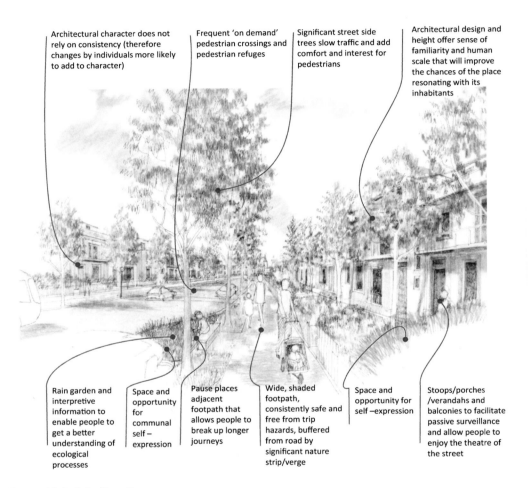

Architectural character does not rely on consistency (therefore changes by individuals more likely to add to character)

Frequent 'on demand' pedestrian crossings and pedestrian refuges

Significant street side trees slow traffic and add comfort and interest for pedestrians

Architectural design and height offer sense of familiarity and human scale that will improve the chances of the place resonating with its inhabitants

Rain garden and interpretive information to enable people to get a better understanding of ecological processes

Space and opportunity for communal self – expression

Pause places adjacent footpath that allows people to break up longer journeys

Wide, shaded footpath, consistently safe and free from trip hazards, buffered from road by significant nature strip/verge

Space and opportunity for self –expression

Stoops/porches /verandahs and balconies to facilitate passive surveillance and allow people to enjoy the theatre of the street

Figure 18.3 Suburban Street

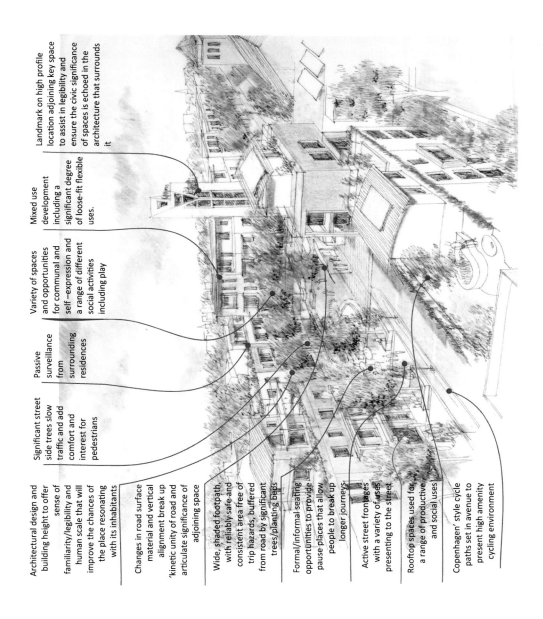

Landmark on high profile location adjoining key space to assist in legibility and ensure the civic significance of spaces is echoed in the architecture that surrounds it

Mixed use development including a significant degree of loose-fit flexible uses.

Variety of spaces and opportunities for communal and self –expression and a range of different social activities including play

Passive surveillance from surrounding residences

Significant street side trees slow traffic and add comfort and interest for pedestrians

Architectural design and building height to offer sense of familiarity/legibility and human scale that will improve the chances of the place resonating with its inhabitants

Changes in road surface material and vertical alignment break up 'kinetic unity of road and articulate significance of adjoining space

Wide, shaded footpath, with reliably safe and consistent area free of trip hazards, buffered from road by significant trees/planting beds

Formal/informal seating opportunities to provide pause places that allow people to break up longer journeys

Active street frontages with a variety of uses presenting to the street

Rooftop spaces used for a range of productive and social uses

Copenhagen' style cycle paths set in avenue to present high amenity cycling environment

Figure 18.4 City Centre Street

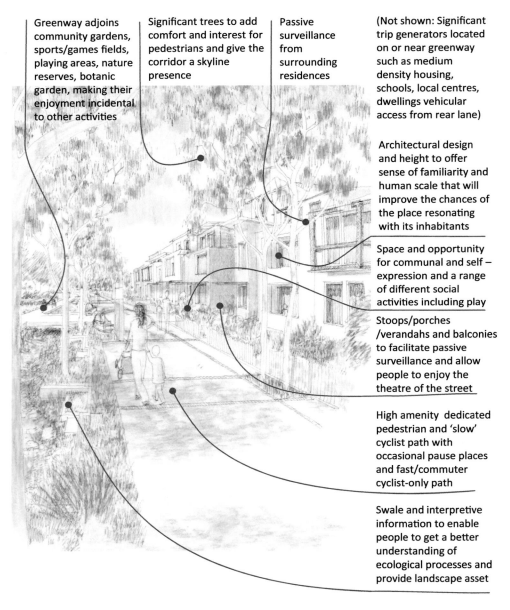

Greenway adjoins community gardens, sports/games fields, playing areas, nature reserves, botanic garden, making their enjoyment incidental to other activities

Significant trees to add comfort and interest for pedestrians and give the corridor a skyline presence

Passive surveillance from surrounding residences

(Not shown: Significant trip generators located on or near greenway such as medium density housing, schools, local centres, dwellings vehicular access from rear lane)

Architectural design and height to offer sense of familiarity and human scale that will improve the chances of the place resonating with its inhabitants

Space and opportunity for communal and self – expression and a range of different social activities including play

Stoops/porches /verandahs and balconies to facilitate passive surveillance and allow people to enjoy the theatre of the street

High amenity dedicated pedestrian and 'slow' cyclist path with occasional pause places and fast/commuter cyclist-only path

Swale and interpretive information to enable people to get a better understanding of ecological processes and provide landscape asset

Figure 18.5 Greenway

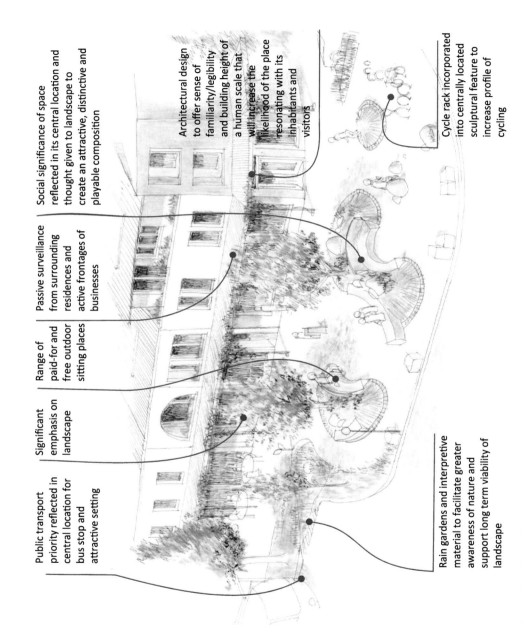

Public transport priority reflected in central location for bus stop and attractive setting

Significant emphasis on landscape

Range of paid-for and free outdoor sitting places

Passive surveillance from surrounding residences and active frontages of businesses

Social significance of space reflected in its central location and thought given to landscape to create an attractive, distinctive and playable composition

Architectural design to offer sense of familiarity/legibility and building height of a human scale that will increase the likelihood of the place resonating with its inhabitants and visitors

Cycle rack incorporated into centrally located sculptural feature to increase profile of cycling

Rain gardens and interpretive material to facilitate greater awareness of nature and support long term viability of landscape

Figure 18.6 Local Centre

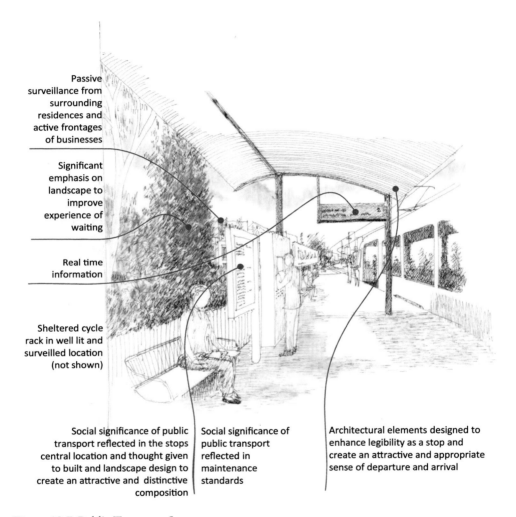

Passive surveillance from surrounding residences and active frontages of businesses

Significant emphasis on landscape to improve experience of waiting

Real time information

Sheltered cycle rack in well lit and surveilled location (not shown)

Social significance of public transport reflected in the stops central location and thought given to built and landscape design to create an attractive and distinctive composition

Social significance of public transport reflected in maintenance standards

Architectural elements designed to enhance legibility as a stop and create an attractive and appropriate sense of departure and arrival

Figure 18.7 Public Transport Stop

Reference

Appleyard, D (1981) *Livable Streets*, Berkeley: University of California Press

19 Conclusions

The buildings and spaces that surround us are more than just a backdrop to our lives—they are players in our lives whether we know it or not. They trap us when they dissuade us from experiencing things that would enhance our lives and influence us to choose unhealthy and unrewarding behaviours that leave our needs unmet and our potential unfulfilled. They liberate when they facilitate us to gather the wealth of experience and positive interactions necessary to understand what our needs are, meet those needs and support us to express our humanity.

The projects covered in this book reveal that with creativity and care (and maybe some luck) it is possible to create places that help people change their relationship with their surroundings and access a wider range of rewarding and nurturing opportunities. Such a relationship can cultivate realistic and achievable hope, a feeling that people have been listened to, that they are empowered and have a say in determining their own futures. Such places improve people's chances of developing their talents and personality, living lives that resonate with their highest ideals and gain satisfaction from their contribution to their well-being and that of their community.

The projects in this book reveal that perhaps the most important factor for this to happen is unlocking the emotional capital of inspired and inspiring people. Their care and willingness to invest their skill, time and reputation, and to find their way around problems that would stifle conventional development, has made these interventions possible in often very difficult circumstances.

However, such projects remain the exception rather than the rule, typically only reaching fruition in places where conditions are particularly favourable and have been overlooked by 'big development'. If compassionate design is to escape its niche, then more structural change is needed to create conducive circumstances for the creativity and emotional capital born of a connection to place and a commitment to humanity to influence what gets built.

From this perspective, the role of urban designers is to use their creative skills to inspire, encourage and create the space for people to 'spread their wings' and explore their potential in a way that does not diminish the ability of other people, elsewhere or not yet born, from achieving their potential.

Conceptually this space provides a wide variety of pathways for people to choose how best they achieve a sense of satisfaction in their life. These pathways make 'needs satisfaction' easier but not necessarily easy, recognizing the importance of setting and meeting challenges. Achieving this has hardware, software and orgware dimensions. The hardware characteristics bias interacting, walking, cycling, playing/having fun and experiencing nature with safeguards that ensure 'wants-driven' activities are facilitated but cannot appropriate that space from 'needs-driven' activities. The software of the people who experience these places is characterized by an awareness of their individual and collective needs that helps them to value the experiences offered by the hardware. These people are bolstered by confidence that they can achieve their potential and overcome difficulties. Finally this hypothetical space has an orgware dimension, where the laws and administrative landscape explicitly value and facilitate the hardware and software of meeting needs.

When these dimensions are aligned, activities that support well-being are more likely to be chosen, not because people *have* to choose them, but because they *want* to. Such nurturing environments reveal to us the beauty in nature, buildings and spaces and the people we share those places with. They invite us to 'let the play out', to be an artist, designer, gardener, athlete, performer, naturalist, play leader or community organiser, or just to appreciate our surroundings as our interests and talents take us.

However achieving this will be challenging. It may require departures from standard professional practice. Institutional resistance may be significant. Raising awareness will increase expectations and add to the pressure to deliver. Engaging people is time consuming. A respectful dialogue between professionals and the community they serve demands the emotional capital and attentional capacity of both parties, denying these resources to other activities from which we might otherwise benefit. Empowering the community and challenging boundaries will always have an element of trial and error. Enabling people to make informed decisions with appropriate checks and balances will constrain development and slow it down in many circumstances. That is to say nothing of the complexities of ensuring different perspectives and priorities can be reconciled. These will all bring costs and take many of us from our comfort zones.

However we also need to consider the costs of *not* addressing the impacts of living in neglectful cities. As explored in Chapter 4, neglectful cities offer few and thinly spread opportunities for people to meet their needs. The lives of the inhabitants of such places are more likely to be blighted by the cumulative effects of social isolation, physical inactivity, stress and exposure to contaminants that will echo through generations. This imposes significant and avoidable costs on healthcare systems around the world, to say nothing of the profound tragedy of lives less rich and less happy than they could have been simply because of the design decisions we make. If doing nothing means towns and cities stay places that stifle many of their inhabitants' human potential, then the question we need to ask ourselves shouldn't be "how can we afford to make the changes necessary to design the compassionate city?" but "how can we afford not to?"

Index

Page numbers in italic indicate a figure and page numbers in bold indicate a table on the corresponding page.